Ready, Set, Dough!

ALSO BY MELANIE BARNARD

Parties!
Low-Fat Grilling
Marinades
Everybody Loves Meatloaf
American Medical Association Family Cookbook
Short and Sweet
A Flash in the Pan

SET, UGH!

Melanie Barnard

Broadway Books   New York

PRINTED IN THE UNITED STATES OF AMERICA

BROADWAY BOOKS and its logo, a letter B bisected on the diagonal, are trademarks of Random House, Inc.

Visit our website at www.broadwaybooks.com

Library of Congress Cataloging-in-Publication Data
Barnard, Melanie.
   Ready, set, dough! / Melanie Barnard.
      p.   cm.
   Includes index.
   1. Dough.   2. Cookery

TX769.B237 2004
641.8'15—dc22

2003055476

Book design by Elizabeth Rendfleisch
Illustrated by Nicole Kaufman

ISBN 0-7679-1424-4

First edition published 2004

1 2 3 4 5 6 7 8 9 10

For Grandma and Nana, who started it all. And for Emily and Kevin, the next generation, whose little hands are already busy mixing and rolling. Happily, both have inherited the "piecrust gene."

Acknowledgments

No book is the work of a single author. This one, especially, has many people and much history in its making. It started, of course, with a love of baking in all forms (except cake decorating, which takes an artist, which I am not), a love that was nurtured from the very beginning by two grandmothers and a mother who taught me much, but who most of all taught me that baking, family, and love are forever intertwined. They are to be thanked today and every day.

My agent, Judith Weber, embraced this idea from its infancy and quickly came up with its terrific title.

My editor, Jennifer Josephy, Laura Marshall, Sonia Greenbaum, Allyson Giard, and everyone at Doubleday Broadway took the idea and the title and transformed it into a wonderfully readable, doable, fun book.

My old friend, the late Richard Sax, demystified and taught me respect for our American heritage of baking.

My longtime writing partner and friend, Brooke Dojny, supports me in all my endeavors, and is always there to pick up the spatula and the pen every single time.

The people who market such wonderful baking doughs are doing their part to keep the ovens of America baking, from the giants of Pillsbury and Pepperidge Farm to the doughs from boutique bakeries from coast to coast.

Thank you, one and all.

Contents

Ready, Set, Dough!

Introduction

I love to cook. But I love to bake even more. Though the two are related, they are also quite different. Cooking is an art, but baking is an art and a science. While a stew or a sauté can be adjusted and changed "en route" as it were, baking needs a precise road map from the very beginning.

Cooking starts with whatever is in my fridge augmented by what looks good at the market every morning (yes, I'm there every morning). Baking, like cooking, is guided by the seasons—gingerbread cookies in winter, strawberry shortcake in spring, peach pie in summer, and apple crisp in autumn, but it is not likely to be a free-for-all from the refrigerator. I can't remember the last time I measured anything for a stew or a soup or a roast or a grill. But the first items I get out when baking are the kitchen scale and the measuring utensils.

After all these years, cooking is pretty much a sure thing. I can taste along the way and it will turn out just fine, especially if I have a few herbs and a dab of butter on hand. But baking still gets the adrenaline pumping—the piecrust rolls out beautifully some days, but other days it shreds like tissue. Cookies can be crisp-edged and tender-centered, but they can also be shoe leather. Some brownies are sheer decadence while others are mere ho-hums. Shortcakes can be feathery or they can be hockey pucks. And as for puff pastry or phyllo dough, I made those from scratch once or twice—every serious amateur baker makes these once, but usually only once. The effort-to-failure ratio is just too high. And in all cases of baking, you don't know whether you've won or lost until the final opening of the oven door.

I come from a long line of home bakers. From Sicily, Nana brought her legendary fig bars—for years I remained convinced that they were the inspiration for Fig Newtons. From her Pennsylvania Dutch gene pool, Grandma passed on to my mother and then to me the innate ability to make a good piecrust, though no one in the family wields a rolling pin better than Grandma did. Grandma and Mom baked from scratch, though Mom flirted awhile with cake mixes when they first came out before soon returning to the old faithful 1,2,3,4 cake (1 part butter, 2 parts sugar, 3 parts flour, and 4 eggs). She made brownies from a mix once, and she even gave frozen bread dough a try. But none of these held a candle to her home-made standards.

I learned the art and science of baking at these women's apron strings, and they taught me that there were only a few formulas and simple ingredients that went into any dough, and that it was making the basic dough that mattered. Piecrust is nothing but flour, shortening (they didn't hold with fancy butter piecrusts), water, and salt. Cookie dough is the same combination in different pro-portions, with sugar and vanilla added to the mix. And brownie dough includes eggs and chocolate, of course. Bread is yeast, flour, water, and salt, and biscuits differ, with baking powder as the leavener and shortening added to the blend. None of my ancestral bakers made phyllo or puff pastry—we didn't have any Greek or French neighbors in Erie, Pennsylvania.

When I started baking in earnest in the '60s, Pepperidge Farm marketed "patty shells" in the freezer section of the market, and alongside them were long boxes of "fillo." Since chicken à la king and beef Wellington were among the hit company dishes of that decade, and baklava was a truly exotic dessert with sure-fire kudos, I bought both, and it opened up a small world of baking from prepared doughs.

Pepperidge Farm expanded to puff pastry sheets, and soon thereafter Pillsbury began to market a whole new line of refrigerated cookie, biscuit, and piecrust doughs in the refrigerated section of the store. I read the ingredients list, and there were only a few unrecognizable items that I researched and learned were harmless and necessary only for a reasonable refrigerator shelf life. The only real flaw, I found, was in the cookie dough, where pure vanilla was not used; I think vanilla is essential in practically every cookie dough.

In the last few years, other companies, from consumer giants like Nestlé to boutique bakeries from New York to California, have brought fresh refrigerated or frozen baking doughs to market, in response no doubt to home cooks who love homemade baking but fear making dough. My grandma maintained that you either inherited the "piecrust gene" or you didn't—it couldn't be learned.

Through professional curiosity, and because I'm like everyone else who has more enthusiasm and appetite than I have time in the kitchen, I've tried practically all of these prepared doughs. And I'm a convert. Instead of treating these doughs as a finished product, I now look at them as the basic homemade product pre-pared without my usual flour-flying mess and mixer/beater cleanup.

I then can fast-forward to the fun part—turning sugar cookie dough into mocha pinwheels, brownies into baked fudge, piecrust into pandowdy, pizza dough into calzones, breadsticks into bagels, biscuits into doughnuts, puff pastry into pithiviers, and phyllo into flowers.

The hard part is already done. The measuring and weighing and angst are over. Now I'm free to be . . . a baker without limits. And so can you. Read on.

Basics of Baking

EQUIPMENT

• Baking Sheets The best baking sheets are those that are made of heavy-weight, shiny metal. Thin baking sheets often warp in the heat of the oven, and very dark metal sheets get too hot and promote burning. On the other hand, insulated sheets keep the heat at such a low temperature that the bottoms of cookies may not even brown at all. Nonstick sheets still need to be greased for really delicate cookies, so I don't bother with them either. Nonstick silicone baking-sheet liners, or Silpat, are reusable and eliminate the need for greasing anytime. A baking sheet may or may not have a rim, but a rimmed baking sheet is only necessary when the recipe specifically indicates the need.

• Baking Pans The standard-size baking pans are 8 inches square, 7 x 11 inches, or 9 x 13 inches. I prefer baking bar cookies in 8-inch square metal baking pans. If a recipe is to be doubled, it is often possible to bake in a 9 x 13-inch pan, but the baking heat is more even throughout if two smaller pans are used. Many old recipes call for a 9-inch square pan, but these are increasingly hard to find today, having been replaced by the 8-inch square pan. A 7 x 11-inch pan is approximately the same size as the 9-inch square pan. Metal pans are generally preferred over glass for bar cookies that bake for less than 30 minutes, since the browning is more intense in metal. Glass is fine for bars baked longer than 30 minutes.

• Baking Dishes The standard-size ovenproof clear glass baking dishes (such as Pyrex) are 9 inches square or 9 x 13 inches, or pie plates of 8, 9, or 10 inches in diameter. I prefer glass for piecrusts, since the browning is more even during high temperatures and most pies spend a longer period of time in the oven. Fancy crockery baking dishes are not as satisfactory as simple clear glass.

• Springform Pans These are metal pans with diameters that measure from 6 to 12 inches, with the most common being 8-, 9- and 10-inch pans. The pan sides release from the bottom by means of a "spring." These pans are essential for cheesecakes, but are also great for mousse cakes, layered and filled desserts, and thick brownies.

• Tube Pans One-piece tube pans, often called Bundt pans, usually have fluted tops, which make attractive cakes. The drawback is that the cake may be difficult to remove from the pan intact. Two-piece tube pans, or angel food cake pans, have a base with a tube that separates from the sides of the pan, making it easy to remove the cake. The drawback is that a really wet dough may seep through the bottom of the pan during baking. Tube pans come in a variety of sizes, with a 9-inch diameter (measured at the widest point) most common.

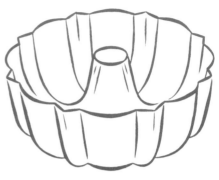

• Mixing Spoons and Spatulas Use good, sturdy large metal or wooden mixing spoons. Useful spatulas are a wide one to transfer cookies from the baking pan to the rack, and a small, narrow offset spatula to use for spreading doughs and frostings.

• Measuring Cups and Spoons Not all measuring utensils are created equal. Liquid measures have a spout, and dry measures usually come in stackables of $\frac{1}{4}$-, $\frac{1}{3}$-, $\frac{1}{2}$-, and 1-cup sizes. Use the right type of cup—dry measuring cups are not accurate for liquids. Measuring spoons are not necessarily equal, either. It's worth it to pay a bit more for these items, since they are more likely to be accurate and will last a lifetime.

• Mixer and Whisk There are a few recipes in this book that need mixing. This can be accomplished with an electric hand mixer or a sturdy hand whisk. No need for a pricey, heavy stand mixer here.

• Rolling Pin I like a good, heavy, wooden rolling pin, 14 to 16 inches long.

• Kitchen Scale Not necessary, but a really nice thing to have for baking, especially if you are substituting locally made dough for the national branded packaged doughs.

Ingredients to Have on Hand

These are the ingredients used most often in the recipes in this book. They are basic staples that I almost always have on hand in my kitchen.

PANTRY SHELF

Vanilla extract   **Big bottle of pure extract**

Almond extract   **Pure extract**

Apple pie spice blend   **Mixture of cinnamon, nutmeg, and allspice**

Pumpkin pie spice blend   **Mixture of cinnamon, ginger, nutmeg, and allspice**

Ground cinnamon

Whole nutmegs and a nutmeg grater

Other ground spices   **Chinese five-spice powder, allspice, ginger, and cloves**

Candied ginger

Nonstick baking spray   **Plain, not flavored**

Granulated sugar

Confectioners' sugar

Brown sugar   **Light and dark**

Molasses

Honey   **Try some new boutique flavors, such as lavender.**

Maple syrup   **The real thing**

Bittersweet or semisweet chocolate   **Many good brands are available in the market. Do not use chocolate chips unless directed in the recipe, as they do not melt in the same manner.**

White chocolate   **Use a high-quality baking bar, not chips, as they do not melt in the same manner.**

Unsweetened cocoa powder   **Dutch process or regular**

Instant coffee powder   **The best quality you can find**

Almond paste in a tube   **Softer than almond paste in a can**

Yellow cornmeal

Raisins   **Look for plump, moist raisins.**

Mixed chopped dried fruit (fruit bits)   **Found with the raisins.**

Lekvar (prune butter)   **Found in the jam section.**

Peanut butter   **Use a good brand of processed peanut butter. "Natural" peanut butter is good for sandwiches, but not for baking, since it separates upon standing.**

Apple butter   **Found in the jam section**

Jams and preserves   **Several flavors**

REFRIGERATOR

Butter   Unsalted is preferred for baking. Margarine is not a substitute.

Eggs   Large

Lemons   Look for firm skins.

Milk   Whole milk is preferred for baking, but low-fat milk is fine unless otherwise stated.

Heavy cream   Not whipping cream

FREEZER

Premium vanilla ice cream   Low-fat ice cream or frozen yougurt is fine for sundaes, but for use as an ingredient in desserts, ice cream with a high butter-fat content is preferred for its slow and even melting qualities.

Tips on Using Prepared Dough

GENERAL

• The microwave oven is the enemy of any kind of dough. Do not thaw (uneven), bake (no browning), or reheat (turns soggy, then dry) any prepared dough in the microwave.

• Home convection ovens are generally standard ovens with a fan system that blows the air, thus increasing its heat and flow to foods, especially cookie sheets stacked on racks. However, few home convection ovens do this well, and may indeed result in "hot spots" that are difficult to control. The recipes in this book are written for a standard home oven.

• When baking two sheets of cookies at the same time, place them as close to the center of the oven as possible, but at least 2 inches apart. Rotate the pans top and bottom, and also back to front about halfway through the baking time.

• Unless otherwise stated, the oven rack should be positioned in the center, or just below the center, for baking.

• Be sure that the oven is properly preheated for baking.

• Keep refrigerated doughs well chilled and frozen doughs quite frozen, and thaw according to package directions.

• Use the dough shortly after opening the packages, since leaveners are activated by opening and some doughs dry out quickly.

• Pay attention to "use by" dates on prepared dough packages. The dough will not function properly after these dates.

PIECRUST DOUGH

• Though you can buy frozen pie shells and boxed piecrust mix, to my mind the only piecrusts worth buying are the folded crusts found in the refrigerated biscuit and bread-dough section of the market. They come two to a 15-ounce package, and can be frozen unbaked and unopened for about a month—any longer and they tend to become brittle. Thaw in the refrigerator, and keep all piecrusts chilled until ready to use.

• Bake pies in ovenproof glass pie plates, not metal pans or ceramic dishes. Most pies are baked in standard 9-inch pie plates. Pyrex is the most reliable brand for sizing, and refrigerated folded piecrusts fit nicely into these pie plates.

• Leave the piecrust in the refrigerator until you are ready to shape it, since it is much easier to work with when well chilled. Carefully unfold the crust and lay it flat or ease it into the pie plate without stretching it. Use your fingers to firmly press any breaks in the folded seams.

• The easiest way to flute a piecrust is to flatten the edges over the top of the pie plate with the tines of a fork to make a striped design. Even prettier and better for holding a filling is to pinch the edge with the forefinger and thumb of each hand, rippling the pinches to form a wavy pattern.

• For unfilled or "blind"-baked piecrusts, shape the crust as directed, then place it in the freezer for at least 30 minutes until partially frozen. Bake directly from the freezer. The chilling time will help to prevent the crust from shrinking during baking, and eliminates the need for weighting the shell with beans or pie weights.

• Prebaked or blind-baked piecrusts can be stored at room temperature for 24 hours before using. If the weather is very humid, cover the crust tightly so it won't absorb moisture and lose flakiness.

• The piecrusts in this book are baked in a different manner from what is suggested on the box. In making most fruit pies, I've found that starting at a high temperature sets the crust to prevent shrinkage, then gradually lowering it promotes even browning and gives the filling enough time to cook. This is the way my grandma made her pies, and it's good enough for me.

• Brushing an unbaked or prebaked pie shell with a "sealant" such as jam or beaten egg whites helps to keep the filling from making the crust soggy.

• Unless otherwise directed, let a prebaked shell cool completely before filling.

• Brushing the top of a double-crust pie with milk and sprinkling with sugar gives it a crackly and beautifully browned top. Brushing with beaten egg or yolk gives a softer crust and a golden sheen.

• Patting or gently rolling fresh or dried herbs or spices into the piecrust adds a new flavor dimension to sweet or savory dishes.

PUFF PASTRY

• Classic homemade puff pastry is difficult and time-consuming to make, but it does feature all butter, which the national brand of commercial puff pastry does not. If you can buy all-butter puff pastry in specialty stores or from a bakery, all the better. However, Pepperidge Farm puff pastry sheets and shells, the prevailing national brand, are quite wonderful—high rising, light, and very flaky. Since most fillings are buttery, fruity, or creamy, there is plenty of distinctive flavor in any recipe in this book that calls for puff pastry.

• Pepperidge Farm frozen puff pastry comes two sheets to a 17.3-ounce box, while pastry shells come six to a 10-ounce box. Keep them frozen until about 6 hours before using, then thaw them in the box in the refrigerator. Or thaw them in the box at room temperature for about 30 minutes, but do not let the pastry come to room temperature. It is much easier to work with puff pastry if it is well chilled. Thawed pastry can be stored in the refrigerator, tightly covered, for 2 days.

• In most recipes, after shaping the puff pastry place it in the freezer for at least 15 minutes, then bake it directly from the freezer. This short chilling time firms the pastry and gives it extra puff in the oven.

• When rolling puff pastry, roll it evenly from the center, both horizontally and vertically, to an even thickness. If possible, chill the rolling pin for about 15 minutes before using.

• Lightly flour a work surface for puff pastry, but don't add any more flour than necessary for maximum puff and tenderness. If possible, work on a cool surface, such as marble, granite, or stainless steel.

• If desired, gently roll fresh or dried herbs, spices, or seeds into puff pastry for extra flavor as a top crust.

- When cutting puff pastry, use a sharp knife and a downward cut, not a sawing motion. Ragged edges will inhibit the puff.

- Brushing the top of puff pastry with beaten egg or egg white will promote a richly browned, crisp crust.

- When brushing the top of unbaked puff pastry with liquid, be sure that it does not drip off the side onto the baking sheet, which will greatly inhibit the puff.

- Sometimes inhibiting the puff is desirable. In this case, prick the unbaked pastry all over before placing it in the freezer. For a really flat pastry, place a baking sheet directly on top of the unbaked pastry. Bake halfway, then remove the baking sheet and finish baking as directed.

- Assemble cream- or fruit-based puff pastry desserts shortly before serving so the pastry stays crisp. Serve puff pastry–topped pot pies shortly after baking for the same reason. If the filling is relatively dry, such as nuts or almond paste, the baked pastry can be stored for 1 day. Blind-baked puff pastry can be stored, covered, in a dry place, for up to 1 day before assembling with fillings.

PHYLLO DOUGH

- Fresh phyllo dough can be found in Greek or Middle Eastern markets, but frozen dough is much more readily available in grocery stores or supermarkets and is of very high quality.

- The most common size box is 1 pound , and contains more than three dozen 12 x 17-inch sheets of phyllo. Occasionally you can find 8-ounce boxes, which are preferable, since it is rare that you will use 1 pound of phyllo at a time.

- No matter what the box says, it is nearly impossible to refreeze phyllo dough, and the leftover dough doesn't keep well in the refrigerator for more than a day even if it is wrapped absolutely airtight.

- Thaw phyllo dough overnight in the box in the refrigerator. Don't try to thaw it at room temperature or use it before it is completely thawed, as the results will be disastrous.

- Phyllo dough is flour and water rolled to a parchment-thin sheet. Because it has no fat, it dries out in the air in a matter of minutes. However, after it is brushed with melted butter, the unbaked pastry can be held, covered, in the refrigerator for several hours, and can even be frozen successfully.

- Baked phyllo dishes can be refrigerated or frozen, but they will be a bit soggy after thawing, even if recrisped in a 300-degree oven.

- Have all recipe ingredients, including melted butter, ready before opening the box of phyllo dough so that you can proceed quickly after the box is opened.

- To use phyllo dough, unwrap the stack of sheets and place the stack on a large tea towel. Immediately cover the top of the stack with another large tea towel, covering the stack completely. The towel can be very lightly dampened, but should not be wet. Do not use paper towels.

- Brush each layer of phyllo with melted butter and sprinkle with crumbs if the recipe directs it. The brushing will moisten the dough and make it easy to work with.

- Don't worry if you break or wrinkle a sheet of phyllo. All recipes use multiple layers and imperfections won't show at all.

- If you are planning to slice or cut the finished phyllo pastry into neat slices or shapes, score the top layers before baking or the ultracrisp baked top will shatter when you try to cut it.

- Do not use very wet fillings in strudels or rolled phyllo dishes or they will seep into the pastry and cause it to become soggy. If the filling is wet, sprinkle the phyllo sheets with bread or graham cracker crumbs to absorb some of the moisture.

COOKIE DOUGH

- Almost all refrigerated cookie doughs come in an 18-ounce package, and the recipes in the book are geared to this size package. Some doughs are sold in tubes, while others are sold in packages, premeasured into cookie sizes.

- Regardless of whether the doughs come in a tube or a package, they are treated as basic dough in this book, and are almost always mixed with other ingredients in a bowl before using. When the recipe calls for half a tube, it is easiest to cut it crosswise with a sharp knife, and with premeasured cookie dough, just count out one-half or one-third according to the recipe yield.

- Extra unused cookie dough can be refrigerated, tightly covered, for up to 3 days or frozen up to 1 month.

- The recipes in this book treat cookie dough as just that—the basic dough to be enhanced and flavored for classic cookie flavor, shapes, and textures.

- None of the recipes call for doughs that contain candies, seasonal shapes or color stamps, or extra sprinkles, as their use is limited as a basic dough.

- There are many variations of chocolate chip cookie dough (with nuts or white chocolate chips) and oatmeal cookie dough with or without raisins. All are of good quality.

- Almost all recipes in this book call for the addition of vanilla extract. The only real drawback to most prepared cookie doughs is the use of artificial vanilla, so the addition of the real thing makes a huge difference.

• Pillsbury and Nestlé are the major national marketers of cookie dough. Store brands are less reliable for good flavor, but you may find one you really like in your market, so try a few. Small regional bakeries are now marketing cookie dough in their areas, and several boutique manufacturers also sell refrigerated cookie dough by mail.

• When breaking up and mixing cookie dough, let it stand out of the refrigerator for a few minutes, then break it into small, approximately 1-inch chunks for easiest mixing with other ingredients. For most recipes, it's easiest and quickest to use your hands to mix the dough—which also makes this a great task for children.

• If slicing or using cookie dough directly from the roll or the package, it is easiest to work with if it is well chilled.

• If you want rounded cookies, chill shaped cookies for a few minutes before baking. If you like flatter cookies, bake them right after mixing and shaping.

BROWNIE DOUGH

• Refrigerated brownie dough comes either in premeasured squares, to be placed in an 8-inch square baking pan or in its own baking pan; both types almost always weigh 18 ounces. The recipes in this book are based on this size package.

• Much preferred are the premeasured brownies that have a few chocolate chips on top. The national brand most often seen is Nestlé, but smaller bakeries, store brands, and Pillsbury also make brownie dough. In most recipes in this book, Nestlé brownies produced the best, most chocolaty results.

• The addition of egg to brownie dough greatly changes the properties of the dough, making it much more cakelike and versatile for many recipes.

• Brownie dough should be separated into small pieces of about 1 inch before mixing with additional ingredients. The dough can be mixed with a large spoon or by hand, though your hands will get very messy and chocolaty—not a particularly bad thing, since licking is the time-honored way to wipe dough off hands.

YEAST BREAD DOUGH

• Pillsbury is the largest national brand of yeast bread doughs, packaged in tubes, and all of very good quality. You may also find locally marketed fresh yeast dough, especially pizza and bread dough, in the refrigerator section of the store or purchased directly from bakeries or pizza shops. Frozen bread dough is not as good as the refrigerated doughs. The recipes in this book are geared to the size tube from Pillsbury, but you can weigh other doughs if you need to substitute.

• Do not freeze unbaked yeast dough.

• Pay attention to the "use by" date on the tube, since the yeast may lose potency after that time. If the tube "explodes" as you open it, the yeast may well have lost its oomph and spent itself.

• Refrigerated doughs do not need an extra rising time before baking. They are ready to go. As soon as the tube is opened, the yeast is activated, so plan to use the dough right away.

• If you have trouble shaping or rolling a yeast dough, let the opened dough rest for a few minutes to relax the gluten in the flour and make the dough easier to roll or shape.

• Brushing shaped dough with beaten egg white will promote a crisp, shiny crust. Brushing with beaten egg or yolk will promote a slightly softer, golden crust. Brushing with melted butter will promote a rich, soft, and golden brown crust.

• Many recipes call for the dough to begin baking at a higher temperature, then quickly reducing the temperature to finish baking. The high initial temperature helps to promote the rising and setting of a good crust.

• Pizza dough (10-ounce tube)—most recipes call for sprinkling the pan with yellow cornmeal, which adds texture and promotes a crisp, richly browned bottom crust. This dough is a bit chewier than bread or roll dough. Fresh pizza dough is available in tubes, but also can be purchased from local pizzerias, either directly, or through supermarkets. If the dough weighs a bit more than 10 ounces, that is fine.

• Breadstick dough (11-ounce tube)—similar to pizza dough, but not quite as chewy. Only plain, unflavored breadstick dough is used in this book.

• French bread dough (11-ounce tube)—does not really approximate authentic French bread, but makes a lovely homestyle loaf. This dough is slightly softer than pizza dough, but bakes to a crisp though thin crust.

• Dinner roll dough (11.3-ounce tube)—similar to French bread dough with a fragrant yeasty aroma.

• Crescent roll dough (8-ounce tube or 15.5-ounce tube large rolls)—richer with shortening and more flaky than bread dough, this is more of a cross between puff pastry and bread dough. It rises well during baking and has a rich, tender, and well-browned crust. Most suitable for sweet rolls and savory braids or rich little hors d'oeuvres. I tested the reduced-fat version, but liked the regular version better.

- Cinnamon sweet roll dough (12.4-ounce tube or 7.3-ounce tube)—sweet roll dough coiled around a cinnamon sugar filling, with a little can of confectioners' sugar icing in the tube. In some recipes, the confectioners' sugar can be used as an icing, but in others it is not needed and can be refrigerated to ice cookies or bars if desired. The cinnamon rolls are pleasantly and mildly spiced and rise to a tender, pale golden roll. This dough is also a good choice to top a fruit cobbler or serve as the basis for a simple sticky bun. Also available are orange-flavored cinnamon buns, though I think the plain are more versatile and fresh tasting.

BISCUIT DOUGH

- Pillsbury is the major national marketer of biscuit doughs, with many varieties and sizes, all coming in tubes. Frozen biscuit dough is actually partially baked and not interchangeable with refrigerated dough in a tube.
- Many home bakers think that biscuits made with shortening are better than those made with butter, so refrigerated doughs are very close to homemade dough.
- Buttermilk or flaky doughs are richer and have more shortening than other doughs.
- In general, the larger the biscuit tube, the richer the dough. The "grand" size is the richest.
- For recipes in which extra shortening or butter will be added, such as frying doughnuts or hush puppies, or for toppings for pot pies, the less rich dough is preferred.
- For recipes in which the biscuit is the star or for fruit cobbler, the richer biscuits are preferred.
- Do not freeze unbaked biscuit dough.
- Watch the "use by" date, since the baking-powder leavening may lose its power after that date. If the tube "explodes" and the dough seems fragmented, sticky, and puffy when you open the tube, the dough is too old.
- The leavener in biscuit dough is activated when the tube is opened, so plan to bake the biscuits right away.
- Many recipes call for starting the baking at a higher temperature, then reducing it to complete the baking. This promotes a quick rise and sets a golden crust on the biscuits.

• Brushing the top of the unbaked biscuits with beaten egg or egg white promotes a crisp top crust. Brushing with melted butter promotes a rich, soft top.

• Types of biscuits that are readily available include buttermilk and old-fashioned (quite flaky), corn bread, golden layers, whole wheat, Southern-style (puffier and lighter), honey butter, and cinnamon sugar. My favorites and most versatile are buttermilk, golden layers, and corn bread. Tube and portion sizes range from 7.5 ounces (smallest size and least rich) to 17.5 ounces (large size and most rich). Some biscuit dough comes in reduced-fat varieties as well, which were tested in the recipes with little difference, though I prefer the regular varieties.

MAIL-ORDER SOURCES FOR DOUGH

Dancing Deer Baking Company sells dough in a 4-pound tub for scooping out to make wonderful chocolate chip cookies. Call 888-699-3337.

David's Cookies sells frozen dough in 3-pound tubs with flavors such as chocolate chip, peanut butter, sugar, and oatmeal raisin. Call 800-217-2938, or see davidscookies.com.

Downtown Bakery and Creamerie sells spicy frozen gingersnap dough that can be thawed and used interchangeably with refrigerated dough. Call 707-431-2719.

Maury's All Natural Cookie Dough makes several flavors, but the oatmeal raisin is stellar from this New York City bakery. Available in some supermarkets in the New York area, or call 866-266-5927.

Neija's produces several high-quality cookie doughs with excellent add-ins, such as Belgian chocolate and spiced nuts in chocolate "chip" cookie dough. Call 877-962-5527.

Poppie's Dough also markets excellent flavored doughs, such as chocolate and white chocolate macadamia or cranberry white chocolate chunk. Call 888-767-7431.

pies

Pies are my **favorite** things to bake. In fact, I like them so much that when it is the "high pie season," which is August in my part of the country, I host an **annual pie party** in the backyard. There are peach, cherry, plum, blueberry, pecan, lemon meringue, and choco-late custard pies. I even bake a couple of apple, strawberry, and pumpkin pies, though it isn't really apple, strawberry, or pumpkin pie season. About forty people come for about eighteen pies. Now I know that this translates to almost **one-half pie per person,** but somehow I never end up with more than a total of about eight slices as leftovers. Perhaps pies are other people's favorite things to eat, too.

all-american cider apple pie

Apples are featured desserts in countries from Germany to France, but only America has a real apple pie—double-crusted and overstuffed with fruit. The Pilgrims, who brought apples to America in the first place, served the pie as breakfast—a very, very good idea! Today's American apple pie has as many variations as there are bakers. In the Midwest, a warm wedge is often served à la mode, with vanilla ice cream melting down the sides, and in Vermont, apple pie is usually accompanied by a wedge of Cheddar cheese. Apple pies can have streusel toppings, but the classic, old-fashioned version always is double-crusted.

This recipe originated with my Pennsylvania Dutch grandma, who sweetened the pie with "boiled" cider. She always brushed the top crust with milk, then sprinkled it with sugar, which resulted in a particularly crisp, rich golden brown crust.

1 cup high-quality apple cider

$3/4$ to 1 cup sugar, depending upon the tartness of the fruit

3 tablespoons all-purpose flour

1 teaspoon ground cinnamon

$1/2$ teaspoon ground mace

$1/8$ teaspoon salt

$2^1/2$ pounds (about 6 large) tart apples, such as Granny Smith

$1/2$ pound sweet apple (about 1 large), such as Golden Delicious

1 tablespoon lemon juice

One 15-ounce package refrigerated folded piecrusts

$1^1/2$ tablespoons unsalted butter

1 tablespoon milk or light cream

1   Preheat the oven to 425°F. In a small saucepan, boil the cider until it is reduced to $1/4$ cup. Let the cider cool. Measure and set aside about 2 teaspoons of the sugar.

2   In a large mixing bowl, stir together the remaining sugar, flour, cinnamon, mace, and salt. Peel and core the tart and sweet apples, and slice them about $1/4$ inch thick. (You should have about 8 cups apples.) Add the apples to the sugar mixture along with the reduced cider and the lemon juice. Toss until the apples are coated with the sugar mixture.

3   Keeping one crust refrigerated, unfold the other crust, and ease it into a 9-inch deep pie plate. Heap the apple mixture into the piecrust, mounding it a bit in the center. Cut the butter into small pieces and scatter it over the apples. Unfold the remaining piecrust and place it over the apples—it will just cover the apples and reach the bottom crust. Use your fingers to pinch the crusts together and flute or crimp decoratively. Use a small knife to cut eight 2-inch slits in the pie. Brush the top of the crust (not the edges) with milk, then sprinkle with the reserved 2 teaspoons sugar.

4   Bake the pie for 30 minutes, then reduce the oven temperature to 400°F. Bake for 15 minutes. Reduce the temperature to 375°F. Carefully remove the pie from the oven, place a 14-inch square of aluminum foil on the rack, fold up the edges of the foil to form a rim, then move the rack to the center of the oven. (The foil will keep the pie juices from bubbling over onto the oven floor.) Place the pie on the foil and bake until the juices are bubbling and the crust is rich golden brown, about 15 minutes more.

5   Cool the pie on a rack, then serve warm or at room temperature.   *(continued)*

All-American Cider Apple Pie **Tips**

- Make apple pies in the fall and winter when apples are crisp and fresh.
- Choose firm, crisp apples with no bruising. The best, of course, are those that are local to your region. If you buy them in the supermarket, Granny Smiths are the most reliable tart apple, and Golden Delicious provide the perfect balance with their perfumy sweetness.
- A good apple pie should have lots of juices and a clear apple taste, so the thickener is best kept to a minimum. If you want a firmer pie, or if the apples are really juicy, increase the flour to 4 tablespoons.

All-American Cider Apple Pie **Variations**

- Toss $1/3$ cup raisins or dried cranberries with the apples. Use only $3/4$ cup sugar, since dried fruit is sweet.
- Substitute $1/2$ cup brown sugar for $1/2$ cup granulated sugar for a more caramel-apple flavor.
- Add 1 to 2 tablespoons brandy or rum to the apples for a bit of a kick.

night sky blueberry pie

Lots of berries are tempting to bake in a piecrust, but blueberries are the hands-down choice, since their flavor is enhanced and released by even a light cooking.

The brilliant, midnight-blue sky color of simmered blueberry juices looks really beautiful bubbling out of a decoratively cut top crust. So, the vents in this crust are cut out with small star or crescent-shaped cookie cutters. Save the cutouts, sprinkle them with cinnamon sugar, and bake along with the pie, then sprinkle the pie or garnish the plate with these crisp little stars and moons.

> $^3/_4$ **cup sugar**
>
> **5 cups fresh or frozen blueberries, stems discarded**
>
> $^1/_4$ **cup all-purpose flour**
>
> **1 tablespoon lemon juice**
>
> **1$^1/_2$ teaspoons grated lemon zest**
>
> **1 teaspoon ground cinnamon**
>
> **One 15-ounce package refrigerated folded piecrusts**
>
> **1 tablespoon milk or light cream**

1   Preheat the oven to 425°F. Measure out and reserve 2 teaspoons of the sugar.

2   In a large mixing bowl, stir together the blueberries, remaining sugar, flour, lemon juice, lemon zest, and cinnamon.

3   Keeping one crust refrigerated, unfold the other crust and ease it into a 9-inch pie plate. Heap the blueberry mixture into the crust. Unfold the remaining crust and place it on a lightly floured counter. Use lightly floured small cookie cutters in star or crescent shapes (or any shape you like) to cut out 4 or 5 shapes from the top of the crust, leaving at least a 2-inch margin uncut. Reserve the cutouts, and place the top crust over the blueberry mixture. Use your fingers to pinch the crusts together and flute or crimp decoratively. Brush the top crust with the milk and sprinkle with the reserved sugar.

(continued)

4   Bake the pie for 30 minutes, then reduce the oven temperature to 400°F. Bake for 15 minutes. Reduce the temperature to 375°F. Carefully remove the pie from the oven, place a 14-inch square of aluminum foil on the rack, fold up the edges of the foil to form a rim, and move the rack to the center of the oven. Place the pie on the foil and bake until the juices are bubbling and the crust is rich golden brown, about 15 minutes more.

5   Cool the pie on a rack, then serve warm or at room temperature.

Night Sky Blueberry Pie Tips

- Frozen blueberries are fine if fresh are not available, but be sure to use them directly from the freezer before they thaw and become mushy. Blueberries are a fruit that freeze particularly well for pies.
- To freeze your own, spread fresh blueberries in a single layer on a rimmed baking sheet. Place in the freezer for at least 1 hour until frozen. Spoon the blueberries into freezer-weight zippered plastic bags. Freeze up to 4 months.
- Blueberry pie can have a lattice topping, but the royal purple juices just look better bubbling out of a full top crust.

Night Sky Blueberry Pie Variations

- Add 1 tablespoon grated orange zest to the lemon zest in the recipe.
- Brush the bottom of the unbaked and unfilled piecrust with 2 tablespoons orange or lemon or ginger marmalade before filling.
- Stir 2 tablespoons finely chopped candied ginger into the blueberry filling.

old-fashioned peaches and cream pie

Georgia is nationally acknowledged as peach country, but great peaches are grown and picked in many other regions from California to Connecticut, too. No matter where you buy them, the best peaches are "tree-ripened." Those hard rocks found in most supermarkets will usually (but not always) soften up nicely, but soft is not the same thing as ripe. Whether golden or blushed with a rosy tinge, the color is of little importance. Tree-ripened peaches announce themselves with an unmistakably lush, perfumed aroma, and a local peach is likely to be a little fuzzy-skinned (peaches destined to be shipped are the unfuzzy variety that holds up better in a box). So, fuzz and smell are the criteria by which peaches should be chosen.

Tradition holds that peach pie is lattice-topped, probably because peaches, unlike blueberries, are large enough to keep their shape in the lattice and soft enough, unlike apples, to allow the lattice to be evenly placed on the pie. Though flour or cornstarch are sometimes used to thicken peach pie, my favorite thickener for peach pie is quick-cooking tapioca, which cooks up clear but not artificially glossy.

1 cup sugar

3 tablespoons quick-cooking tapioca

1 tablespoon lemon juice

$3/4$ teaspoon ground cinnamon

$1/2$ teaspoon grated nutmeg, preferably freshly grated

$1/2$ teaspoon grated lemon zest

3 pounds ripe peaches, peeled and sliced about $1/2$ inch thick
   (about 7 cups)

One 15-ounce package refrigerated folded piecrusts

3 tablespoons heavy or light cream

1   Remove and reserve 2 teaspoons of the sugar. In a large mixing bowl, stir together the remaining sugar, tapioca, lemon juice, cinnamon, nutmeg, and lemon zest. Stir in the peaches. Let the mixture stand for 15 minutes to soften the tapioca.

(continued)

2   Preheat the oven to 425°F.

3   Keeping one crust refrigerated, unfold the other crust and ease it into a 9-inch deep-dish pie plate. Spoon the peaches and juices into the crust, spreading evenly. Dribble with 2 tablespoons of the cream.

4   Unfold the remaining crust and place it on a lightly floured surface. Use a small, sharp knife or a pastry wheel or pizza cutter to cut the crust into $1/2$- to $3/4$-inch wide strips. Lay the longest strip vertically in the center over the fruit. Lay another long strip horizontally in the center over the fruit. Now alternate and crisscross vertical and horizontal strips, about $1^1/2$ inches apart, on either side of the center so that there is a total of 5 vertical and 5 horizontal strips. Flute the edge of the bottom crust, pinching in  the ends of the strips. Use any extra top crust to patch and build up the fluted edges. Brush the lattice with the remaining 1 tablespoon cream and sprinkle with the reserved 2 teaspoons sugar.

5   Bake the pie for 30 minutes, then reduce the oven temperature to 400°F. Bake for 15 minutes. Reduce the temperature to 375°F. Carefully remove the pie from the oven, place a 14-inch square of aluminum foil on the rack, fold up the edges of the foil to form a rim, and move the rack to the center of the oven. Place the pie on the foil and bake until the juices are bubbling and the crust is rich golden brown, about 15 minutes more.

6   Cool the pie on a rack, then serve warm or at room temperature.

Old-Fashioned Peaches and Cream Pie **Tips**

- To peel peaches, place them in a pan of boiling water for 30 to 45 seconds. Remove with tongs and run under cold water. Use a small knife to loosen the skin, then slip the peel from the peaches.
- If available, use two varieties of peaches for a more complex flavor.
- Make peach pie in the summer, when fresh, ripe peaches are available. Don't bother with canned or frozen peaches for pie.

Old-Fashioned Peaches and Cream Pie **Variations**

- Nectarine pie—related to peaches, nectarines are smooth-skinned (no need to peel), slightly firmer and sweeter than peaches. A couple of nectarines can be substituted for peaches in a pie, but if you make a whole nectarine pie, reduce the sugar to $3/4$ cup to compensate for the increased sweetness.
- Blueberry-peach pie—fruits that have the same season often team up well in a pie, and this is especially true of peaches and blueberries. Substitute 1 cup blueberries for 1 cup of the peaches (about 2 peaches).
- For a Southern taste, add 2 tablespoons bourbon or dark rum to the peaches.
- Substitute $1/2$ cup light brown sugar for $1/2$ cup granulated sugar for a more caramelized flavor.

plum streusel pie

According to the nursery rhyme, the plum pie seemed to have had a top crust, or Little Jack Horner wouldn't have had any pastry to stick his thumb through. In reality, the Christmas pie in question was probably a steamed pudding, and the plum was likely a big raisin. So, don't feel a bit guilty about baking your plum pie with a streusel topping. Indeed, plums have a natural tartness and a soft texture that pairs nicely with a sweet, crunchy topping.

Prepared sugar cookie dough, crumbled together with cinnamon and nuts, makes a wonderfully easy and delicious pie streusel. Couple this with the fact that plums need no peeling or even much chopping, and you have a spectacular late summer fruit pie with almost no effort.

There are dozens of plum varieties on the market, but the only one that really differentiates itself is the small Italian prune plum, which has a firmer texture and deeper flavor than larger plums. A combination of varieties, including the prune plum, makes the most interesting pie.

One-half 15-ounce package refrigerated folded piecrusts

1 pound Italian prune plums, pitted and quartered

1 pound purple or red plums (any variety, such as Damson or
    Santa Rosa), pitted and thickly sliced

3 tablespoons all-purpose flour

1^1/$_2$ teaspoons ground cinnamon

^{1}/$_4$ teaspoon ground cloves

One-third 18-ounce tube refrigerated sugar cookie dough, well
    chilled

^{1}/$_2$ cup coarsely chopped walnuts

1   Keeping one crust refrigerated for other uses, unfold the remaining piecrust and ease it into a 9-inch pie plate. Flute or crimp the edges. Prick the bottom of the piecrust 8 or 10 times with the tines of a fork. Place the crust in the freezer for at least 20 minutes or up to 2 hours.

2   Preheat the oven to 450°F. Bake the crust, directly from the freezer, until pale golden and crisp, 10 to 12 minutes. Let the piecrust cool slightly on a rack. Reduce the oven temperature to 400°F.

3 In a large mixing bowl, combine the plums, flour, $\frac{1}{2}$ teaspoon of the cinnamon, and the cloves. In another bowl, crumble the cookie dough with the walnuts and remaining 1 teaspoon cinnamon so that small clumps form. Spoon the plum filling into the pie shell. Crumble and sprinkle the topping over the fruit.

4 Bake the pie until the filling is bubbly and thickened, and the topping is rich golden brown and crisp, about 40 minutes.

5 Let the pie cool on a rack, then serve warm or at room temperature.

Plum Streusel Pie Tips

- Prebaking the bottom crust helps to keep it crisp after the fruit is added.
- The bottom crust may be baked several hours ahead, the plum filling and streusel topping made ahead as well. Assemble the pie when you are ready to bake it.
- Keep the cookie dough well chilled so that it will crumble easily.
- You may use preformed, ready-to-bake sugar cookies from an 18-ounce package in place of the dough in a tube. Use 7 cookies.
- Choose plums that are firm but not rock hard. Hard plums may "soften" at home, but they are likely also to become mushy or mealy in texture.

Plum Streusel Pie Variations

- Other nuts, such as pecans, almonds, or hazelnuts, can be used in place of the walnuts.
- Oatmeal cookie dough may be used in place of the sugar cookie dough.
- Blueberries or thinly sliced apples also make a lovely streusel pie. The proportions are the same as for the plum pie.

sticky pecan pie

This is a fairly standard pecan filling, but the baking method is radically different. The pie starts out at a high temperature, then the oven temperature is immediately reduced to very low, and the baking time is about doubled from the usual. The result is, however, quite simply the best pecan pie you've ever tasted—a chewy, crunchy, caramelized filling in a richly browned flaky crust. Serve it with a dollop of whipped cream or a scoop of vanilla ice cream, for the perfect nut dessert.

One-half 15-ounce package refrigerated folded piecrusts

3 large eggs

1 cup sugar

1 cup dark corn syrup

1^1/$_2$ teaspoons vanilla extract

^{1}/$_4$ teaspoon salt

3 cups broken pecan halves

1   Preheat the oven to 450°F. Keeping one crust refrigerated for another use, unfold the other crust and ease it into a 9-inch pie plate. Flute or crimp the edges, then place the pie plate in the freezer for 5 minutes while preparing the filling.

2   In a large mixing bowl, whisk the eggs, then whisk in the sugar, corn syrup, vanilla, and salt until well blended. Stir in the pecans. Pour the mixture into the prepared pie shell, spreading the nuts evenly.

3   Place the pie in the oven and bake for 10 minutes. Reduce the oven temperature to 275°F. Bake for 1^1/$_4$ hours more, without opening the oven, until the pecan filling is richly browned.

4   Cool the pie on a rack, then serve at room temperature.

Sticky Pecan Pie Tips

- Yes, pecans have a season, and it is autumn. If you can get a "fresh" batch (often sold as charity fund-raisers in my area), you will really taste the difference.
- Don't chop the nuts too finely, and don't use a food processor. Just coarsely break the pecan halves in pieces by hand.
- Pecan pie can be baked a day ahead and kept, lightly covered, at room temperature.

Sticky Pecan Pie Variations

- Other nuts, or combinations of nuts such as walnuts or hazelnuts, can be substituted for about half of the pecans.
- About $1/2$ teaspoon ground cinnamon can be added to the filling.
- One tablespoon unsweetened cocoa can be added to the filling for a chocolate version.

spiked and spiced pumpkin pie

It was an honor to call the esteemed food writer the late Richard Sax a friend. This pumpkin pie recipe is based on one in his definitive work, *Classic Home Desserts*. It is a tad less eggy, a bit richer than most, and somewhat spicier than most. It is the best pumpkin pie I've ever tasted, which also might have a little to do with the shot of bourbon in it.

Some pumpkin pie recipes call for filling an unbaked crust, while others completely pre-bake the crust before filling. Here, I've found the middle-of-the-road approach is best. The crust is baked until pale golden, which is enough to firm the pastry. It is then filled and baked at a moderately high temperature, which finishes the pastry and sets the custard with a lovely dark, caramel top. The large amounts of sugar and pumpkin in relation to the eggs assure that the custard will not weep even at the high temperature. A dollop of unsweetened whipped cream is always a festive touch for pumpkin pie.

One-half 15-ounce package refrigerated folded piecrusts

1^3/$_4$ to 2 cups pure pumpkin puree

^{2}/$_3$ cup packed light brown sugar

^{1}/$_3$ cup granulated sugar

1 tablespoon all-purpose flour

1 tablespoon pumpkin pie spice blend

^{1}/$_2$ teaspoon salt

Pinch of freshly ground black pepper

1 cup heavy cream

^{1}/$_3$ cup milk

2 eggs, lightly beaten

3 tablespoons bourbon

1 teaspoon vanilla extract

1   Keeping one crust refrigerated for another use, unfold the other crust and ease it into a deep 9- or 10-inch pie plate. Flute or crimp the edge. Prick the bottom of the pie crust 8 or 10 times with the tines of a fork. Place the crust in the freezer for at least 20 minutes or up to 2 hours.

2   Preheat the oven to 450°F. Bake the crust, directly from the freezer, until pale golden and crisp, 10 to 12 minutes. Let the piecrust cool slightly on a rack. Reduce the oven temperature to 400°F.

3   In a mixing bowl, whisk together the pumpkin, brown and granulated sugars, flour, spice blend, salt, and pepper. Whisk in the cream, milk, eggs, bourbon, and vanilla until smooth. Open the oven door and partially pull out the rack. Place the pie plate on the rack, then pour in the pumpkin filling. Slide the rack back into the oven and shut the door.

4   Bake until the filling is almost set, but still wobbly in the center, 40 to 45 minutes.

5   Let the pie cool on a rack, then serve at room temperature or lightly chilled. Store leftover pie in the refrigerator.

Spiked and Spiced Pumpkin Pie Tips

- Custards baked at high temperature usually need a water bath to keep them from curdling. However, baking in a crust does the trick for many custard pie recipes.
- Be sure to use a deep pie dish, especially if it is a 9-inch pie. The filling is generous.
- Since the filling will nearly fill the pie plate, the dish is first placed on the oven rack, then the filling is poured in—thus eliminating the need to lift and carry the liquid-filled piecrust.
- If you don't have pumpkin pie spice blend, a pleasing mixture of traditional spices, use the following: $1\frac{1}{2}$ teaspoons ground cinnamon, $\frac{1}{2}$ teaspoon grated nutmeg, $\frac{1}{2}$ teaspoon ground ginger, $\frac{1}{4}$ teaspoon ground allspice, and $\frac{1}{4}$ teaspoon ground cloves. The pepper is subtle but important—don't leave it out.

(continued)

- If you use canned pumpkin (which about 99 percent of us do), be sure it is plain puree, not sweetened pie filling—the cans look very similar.

- Most old-fashioned pies call for 2 cups pureed pumpkin. If you make your own, use this amount. However, today's canned pumpkin comes in a 15-ounce can, which measures about $1^3/_4$ cups. That's okay—don't buy another can unless you have use for the extra pumpkin.

- Uses for extra canned pumpkin include stirring a few tablespoons into creamed soups, mashed potatoes, custard sauces, softened ice cream, puddings, or pancake batter. Heat with an equal amount of maple syrup and use as a topping for waffles or pancakes.

Spiked and Spiced Pumpkin Pie Variations

- Substitute orange juice for the bourbon.

- Substitute 2 cups mashed sweet potatoes for the pumpkin puree—the pie will have a different but equally pleasing taste.

- For an even deeper caramel flavor, substitute dark brown sugar for the light brown sugar.

mile-high lemon meringue pie

There are as many recipes for this American classic as there are people who love it. In my informal survey, lemon meringue ranks up there with apple as the favorite pie of the men in my life, while women go more for Key lime pie, though apple is still tops in everyone's book. So, perhaps the way to a man's heart is indeed a lemon meringue pie. If so, this is the one you are looking for. It is quite tart with a mile-high meringue, thanks to the extra egg white.

Lemon meringue pie is not hard to make, but it is key to have the crust completely cooled, the filling hot, and the meringue ready to spread.

One-half 15-ounce package refrigerated folded piecrusts

2 tablespoons lemon or orange marmalade

FILLING

1 cup sugar

1/3 cup cornstarch

1/2 teaspoon salt

1/4 teaspoon grated nutmeg

2 cups water

1/2 cup fresh lemon juice

1 1/2 tablespoons grated lemon zest

4 large egg yolks, at room temperature

2 tablespoons unsalted butter

MERINGUE

5 large egg whites, at room temperature

1/4 teaspoon salt

1/4 teaspoon cream of tartar

1/2 cup sugar

1/4 teaspoon almond extract

1   Keeping one crust refrigerated for another use, unfold the other crust and ease it into a deep 9-inch pie plate. Flute or crimp the edges. Prick the bottom of the crust 8 or 10 times with the tines of a fork. Place the pie plate in the freezer for at least 30 minutes or up to 2 hours.

(continued)

2   Preheat the oven to 450°F. Bake the crust, directly from the freezer, until richly golden and crisp, 12 to 14 minutes. Let the crust cool completely on a rack. Brush the bottom of the crust with the marmalade.

3   For the filling: In a heavy saucepan, whisk together the sugar, cornstarch, salt, and nutmeg. Whisk in the water, lemon juice, and lemon zest. Bring to a boil over medium heat, stirring or whisking almost constantly, about 5 minutes. Boil and whisk for 1 minute. Place the egg yolks in a small bowl and whisk in about 1 cup of the hot lemon mixture until blended. Whisk the egg mixture back into the saucepan, reduce the heat to low, and cook, stirring gently, until the custard is thickened, 1 to 2 minutes. Do not allow to come to a full boil. Remove the pan from the heat and stir in the butter until melted and smooth. Let the filling cool for about 10 minutes while you make the meringue.

4   Preheat the oven to 350°F. Position the rack in the center of the oven.

5   For the meringue: In a large, grease-free bowl of an electric mixer, beat the egg whites at medium speed until they are frothy. Add the salt and cream of tartar, and beat until soft peaks form, 3 to 5 minutes. Gradually beat in the sugar, 2 tablespoons at a time, until the meringue stands in firm, shiny, moist peaks when the beaters are lifted, 3 to 4 minutes. Beat in the almond extract.

6   Pour and spread the warm filling in the cooled piecrust. Spoon the meringue over the filling in big dollops, spreading to completely cover the filling. Spread the meringue to the edges of the piecrust to seal in the filling. Use a blunt knife or thin spatula to mound the meringue in the center, swirling and making small peaks all over.

7   Immediately place the pie in the oven and bake until the meringue is pale golden and the peaks are richly golden, 12 to 15 minutes.

8   Cool the pie completely on a rack, then serve at room temperature or chilled. Store leftover pie in the refrigerator.

Mile-High Lemon Meringue Pie **Tips**

- The filling needs to be hot in order to lightly "poach" the meringue that comes in contact with the filling, thus sealing the meringue to the filling and keeping it from slipping off—a common problem with meringue pies.
- Brushing the bottom of the pie shell with the marmalade helps seal it from the hot filling.
- Baking the meringue at moderate heat helps to cook and firm the egg whites, though they may not be completely cooked; so, if undercooked eggs pose a potential health problem for you, cover the cooled filling in the pie crust with whipped cream instead of meringue.
- Don't refrigerate the pie until the meringue is fully cooled, or else beads of moisture may form on the meringue—another common problem with meringue pies.

Mile-High Lemon Meringue Pie **Variations**

- This can be a lime or lemon-lime meringue pie just as easily. Use the same quantities of citrus juice and zest.
- Make individual lemon meringue tarts, using eight 4-inch tart shells. Fully bake the piecrust in the shells, fill each with the filling (there may be some left over), then mound with the meringue and bake as directed.
- Instead of making the meringue, chill the filling in the pie, then top the pie with lightly sweetened whipped cream, and sprinkle with grated lemon zest.

double chocolate cream pie

A cream pie is simply a cooked custard poured into a fully baked piecrust—as easy as a pie gets. But it should be served on the day that it is assembled or the custard may begin to weep and soften the piecrust. This problem is minimized here by brushing the bottom of the baked crust with melted chocolate and letting it firm up before adding the filling. Refrigerate the leftovers, which taste just fine, weepy or not.

Cream pies are like a pudding in a piecrust, and thus probably the ultimate in comfort desserts. There are endless variations on the theme, but somehow "chocolate" and "pudding" are words that always taste the most delicious together. The only real difference between pudding and pie filling is that the latter needs to be thicker so that it will cut into neat (though still soft) slices. This can be accomplished by using extra egg yolks, butter, cornstarch, or more chocolate. I opt for the chocolate—no surprise.

One-half 15-ounce package refrigerated folded piecrusts

6 ounces bittersweet or semisweet chocolate

$^3/_4$ cup sugar

3 tablespoons cornstarch

2 tablespoons unsweetened cocoa powder

2 $^3/_4$ cups half-and-half or whole milk

1 large egg

3 large egg yolks

1 tablespoon unsalted butter

2 teaspoons vanilla extract

1 cup heavy cream, well chilled

1 tablespoon confectioners' sugar

1   Keeping one crust refrigerated for another use, unfold the other crust and ease it into a 9-inch pie plate. Flute or crimp the edges. Prick the bottom of the crust 8 or 10 times with the tines of a fork. Place the pie plate in the freezer for at least 30 minutes and up to 2 hours.

2   Preheat the oven to 450°F. Bake the piecrust, directly from the freezer, until it is richly golden, 12 to 14 minutes. Let the piecrust cool completely on a rack. In a small dish or saucepan, melt

about one-sixth of the chocolate (about 1 ounce) in the microwave oven or over very low heat on the stovetop.

3   Grate about 1 tablespoon of the chocolate and reserve, then chop the remaining chocolate. Melt about 2 tablespoons of the chopped chocolate in the microwave or on the stovetop. Brush the melted chocolate onto the bottom and sides of the cooled pie shell. Let stand until the chocolate is firm.

4   In a medium saucepan, whisk together the sugar, cornstarch, and cocoa, then slowly whisk in the half-and-half. Set the pan over medium heat and cook, stirring or whisking almost constantly, until the mixture thickens and boils for 1 minute. In a small bowl, whisk together the egg and yolks. Whisk in about $1\frac{1}{2}$ cups of the cream mixture to warm the eggs, then whisk back into the saucepan. Cook, stirring, until the custard thickens, but does not completely boil, about 2 minutes. Remove the pan from the heat, add the butter, vanilla, and remaining chopped chocolate. Let stand for about 2 minutes, then gently stir until smooth. Cool the custard for about 15 minutes, then pour into the prepared piecrust. Refrigerate the pie until ready to serve, up to 6 hours.

5   No more than 1 hour before serving, whip the cream and confectioners' sugar to firm peaks, and spread over the top of the pie to completely cover the filling. Sprinkle with the reserved grated chocolate. Refrigerate until ready to serve.

Double Chocolate Cream Pie Tips

- If you want to make the filling and crust several hours ahead of time, keep the crust at room temperature, but refrigerate the filling with a piece of plastic wrap applied directly to the surface in order to keep a "skin" from forming on the surface.
- Once a cornstarch-thickened mixture is cooked, avoid stirring excessively or the cornstarch will tend to break down and thin the custard.
- Though the pie is stored in the refrigerator, it is best served at cool room temperature. *(continued)*

Double Chocolate Cream Pie **Variations**

- For White Chocolate Cream Pie, delete the cocoa and replace the bitter-sweet chocolate with bar white chocolate (not chips).

- For Vanilla Cream Pie, delete the cocoa and chocolate. Increase the cornstarch to 4 tablespoons and cook a whole, split vanilla bean with the half-and-half in the filling. After completing the custard, remove the vanilla bean and scrape the seeds back into the filling.

- For Banana Cream Pie, first brush the baked piecrust with 1 tablespoon apricot or other golden jam or marmalade, then make a layer of 2 thinly sliced bananas. Add the Vanilla Cream or Chocolate Cream filling and whipped cream. Just before serving, top with another thinly sliced banana.

- For a Coconut Cream Pie, first brush the baked piecrust with 1 tablespoon ginger marmalade or other golden jam or marmalade. Fold $^3/_4$ cup toasted coconut into Vanilla Cream filling, then spoon into the piecrust, top with whipped cream, and sprinkle with an additional $^1/_4$ cup toasted coconut.

tarts

Tarts are generally a more **elegant** version of pies. But amazingly, they are also generally **easier** to make. In some cases, a tart is simply a single crust or free-form variation on a fruit pie, serving fewer people and thus more appropriate for a small family. Tarts can be **beautifully** fashioned and topped with glistening berries or served inverted with a caramelized fruit filling under a **crisp crust**. Tartlets are individual tarts, and everyone likes to have a dessert of their own, which is espccially impressive at a **dinner party**

apple-pear galette

A galette is like a thin tart; in France it is usually made with puff pastry. It can be any shape, but this square galette is the easiest when you use frozen puff pastry, with its roughly square sheets. Though they look and taste very elegant, most galettes are ridiculously easy to make. You can use a combination of autumn fruits, but the basic galette can be adapted to any season. Serve it warm from the oven to rave reviews.

1 sheet frozen puff pastry from a 17.3-ounce box, thawed but well chilled

$1/3$ cup finely chopped walnuts

$1/3$ cup sugar

$1/2$ teaspoon ground cinnamon

$1/4$ teaspoon grated nutmeg

2 small tart apples, such as Granny Smith, peeled, cored, and thinly sliced

2 ripe, firm pears, peeled, cored, and thinly sliced

1 tablespoon chilled unsalted butter, cut into 4 pieces

1   Preheat the oven to 400°F. On a large ungreased baking sheet, roll the puff pastry to an 11- or 12-inch square. Use a sharp knife to trim the edges evenly, then cut a $1/2$-inch strip from all four edges. Place the strip on top of the edges to form a border on all four sides. Place the baking sheet in the freezer for 10 minutes.

2   In a mixing bowl, stir together the nuts, sugar, cinnamon, and nutmeg. Sprinkle half of the mixture on the puff pastry, inside the border. Make alternating and overlapping rows of apples and pears on top of the nut mixture. Use your fingers to rub the butter into the remaining nut mixture until crumbly. Sprinkle the nut mixture over the fruit.

3   Bake until the pastry edges are well puffed and rich golden brown, the fruit is tender, and the topping crisp, about 30 minutes.

4 Let the tart cool slightly on the baking sheet, then use a wide spatula to loosen it. Serve warm or at room temperature, cut into squares.

Apple-Pear Galette **Tips**

- It doesn't matter if you roll the pastry to an exact square, since the edges will be trimmed.
- Rolling the pastry on the baking sheet saves transferring it from a board to the sheet.
- If you wish, use two spatulas to transfer the baked galette from the baking sheet to a serving platter or board.

Apple-Pear Galette **Variations**

- Use pears in place of the apples.
- Use quartered apricots and plums in place of the apples and pears. Arrange the fruit quarters in an attractive pattern.
- Other nuts, such as almonds, can be used in place of the walnuts.

nectarine five-spice tarts

When making round puff pastry tarts, start with frozen puff pastry shells, which are already shaped in perfect rounds. Using a rolling pin to lightly flatten the rounds still allows puffing of the edges to form a tart shell, but the shell isn't quite as high as the shell pictured on the box when baked.

One 10-ounce box frozen puff pastry shells, thawed but well
chilled
$1/4$ cup sugar
2 teaspoons Chinese five-spice blend
5 small nectarines, cored and thinly sliced
2 tablespoons unsalted butter, cut into small pieces
1/4 cup peach preserves
1 tablespoon dark rum

1   On a lightly floured surface, roll each of the 6 pastry shells, perforated side up, to a 5- or 6-inch circle. Arrange at least 2 inches apart, on a large ungreased baking sheet. Place the baking sheet in the freezer for at least 10 minutes.

2   Preheat the oven to 400°F. In a small dish, stir together the sugar and five-spice blend. Sprinkle each of the pastry shells with about 2 teaspoons of the sugar mixture. Arrange the nectarines, overlapping in a spoke fashion on the pastry shells, leaving a $1/2$-inch border all around. Scatter the butter atop the fruit and sprinkle with the remaining sugar.

3   Bake until the edges of the tarts are risen and rich golden brown, and the fruit is soft and bubbly, about 20 minutes.

4   While the tarts are baking, heat the preserves and rum in a small saucepan or microwave oven. Brush the warm tarts with the preserves mixture.

5   Let the tarts cool slightly, then serve warm or at room temperature.

Nectarine Five-Spice Tarts **Tips**

- Chinese five-spice blend is a mixture of cinnamon, cloves, anise, ginger, and often licorice root. It is found in the dried-spice section of the market, and is a common aromatic blend in Chinese cooking.
- Nectarines are perfect here, since they don't need to be peeled, and their lovely rosy-golden skins make a very pretty presentation.
- Be sure to roll and bake the pastry shells, perforated side up, since that helps the sides puff while the interior stays flat.
- Don't worry if the pastry shells don't roll to a perfect circle—they will look just as nice with a "homemade" edge.

Nectarine Five-Spice Tarts **Variations**

- Quartered Italian prune plums or peeled and sliced peaches can be substituted for the nectarines.
- Use other spices, such as cinnamon, cloves, or nutmeg, in place of the five-spice blend.
- Bake rectangular tarts by unfolding one sheet (from a $17\frac{1}{4}$-ounce box) of puff pastry along the fold lines, then cutting each piece in half to form 6 square pastry bases.

caramel apple
upside-down tart

This is a classic "tarte Tatin," except that most French versions use puff pastry, which makes an equally delicious upside-down tart. However, I just like apples with a classic piecrust, and prefer more delicate fruit, such as apricots or pears, with puff pastry.

Be sure to use a heavy, deep, ovenproof skillet that will caramelize the apples and distribute the heat evenly. Cast iron is the traditional skillet.

The technique of shaping and partially freezing the pie pastry to form an inverted hollow allows it to be tucked around the hot apples without the risk of burning your fingers.

> **One-half 15-ounce package refrigerated folded piecrusts**
>
> **6 tablespoons unsalted butter, softened**
>
> **$2/3$ cup sugar**
>
> **1 teaspoon ground cinnamon**
>
> **2 pounds (5 or 6) tart apples, such as Granny Smith**
>
> **$1/2$ pound (1 large) fragrant apple, such as Golden Delicious**
>
> **1 tablespoon lemon juice**

1   Line a 9- or 10-inch heavy, deep, ovenproof skillet with plastic wrap. Keeping one crust refrigerated for another use, unfold the other crust and ease it into the lined skillet. Use a knife to make 4 small slits at the folds. Place the skillet in the freezer for at least 15 minutes and up to 2 hours. Using the plastic wrap as an aid, transfer the piecrust to a plate and refrigerate until ready to use.

2   Smear the butter thickly over the bottom of the skillet. Sprinkle evenly with the sugar and the cinnamon. Peel, core, and slice the apples about $3/4$ inch thick. Arrange the apple slices, overlapping and packing together tightly in concentric circles over the sugar. Drizzle with lemon juice.

3   Preheat the oven to 400°F. Place the skillet over medium-high heat and cook, undisturbed, until the juices turn a rich caramel color, about 15 minutes. If the caramel begins to brown unevenly, rotate the skillet on the burner.

4   Place the piecrust, rimmed side down, on the apples so that the pastry covers the apples and tucks in around the rim of the pan. Return to the oven and bake until the apple juices bubble

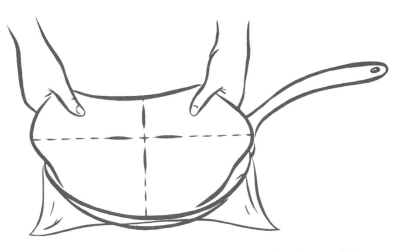

up around the pastry and the crust is rich golden brown, about 25 minutes.

5 Remove the tart from the oven, let it stand for 5 minutes, then use a spatula to loosen the edges. Place a large, rimmed plate on top of the skillet. Holding the plate and the skillet, invert the tart onto the plate. Carefully lift off the skillet. Scrape any apples and caramel clinging to the skillet back onto the tart.

6 Let the tart cool for about 20 minutes, then serve warm or at room temperature.

Caramel Apple Upside-Down Tart **Tips**

- If the handle of your skillet isn't ovenproof at high temperatures, wrap it in a double thickness of heavy-duty aluminum foil before placing it in the oven.
- Remember that the handle of the skillet will be very, very hot when removed from the oven. Drape a potholder or kitchen towel over it to remind yourself not to touch the handle.

Caramel Apple Upside-Down Tart **Variations**

- Sprinkle $1/3$ cup coarsely chopped walnuts over the butter-sugar mixture in the skillet before adding the apples.
- Toss 2 tablespoons Calvados or applejack with the apples before adding to the skillet.
- Thickly sliced firm pears can be used in place of the apples.

apricot tarte tatin

Apples are the traditional fruit for a tarte Tatin, but apricots are especially elegant. This most sophisticated French dessert has but five ingredients and a very simple preparation, especially with the advantage of prepared puff pastry. The key is to buy really good fruit, and watch the pan during the caramelization process.

One-half 17.3-ounce package frozen puff pastry, thawed but well chilled

5 tablespoons unsalted butter, softened

$1/2$ cup sugar

9 medium apricots (about 2 pounds), halved and pitted

1 tablespoon brandy or Amaretto

1   Keeping one sheet of puff pastry refrigerated or frozen for another use, unfold the other puff pastry sheet. On a lightly floured surface, roll the pastry to an 11-inch square, then trim to form a $10^{1}/_{2}$-inch circle. Place the pastry on an ungreased baking sheet and refrigerate it.

2   Preheat the oven to 425°F. Smear the butter in the bottom of a 10-inch heavy ovenproof skillet, then sprinkle with the sugar. Arrange the apricots, cut side up, in tight concentric circles on the sugar. Sprinkle the fruit with the brandy. Set the pan over direct medium-high heat and cook, without stirring, until the juices are golden and caramelized, about 12 minutes. If the juices begin to color unevenly, rotate the pan on the burner.

3   Remove the pan from the heat, place the puff pastry round on the bubbling fruit. Immediately place the tart in the oven and bake until the pastry is puffed and rich golden brown, 20 to 25 minutes.

4   Remove the skillet from the oven (taking care to use a potholder on the handle) and let it stand for 5 minutes. Use a small spatula to loosen the edges, then place a rimmed serving plate on top of the skillet. Holding the plate, invert the skillet onto the plate. Carefully lift off the skillet, then use the spatula to scrape off any fruit or caramel clinging to the skillet and replace it onto the tart.

5 Let the tart cool for about 15 minutes, then serve warm or at room temperature.

Apricot Tarte Tatin Tips

- Buy firm, but not hard apricots of uniform size for the most attractive presentation.
- Be sure to keep the puff pastry round well chilled until you place it on the bubbling tart.
- Remember that the skillet handle is very hot when you remove it from the oven. Use a potholder or oven mitt, then drape a towel or oven mitt over the handle as it cools so you won't be tempted to pick it up.

Apricot Tarte Tatin Variations

- Apricots are a late spring and summer fruit, so in the autumn make a traditional apple or a pear tarte Tatin, and in the winter use thickly sliced oranges or sliced pineapple. The quantity of the fruit should be enough to tightly cover the bottom of the pan.
- Use rum or another liqueur to flavor the tart, or eliminate the liqueur completely.
- Top a warm slice of tarte Tatin with a small scoop of vanilla ice cream to melt and form a cool custard sauce.

citrus custard tart

More delicate and lighter than many custard pies, this tart is full of bright citrus flavor. The custard is poured into a fully baked shell that is brushed with marmalade, then baked in a moderate oven just until the filling is set. Unlike most fruit pies and tarts, this one should be made in the winter or early spring, as this is when oranges and lemons are at their peak.

One-half 15-ounce package refrigerated folded piecrusts

1$^{1}/_{2}$ tablespoons orange or lemon marmalade

4 large eggs

$^{3}/_{4}$ cup sugar

$^{1}/_{3}$ cup fresh orange juice

$^{1}/_{4}$ cup fresh lemon juice

3 tablespoons heavy cream

2 teaspoons grated orange zest

1 teaspoon grated lemon zest

1 Keeping one crust refrigerated for another use, unfold the other crust and ease it into a 9-inch tart pan with a removable bottom. Fold any crust that hangs over the side inward to reinforce the edge of the tart. Press firmly to form the rippled edges, then use a rolling pin or sharp knife to trim the pastry even with the top of the tart pan. Prick the bottom of the tart 4 or 5 times with the tines of a fork. Place the tart shell in the freezer for at least 20 minutes and up to 2 hours.

2 Preheat the oven to 450°F. Bake the tart shell, directly from the freezer, until it is golden and crisp, 12 to 14 minutes. Let cool completely on a rack. Brush the bottom of the tart shell with the marmalade. Reduce the oven heat to 350°F.

3 In a mixing bowl, whisk the eggs until blended. Then whisk in the orange and lemon juices, cream, and orange and lemon zests until blended. Open the oven door and partially pull out the center rack. Place the tart shell in the center of the rack. Pour the custard into the baked pastry shell. Slide the rack back into the oven and close the door.

4   Bake until the filling is just set, 25 to 30 minutes. Let the tart cool completely on a rack, then serve at room temperature. Store any leftover tart in the refrigerator.

Citrus Custard Tart Tips

- Be sure to use fresh lemon juice. The bottled lemon and lime juices found in the produce section are never good substitutes. Frozen lemon juice is fine for most uses, but not when lemon zest is also needed.
- Pouring the filling into the tart on the oven rack eliminates the need to carry a liquid-filled tart shell.
- A knife inserted about 1 inch from the center will come out clean when the custard is done. It will still be soft in the center, but will continue to firm up as it cools.

Citrus Custard Tart Variations

- Lime juice can be substituted for lemon, or the tart can be made with equal quantities lime, lemon, and orange juice and zest, but increase the sugar by 1 tablespoon to compensate for the tartness of the lemon and lime.
- If you really like citrus, increase the grated zest to a total of 3 or even 4 teaspoons.
- You will have leftover heavy cream, no doubt, so whip it and serve sprinkled with a little nutmeg on the top of each serving.

dark and white chocolate soufflé tarts

Soufflés are a bit overrated to my mind. They are spectacular as they come to the table, but even the most richly flavored soufflé gets a little boring after a few bites of fluff. So, I set out to bake a soufflé in a piecrust to add a little textural interest, and it worked perfectly. The key is a sturdy enough soufflé mixture so that it can mound in the crust without running over, and chocolate provides the needed body. The result is a lovely, puffed tart that combines the best of pie and soufflé. The surprise dark chocolate layer in the crust is an added bonus, and extra chocolate is always welcome, of course.

You will need eight 4-inch round tartlet pans with removable bottoms for this recipe. If you don't have them, you can order them from any kitchenware store or website. They are worth the small investment.

One 15-ounce package refrigerated folded piecrusts

3 ounces bittersweet chocolate, coarsely chopped

4 ounces white chocolate baking bar, chopped

2 tablespoons Cognac or brandy

2 eggs, separated

1 egg white

2 tablespoons sugar

1   Working with one crust at a time, and keeping the other one refrigerated, cut the pastry into quarters along the fold lines. Ease each quarter into a 4-inch tart pan with a removable bottom. Remove the excess dough and press and piece it into any areas that are not covered with dough. Press the dough firmly against the sides of the pans. Use a small knife or a rolling pin to trim the pastry to the top of the tart edge. Prick the bottoms of the tarts 2 or 3 times with the tines of a fork. You will have 8 tart shells. Place the tart shells in the freezer for at least 30 minutes or up to 2 hours.

2   Preheat the oven to 450°F. Bake the tart shells, directly from the freezer, until they are pale golden, about 10 minutes. Remove from the oven and sprinkle evenly with the chopped bittersweet chocolate. Let the shells stand while you make the filling. Reduce the oven temperature to 400°F.

3   In a small bowl or saucepan, melt the white chocolate with the Cognac in the microwave oven or over very low heat on the stovetop. One at a time, quickly beat in the egg yolks. Let the mixture cool slightly. In a large mixing bowl, beat the egg whites until frothy, then slowly beat in the sugar until the whites form firm, glossy peaks when the beaters are raised. Stir a spoonful of egg whites into the chocolate mixture to lighten it, then fold the chocolate into the remaining egg whites.

4   Spoon the mixture into the baked tart shells, mounding in the center and using a heaping ¼ cup soufflé mixture for each tart shell. Bake until the soufflé is puffed and golden on the top, 10 to 12 minutes.

5   Remove from the oven and carefully slip the sides off the tart pans, then slide the tarts onto dessert plates. Serve immediately.   *(continued)*

Dark and White Chocolate Soufflé Tarts **Tips**

- The chocolate in this soufflé gives it body and stabilizes it a bit, so it won't immediately fall when taken out of the oven. Further, it is excellent served at room temperature, when the soufflé does collapse a bit, but is still a light, puffy custard.
- The tart shells can be baked ahead of time or just before the soufflé is baked—no need to cool the shells completely.
- Be sure to use a high-quality white chocolate bar. White chocolate chips do not melt in the same way, and can be difficult to use.

Dark and White Chocolate Soufflé Tarts **Variations**

- Sprinkle the bottom of each tart with 1 tablespoon chopped hazelnuts, then flavor the soufflé mixture with hazelnut liqueur or syrup.
- Flavor the white chocolate mixture with rum or orange liqueur, and layer thin slices of orange on the tart shell instead of chopped bittersweet chocolate.
- Reverse the chocolates and make the soufflé with bittersweet chocolate, sprinkling the tart shell with chopped white chocolate.

berries brûlée tart

This is the absolute in sophisticated simplicity. Use fresh, seasonal berries—a mix of raspberry colors makes a particularly pretty tart. Crème fraîche is now widely available in the dairy section of many markets, but regular sour cream is an excellent substitute. The crust can be made ahead of time, and the tart assembled in minutes just before serving.

One-half 18-ounce tube refrigerated sugar cookie dough

1 cup crème fraîche or sour cream

1 tablespoon Grand Marnier or orange juice

2 teaspoons grated orange zest

2 cups raspberries, preferably a mix of red, black, and golden raspberries

$^1/_3$ cup packed light brown sugar

1   Preheat the oven to 350°F. Use your hands to press the dough evenly onto the bottom and sides of a 9-inch tart pan with a removable bottom. Bake until the cookie crust is golden and set, 20 to 23 minutes. Let the crust cool completely on a rack.

2   Preheat the broiler. Position the rack 4 to 5 inches from the heat source.

3   In a small bowl, gently stir together the crème fraîche, Grand Marnier, and orange zest. Spread the mixture over the bottom of the baked crust. Sprinkle evenly with the berries. Press the brown sugar through a sieve to sprinkle evenly over the tart. Broil, watching carefully to prevent burning, until the sugar is melted and bubbly, 1 to 2 minutes.

4   Serve the tart immediately, cut into wedges.

(continued)

Berries Brûlée Tart Tips

- Be sure to position the tart between 4 and 5 inches from the broiler heat source—any closer, the sugar might burn; farther away, it might not melt quickly enough. Watch carefully, since the broiler cooks quickly.
- The cookie crust can be made a day ahead and stored, covered, at room temperature. The crème fraîche filling can be made a few hours ahead and refrigerated. But the tart should be assembled and broiled shortly before serving.
- Do not overstir crème fraîche or sour cream, since this may cause it to thin out.

Berries Brûlée Tart Variations

- Other berries or combinations, such as blueberries and/or strawberries, can be substituted for the raspberries.
- Substitute Amaretto or another liqueur, or a flavored syrup for the Grand Marnier.
- Substitute 1 teaspoon grated lemon zest for the grated orange zest.

fruit and nut holiday tart

If you like apple pie, you will love this festive holiday variation. Add it to your Thanksgiving pie repertoire, or serve it for Christmas dinner. But my favorite way to enjoy it is for breakfast, with a ladle of cream or eggnog spooned over it.

6 tablespoons sugar

1 small clementine or seedless orange, quartered

$1/2$ pound (1 large or 2 small) tart apples, such as Granny Smith, peeled, cored, and diced

$1/4$ cup golden raisins

$1/4$ cup dried cranberries

$1/4$ cup lemon- or orange-flavored prunes, snipped into small pieces

$1/4$ cup snipped dried apples

$1/3$ cup apple cider or orange juice

1 tablespoon lemon juice

1 teaspoon grated lemon zest

1 teaspoon apple pie spice blend

$1/3$ cup chopped walnuts

One-half 15-ounce package refrigerated folded piecrusts

1 tablespoon whole milk or light cream

1 Measure and reserve 2 teaspoons of the sugar. In a food processor, pulse to chop the clementine into small pieces. Place the chopped clementine in a medium saucepan. Add the apples, raisins, cranberries, prunes, dried apples, and remaining sugar. Stir to mix. Add the cider, lemon juice and zest, and spice blend. Bring to a boil, stirring often. Reduce the heat to medium-low and simmer, uncovered and stirring occasionally, until the mixture is thickened, about 10 minutes. Set aside to cool completely. Stir in the nuts.

2 Preheat the oven to 425°F. Keeping one crust refrigerated for another use, unfold the other crust and place it on a baking sheet. Spoon the cooled filling onto the crust, leaving a $1^1/2$-inch

border. Fold the pastry border back over the filling to make an uneven rustic edge of about 1$\frac{1}{2}$ inches. Brush the border with the milk and sprinkle with the reserved 2 teaspoons sugar.

3 Bake for 20 minutes. Reduce the oven temperature to 400°F and bake until the filling is bubbly and the crust is rich golden brown, 15 to 20 minutes more.

4 Serve the tart warm or at room temperature, cut into wedges.

Fruit and Nut Holiday Tart Tips

- The filling can be made a day ahead and refrigerated. Return it to room temperature before completing the tart.
- The tart is best served on the day of baking, but it is also good the next morning, straight from the refrigerator or warmed slightly in the oven.
- Use "fresh" soft dried fruit; squeeze the package a bit before buying as a test.

Fruit and Nut Holiday Tart Variations

- Other spices, nuts, and dried or fresh fruits, especially pears, can be used in the same proportion here.
- It's just as easy to make a double recipe of filling, so consider making two tarts—one for dinner and one for breakfast.
- Serve the warm tart with a ladle of chilled prepared dairy eggnog poured over, or serve it with a small scoop of eggnog ice cream.

summer peach tart

Though peaches are available nearly year round, the only ones worth buying are ripe, plump, and fragrant fruit. And those are only available in the summer. Peaches, like many summer fruits, must be picked at their peak. (Although they may "soften" off the tree, they won't ripen or improve in any other way during transit and storage.) So this is a tart for summer only, and you may dress it up with a mint sprig—the classic culinary "accessory" of the summer season.

> 1 pound ripe peaches, peeled, cored, and sliced
>
> 1/2 cup sugar
>
> 1 tablespoon flour
>
> 2 teaspoons amaretto
>
> 2 teaspoons lemon juice
>
> 1 teaspoon grated lemon zest
>
> One-half 15-ounce package refrigerated folded piecrusts
>
> 1 tablespoon whole milk or light cream
>
> 1 mint sprig

1   Preheat the oven to 425°F. Place the peaches in a mixing bowl. Measure and reserve 2 teaspoons of the sugar, then add the remaining sugar to the peaches along with the flour, amaretto, lemon juice and zest. Toss to mix well. Set aside while you prepare the crust.

2   Keeping one crust refrigerated for another use, unfold the other crust and place it on a baking sheet. Spoon the filling onto the crust, heaping it in the center and leaving a 1½-inch border. Fold the pastry border back over the filling to make an uneven rustic edge of about 1½ inches. Brush the pastry border with milk and sprinkle with the reserved 2 teaspoons sugar.

3   Bake for 20 minutes. Reduce the oven temperature to 400°F and bake until the filling is bubbly and the crust is rich golden brown, 15 to 20 minutes more.

4   Serve the tart warm or at room temperature, cut into wedges.   *(continued)*

Summer Peach Tart **Tips**

- Bake the tart as soon as the pastry is filled so that the bottom does not become soggy.
- Don't worry about making a fancy border. The beauty of the tart is its freeform shape.
- Look for peaches that are plump and slightly soft, but not mushy. A ripe peach will have a fragrant perfume.

Summer Peach Tart **Variations**

- Substitute peeled and sliced apricots for the peaches.
- Substitute plums for the peaches, increasing the flour to $1^1/_2$ tablespoons.
- Substitute peeled, cored, and sliced pears for the peaches.
- Add $^1/_3$ cup blueberries to the filling.

chocolate mint strawberry tart

Unbelievably easy, this tart is one of my most often baked desserts, since it combines pastry, chocolate, and strawberries—an all-time favorite combination. It looks bakery-perfect and tastes homemade-terrific. Look for small strawberries, especially the increasingly available French fraises des bois, but most important is that the berries are of uniform size for the prettiest presentation.

One-half 15-ounce package refrigerated folded piecrusts

8 ounces bittersweet chocolate

1 cup heavy cream

2 tablespoons white crème de menthe

1 pint small strawberries (about 30 berries), hulled

2 tablespoons strawberry jelly

8 small sprigs fresh mint

1 Keeping one crust refrigerated for another use, unfold the other crust and ease it into a 9-inch tart pan with a removable bottom. Fold any crust that hangs over the side inward to reinforce the edge of the tart. Press firmly to form the rippled edges, then use a rolling pin or sharp knife to trim the pastry even with the top of the tart pan. Prick the bottom of the tart 4 or 5 times with the tines of a fork. Place the tart shell in the freezer for at least 20 minutes and up to 2 hours.

2 Preheat the oven to 450°F. Bake the tart shell, directly from the freezer, until it is golden and crisp, 12 to 14 minutes. Let cool completely on a rack.

3 In a small bowl set over hot water or in a microwave oven, gently melt the chocolate. Stir in ⅓ cup of the cream and 1 tablespoon of the crème de menthe until the mixture is smooth. Spread the chocolate over the bottom of the tart shell. (Refrigerate the remaining ⅔ cup heavy cream.)

4 Arrange the berries in concentric circles, hulled side down, in the lukewarm chocolate. Refrigerate the tart until the chocolate is set, 15 to 20 minutes. In a small saucepan or

microwave oven, melt the jelly with the remaining 1 tablespoon crème de menthe. Carefully brush the berries with the jelly, trying to avoid brushing the jelly on the crust or the chocolate. Refrigerate until ready to serve, up to 3 hours.

5 Shortly before serving, whip the reserved heavy cream to soft peaks.

6 To serve, cut the tart into wedges and serve each with a spoonful of softly whipped cream and garnished with a mint sprig.

Chocolate Mint Strawberry Tart Tips

- Strawberries should be rinsed before they are hulled, since the cut from the hull allows the berries to soak up water.
- Use strawberries within a day of purchase, since they have a rather short shelf life.
- Choose berries that smell fragrant—the best indicator of good taste.

Chocolate Mint Strawberry Tart Variations

- Use raspberries in place of the strawberries and brandy in place of the crème de menthe.
- Use lemon juice–sprinkled sliced bananas in place of the strawberries, and brush with orange marmalade melted with rum. This fruit should be added no more than 1 hour before serving.
- Use quartered apricots in place of the strawberries, and brush with apricot jelly melted with brandy.

anise fig and mascarpone puff tarts

MAKES 6
SERVINGS

Fresh figs are beautiful to the eye and delicate to the palate. They should be enjoyed only during the fleetingly short fall and early winter seasons, when they are at their best. Although figs can be simmered or baked, I think their gentle flavor is best enhanced with only a very short warming under the broiler—a reminder of the sun-ripening lushness of their native climates. Puff pastry makes a more elegant base for these tarts than traditional pie pastry.

8 ounces mascarpone cheese

2 tablespoons Pernod or other anise liqueur or syrup

5 tablespoons sugar

1 sheet frozen puff pastry from a 17.3-ounce package, thawed but well chilled

12 ripe, firm figs, stemmed and quartered

1   In a small bowl, stir together the mascarpone, Pernod, and 4 tablespoons of the sugar. Refrigerate for at least 30 minutes to dissolve the sugar.

2   Preheat the oven to 425°F. Unfold the puff pastry and cut along the fold lines to make 3 rectangles. Cut each rectangle in half. Place, at least 1 inch apart, on an ungreased baking sheet. Sprinkle with a total of 2 teaspoons of the remaining sugar. Prick each rectangle 6 or 7 times with the tines of a fork. Place the baking sheet in the freezer for 10 minutes.

3   Bake the pastries, directly from the freezer, for 10 minutes. Then reduce the temperature to 400°F, open the oven door, and quickly make several pricks in the pastry to deflate the puff a bit. Continue to bake until the pastry is rich golden brown and crisp, about 10 minutes more. Remove the baking sheet from the oven. Change the oven temperature to broil and position the oven rack to about 5 inches from the heat source.

4   Let the pastries cool for at least 3 minutes on the baking sheet, then spread with the cheese and arrange the fig quarters on the cheese. Sprinkle with the remaining 1 teaspoon sugar.

(continued)

5   Return the baking sheet to the oven. Broil until the cheese begins to bubble and the figs and tart edges are beginning to darken, about 1 minute. Serve warm.

Anise Fig and Mascarpone Puff Tarts Tips

- Pricking the pastry before and during baking will hold down the puff, which is preferable in this dessert.
- If you use anise or any other flavored syrup, it is most often found in the baking section or the coffee section of the market, or at many gourmet coffee shops.
- Figs spoil quickly and are often rather expensive, so shop carefully and buy fruit that is firm, but not hard, and has no bruising.

Anise Fig and Mascarpone Puff Tarts Variations

- Whipped cream cheese can be substituted for the mascarpone for a less rich version.
- Use fresh pineapple chunks in place of the figs, and orange or coconut liqueur in place of the Pernod.
- Use apricots in place of the figs, and Cognac in place of the Pernod (though Pernod is nice with apricots, too).

pastry

Pastries, like tarts, are often upscale, richer variations on homespun pies, but they are also part of the **heritage** of many of the great cuisines of Europe. Baklava from Greece, napoleons from France, eccles cakes from England, and strudels from Austria are important elements of those countries' **culinary** attractions. Visitors almost never come home without sampling these famous **creations**, often assumed to be bakery items and difficult to make at home. Prepared doughs such as puff pastry and phyllo not only **shortcut** the time, but guarantee superb results.

double chocolate napoleons

Napoleons, the darlings of fancy French pastry shops, are amazingly easy to make at home, even with the traditional chocolate filigree decoration on the top—all you need for this is a toothpick! The classic napoleon is filled with a rich vanilla pastry cream. This version is classic, with a little added chocolate, of course.

CHOCOLATE PASTRY CREAM

$1/3$ cup sugar

2 tablespoons flour

Pinch of salt

1 cup half-and-half or whole milk

1 vanilla bean, split open lengthwise

2 egg yolks, lightly beaten

3 ounces bittersweet chocolate, coarsely chopped

1 tablespoon unsalted butter

PASTRY AND DECORATION

1 sheet frozen puff pastry from a 17.3-ounce box, thawed but well chilled

3 ounces bittersweet chocolate, coarsely chopped

2 tablespoons heavy cream

2 ounces white chocolate baking bar, coarsely chopped

1   For the pastry cream: In a medium saucepan, stir together the sugar, flour, and salt. Whisk in the half-and-half. Add the vanilla bean. Cook over medium heat, whisking constantly, until the mixture is smooth, thickened, and bubbly, 3 to 5 minutes. Whisk about one-fourth of the mixture into the yolks to warm them, then return the yolks to the saucepan. Cook, whisking, until thickened and the mixture almost begins to bubble around the edges, about 1 minute. Remove from the heat and stir in the chocolate and butter until melted. Let cool, then discard the vanilla bean and refrigerate the pastry cream until well chilled, at least 2 hours or up to 2 days.

2   For the napoleons: Preheat the oven to 425°F. Unfold the puff pastry sheet and use a sharp knife to cut along the fold lines to make 3 strips. Cut each strip into 3 equal rectangles. Place, at least 1 inch apart, on an ungreased baking sheet. Place the baking sheet in the freezer for 10 minutes.

3   Bake the pastries, directly from the freezer, until they are well puffed, golden, and crisp, 15 to 18 minutes. Transfer to a rack to cool completely. Use a sharp knife to split each pastry rectangle in half horizontally. Set aside 6 of the prettiest pastry tops for the decorated top layer of the napoleons.

4   In a small bowl over hot water, or in a microwave oven, melt together the bittersweet chocolate and the cream, stirring until smooth. In another small bowl, melt the white chocolate and stir until smooth. Carefully spread the bittersweet chocolate over the uncut side of the reserved pastry tops. Use a spoon to drizzle the melted white chocolate in 3 crosswise rows over the iced pastry tops. Use a toothpick to draw 3 lines through the white chocolate rows to make a decorative squiggle into the dark chocolate. Place the decorated tops in the refrigerator for a few minutes to set the chocolate.

5   Meanwhile, spread the chocolate pastry cream smoothly onto the cut sides of the remaining 12 pastry rectangles. Stack to make 6 pastries, then top with the reserved decorated pastries.

6   Refrigerate the filled and decorated napoleons for at least 1 hour and up to 6 hours before serving. *(continued)*

Double Chocolate Napoleons Tips

- Don't skip the chilling step, which firms up the pastry cream and keeps the napoleons "glued" together.
- It is especially important here to use a sharp knife to cut the puff pastry into rectangles, so that each will rise to its fullest potential.
- Decorating with the toothpick is much easier than it sounds. Even if you don't have a practiced and steady hand, the artwork will still look great . . . and original.

Double Chocolate Napoleons Variations

- Make a Mocha Napoleon by dissolving 1 tablespoon instant espresso or coffee in the pastry cream, and decorate the tops with chocolate-covered coffee beans.
- Instead of icing the top, simply dust with powdered sugar or cocoa powder.
- Omit the white chocolate drizzles, and decorate the tops of the iced napoleons with raspberries.
- Whip $1^1/_2$ cups heavy cream with 2 tablespoons confectioners' sugar and 1 tablespoon rose water. Fold in $^1/_2$ cup coarsely chopped pistachios. Spread the layers with the whipped cream, then layer with about 1 pound sliced apricots, if desired.

eccles cakes

These little cakes from Lancashire, England, are really pastries. Served in smaller versions (see Variations) as sweet tea cakes, the larger ones are lovely as dessert or for breakfast, in England or America. If you like raisins, you will love these cakes. If you don't like raisins, fill the cakes with whatever chopped dried fruit you fancy.

$1/2$ cup golden raisins

$1/2$ cup dark raisins

$1/2$ cup dried currants

$1/4$ cup finely chopped candied orange peel

2 tablespoons finely chopped fresh ginger

2 teaspoons grated lemon zest

$1/2$ teaspoon grated nutmeg

$1/2$ teaspoon ground cinnamon

$1/8$ teaspoon ground cloves

$1/4$ cup packed dark brown sugar

3 tablespoons unsalted butter, melted

2 tablespoons lemon juice

One 10-ounce box frozen puff pastry shells, thawed but well chilled

1 egg white, beaten until frothy

2 teaspoons granulated sugar

1   In a mixing bowl, stir together the golden and dark raisins, currants, candied orange peel, ginger, lemon zest, nutmeg, cinnamon, and cloves. Stir in the brown sugar, butter, and lemon juice until blended.

2   Preheat the oven to 400°F. Roll each pastry shell to a 6-inch circle. Spoon the filling into the center of each circle. Brush the edges of the circles with the egg white, then fold the edges up and around the filling to enclose it completely. Press and seal the pastry with your fingers. Place the pastries, smooth side up, at least 2 inches apart on an ungreased baking sheet. Brush the tops

with more egg white, taking care not to allow it to drip down the sides, then sprinkle with the granulated sugar. Place the baking sheet in the freezer for 10 minutes.

3   Bake, directly from the freezer, until the pastries are well puffed and rich golden brown, 22 to 25 minutes. (If the pastries begin to brown too much before the end of the baking time, reduce the oven temperature to 375°F.)

4   Transfer the pastries to a rack to cool. Serve warm or at room temperature.

Eccles Cakes Tips

- The cakes can be baked several hours in advance, and reheated on a baking sheet in a 300°F oven for about 5 minutes.
- The egg white "glues" the pastry edges together. If it runs down the top of the pastry onto the baking sheet, it will also glue the pastry to the baking sheet, thus preventing maximum rise. Take care not to drip the egg white onto the baking sheet.
- If your raisins and dried fruit are a bit too dried, plump them a bit by microwaving for a few seconds in a covered dish with about $1/2$ inch water, or apple or orange juice.

Eccles Cakes Variations

- Make 12 to 16 smaller tea "cakes" by using one sheet from a 17.3-ounce box of frozen puff pastry. Roll to about $1/8$-inch thickness, then cut with a $3^1/2$- or 4-inch biscuit cutter. Fill, roll, and brush as for the larger cakes, but reduce the baking time to 15 to 17 minutes.
- Substitute $1^1/2$ cups any other dried fruit, or even fruits and nuts, for the raisins and currants.
- Omit the glazing of the tops, and instead dust the baked pastries with confectioners' sugar.

gianduja pillows

Gianduja is the Italian name for hazelnut-flavored chocolate, a combination especially favored in Switzerland and Italy, where hazelnut-chocolate spreads are as popular as peanut butter in America. The best-known Italian spread, Nutella, is available throughout the United States; it can be found, logically, in the peanut butter section of the grocery store. One taste of the PB alternative, and you will be a convert. Nutella is especially well suited as a filling for these puff pastry "pillows" since, unlike solid chocolate, it remains soft even after the pastries cool to room temperature.

> 1 sheet frozen puff pastry from a 17.3-ounce box, thawed but well chilled
>
> ¾ cup Nutella (hazelnut-chocolate spread)
>
> 1 tablespoon unsweetened cocoa powder
>
> 1 tablespoon confectioners' sugar

1   Unfold the puff pastry and roll on a lightly floured surface to a 12-inch square. Use a sharp knife to cut into sixteen 4-inch squares. Place 1 heaping tablespoon Nutella in the center of each square, spreading slightly to the sides. Moisten the edges of the pastry slightly by running a damp finger over the edges. Fold the pastry over to form triangles. Use the tines of a fork to seal the pastry edges together. Place the pastries, at least 2 inches apart, on an ungreased baking sheet. Place the baking sheet in the freezer for 10 minutes.

2   Preheat the oven to 400°F. Bake the pastries, directly from the freezer, until rich golden brown and well puffed, 15 to 17 minutes. Transfer to a rack to cool slightly, then serve warm or at room temperature. Sprinkle with cocoa and confectioners' sugar.

Gianduja Pillows Tips

- The pastries can be baked ahead and frozen for up to 1 month. They can be reheated directly from the freezer by placing on a baking sheet in a 200°F oven for about 10 minutes until thawed, warmed, and recrisped.
- The pastries can be filled, unbaked, and frozen for up to 2 days. Bake

directly from the freezer, but decrease the baking temperature after 10 minutes to 375°F and increase baking time to 17 to 20 minutes.

- The Nutella jar says not to store in the refrigerator, but I've found it lasts longer if I refrigerate an opened jar.

Gianduja Pillows Variations

- Six ounces of any type of chocolate, including white and dark chocolate chips and peanut butter chips, can be substituted for the Nutella, but the pastries should be served warm while the chocolate is still soft.
- Omit the dusting of confectioners' sugar and instead glaze the pillows with melted chocolate and sprinkle with chopped toasted hazelnuts.

gâteau pithiviers

Though called a gâteau, this is not a cake, but rather a very fancy double-crusted puff pastry frangipane tart. Frangipane is a rich, thick almond custard often used as a fruit tart base in French pastries. Even in a French bakery, this tart is a time-consuming work of art. At home, with the "jump starts" of frozen puff pastry sheets and a tube of almond paste, you can impress just about anyone, French or not, with your almost instant creation.

In France, a similar pastry, called *galette des rois* or "three kings" tart, is a traditional treat for New Year's Eve and the Feast of the Epiphany on January 6. For this tart, a whole almond is buried in the filling, and the person who gets the almond in his or her slice is guaranteed good luck in the year ahead. It's worth a try, any day of the year.

One 7-ounce tube almond paste, broken into 6 or 7 pieces
$1/3$ cup packed brown sugar
3 tablespoons unsalted butter, softened
2 eggs
One 17.3-ounce box frozen puff pastry, thawed but well chilled
1 whole almond, optional
2 teaspoons granulated sugar
8 large or 24 small whole strawberries, preferably with stems

1 In a food processor, puree the almond paste with the brown sugar and butter until smooth, about 30 seconds. In a small dish, beat the eggs until blended. Remove and set aside about 1 tablespoon beaten egg. Add the remaining eggs to the food processor and process until smooth, about 10 seconds. Refrigerate the filling until ready to use, at least 20 minutes or up to 2 hours.

2 On a lightly floured surface, roll one sheet of puff pastry to an 11-inch square. Use a small knife to cut around corners to form an approximately 11-inch circle. Place the circle on a large ungreased baking sheet. Spoon and spread the filling to within 1 inch of the edge. If you are using the whole almond, push it into the filling now.

3 Roll the other sheet of puff pastry to an 11-inch square. As in step 2, cut into an 11-inch circle. Brush the edges of the top and bottom pastry to moisten, then place the top pastry, moistened

side down, over the filling. Press the edges together firmly to seal. Use a pastry wheel, pizza cutter, or sharp knife to cut an even, decorative edge around the circle. Sprinkle the top with the granulated sugar. Use a small, sharp knife to make curved slashes from the center to the pressed edge, like a pinwheel. Place the baking sheet in the freezer for 10 minutes.

4   Preheat the oven to 425°F. Bake the pastry for 15 minutes, then reduce the oven temperature to 350°F and bake until the pastry is rich golden brown, 25 to 30 minutes more. Use two large spatulas to transfer the pastry to a rack to cool slightly, then transfer to a serving board or tray.

5   Serve, warm or at room temperature, cut into wedges. Garnish with the strawberries.

Gâteau Pithiviers Tips

- If you use almond paste in a can, which is firmer than almond paste in a tube, you may need to add another egg or part of a beaten egg. Add the additional egg a little at a time so that the filling will still hold its shape and not run out of the tart.
- Warn your guests (especially children and Grandma) about the almond in the center, so they don't bite down too hard.
- The spiral cutting on the top is both decorative and a way to allow steam to escape, as well as helping to keep the puff from getting out of hand.

Gâteau Pithiviers Variations

- Granulated sugar can be used in place of the brown sugar, though the brown sugar gives a more interesting, slightly caramel flavor to the filling.
- A nontraditional but very delicious chocolate pithiviers is made by adding 3 tablespoons unsweetened cocoa to the filling.
- Other nontraditional decorations or slashes can be made on the top, or you can simply cut a few air vents or make a single 1-inch hole in the center, if you like.

palmiers

Palmiers are the fancy French name for very simple crisp puff pastry "cookies" that are a lovely accompaniment to coffee or tea, but are equally impressive as a garnish for ice cream or sorbet. The basic sugared version can be "spiced" in a variety of ways.

> 2 tablespoons sugar
> 1 sheet frozen puff pastry from a 17.3-ounce package, thawed but
>   well chilled

1   Sprinkle a work surface with $1\frac{1}{2}$ teaspoons of the sugar. Place the pastry sheet on the sugar, then sprinkle the top with another $1\frac{1}{2}$ teaspoons sugar. Roll the pastry to a 13-inch square, then trim evenly to a 12-inch square.

2   Working quickly to prevent the pastry from softening, use the back of a knife blade to lightly score a line down the center of the pastry. Fold the right side over to meet the center line, then repeat with the left side. Sprinkle $1\frac{1}{2}$ teaspoons sugar over the pastry. Again fold the right side, then the left side over to meet the center line to form a rectangle about 12 x $1\frac{1}{2}$ inches. Sprinkle again with the remaining sugar. Use a sharp knife to cut the pastry crosswise into $\frac{1}{3}$-inch slices. Place, cut side up and at least 2 inches apart, on a large ungreased baking sheet. Place the baking sheet in the freezer for at least 15 minutes.

3   Preheat the oven to 400°F. Bake the pastries, directly from the freezer, for 10 minutes. Use a spatula to turn the pastries and bake until rich golden brown, about 5 minutes more. Transfer to a rack to cool.

Palmiers Tips

- A cool work surface makes it easier to work with the pastry.
- The cookies are great warm from the oven, but can be covered and stored for up to 5 days at room temperature.
- Baked pastries can be frozen, then recrisped on a baking sheet for a few minutes in a 300°F oven.

Palmiers **Variations**

- Flavor the sugar with 1 teaspoon ground spice, such as cinnamon, nutmeg, allspice, or Chinese five-spice blend.
- Sandwich 2 palmiers with sweetened whipped cream or ice cream, then serve immediately drizzled with hot fudge sauce for a quick, impressive dessert.

puff pastry bear claws

Bear claws are only one of many fanciful filled shapes for puff pastry, but have long been a bakery favorite, often filled with prune puree. These are great for breakfast or with coffee anytime.

One 17.3-ounce box frozen puff pastry, thawed but well chilled

12 tablespoons lekvar (prune puree), thick fruit preserves, or
sweetened cream cheese

1 egg, beaten with 2 teaspoons water

1 tablespoon sugar

1   On a lightly floured surface, roll one sheet of puff pastry to an 8 x 12-inch rectangle. Cut into 6 rectangles, each 3 x 4 inches. Spread 1 tablespoon lekvar or other filling in the center of each rectangle. Brush the edges of the pastry lightly with the beaten egg, then fold over from the short side, and pinch the edges to enclose the filling. Use a small, sharp knife to make three $1/2$-inch slits from the folded short edge to form the "claws." Repeat using the remaining puff pastry and filling. Place the pastries on ungreased baking sheets, at least 2 inches apart. Brush the tops with additional beaten egg and sprinkle with the sugar. Place in the freezer for at least 15 minutes.

2   Preheat the oven to 400°F. Bake the pastries, directly from the freezer, until rich golden brown and crisp, 20 to 25 minutes. Transfer to a rack to cool. Serve warm or at room temperature.

Puff Pastry Bear Claws Tips

- The filled pastries can be covered and frozen for up to 3 days, then baked directly from the freezer. Bake at 400°F for 5 minutes, then reduce the oven temperature to 375°F and bake for an additional 20 to 25 minutes.
- Be sure that the edges of the pastry are sealed to keep the filling from seeping out during baking.

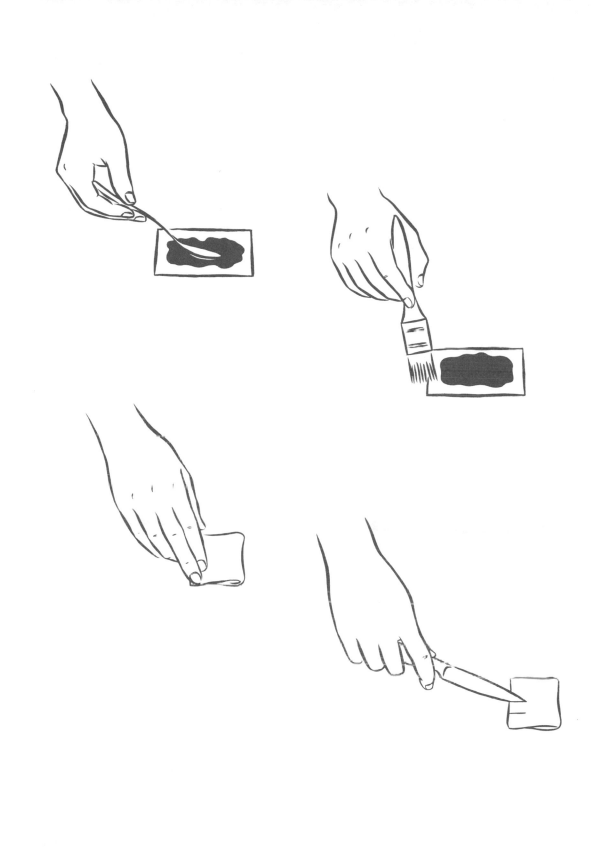

fall fruit strudel

Every pastry shop in Vienna, which vies with Paris as the pastry capital of the world, has strudels. Made with layer upon layer of paper-thin pastry that bakes up crackling-crisp, a slice of warm strudel accompanied by a cup of dark Viennese coffee is one of the highlights of a trip to the former capital of the Austro-Hungarian empire. Unlike some pastries, which can only be "replicated" by a home cook, even the most inexperienced home baker can duplicate strudels with ease. And the filling ideas are nearly endless, though I've found that moderately moist, but not runny or wet, fillings work best. Autumn fruits, such as apples and pears, are not as juicy as the fruits of summer, which might be a reason that apple is the classic filling for a strudel. Here, a combination of apples, pears, and some dried cranberries (for color) make a memorable autumn strudel. Truly, making a cup of Viennese coffee is harder than making the strudel.

2 large tart apples, such as Granny Smith, peeled, cored, and
  thinly sliced (about 2 cups)

1 large pear, peeled, cored, and thinly sliced (about 1 cup)

$1/2$ cup dried cranberries

2 tablespoons brandy or rum, optional

1 tablespoon lemon juice

$1/2$ cup plus 2 tablespoons sugar

2 teaspoons apple pie spice blend

1 teaspoon grated lemon zest

$3/4$ cup unflavored dried bread crumbs

8 tablespoons unsalted butter

$1/4$ cup finely chopped walnuts

6 sheets (12 x 17 inches) frozen phyllo dough, thawed overnight
  in the refrigerator

1   Preheat the oven to 375°F. In a large mixing bowl, toss together the apples, pear, cranberries, brandy, if using, and lemon juice. Add $1/2$ cup of the sugar, spice blend, lemon zest, and $1/4$ cup of the bread crumbs; toss to mix well. In a small skillet, melt 2 tablespoons of the butter. Add the remaining $1/2$ cup bread crumbs and the walnuts. Toss over medium heat just until the nuts

become fragrant and a shade darker, 1 to 2 minutes. Remove from the heat and stir in the remaining 2 tablespoons sugar. In a small saucepan, melt the remaining 6 tablespoons butter.

2   Place a 24-inch long sheet of wax paper on a work surface. Open the box of phyllo and unroll it onto a tea towel. Place one sheet of phyllo on the wax paper, and cover the remaining phyllo completely with a large tea towel.

3   Brush the phyllo sheet with about 1 tablespoon of the butter, then sprinkle with about 1 1/2 tablespoons of the bread-crumb mixture. Place another layer of phyllo on the first one and repeat the brushing of butter and sprinkling of crumbs. Make a total of 6 layers of phyllo, using all of the crumbs and all but about 1 tablespoon of the remaining butter and ending with a phyllo sheet.

4   Spoon the fruit filling along one long side of the phyllo, leaving a 1-inch edge all around. Fold in the edges at the ends, then use the wax paper to begin rolling the strudel, like a jelly roll, from the fruit-filled end and attempting to tuck in the fruit at the ends. Use the wax paper to help transfer the strudel to a large ungreased baking sheet, placing it seam side down. Discard the wax paper. Brush the top of the strudel with the remaining butter. Use a sharp knife to cut through the top layers of strudel, making diagonal cuts about 2 inches apart to score 6 to 8 slices of strudel.

(continued)

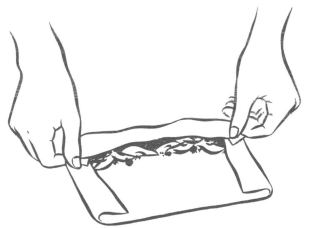

5 Bake the strudel until the phyllo is rich golden brown and crisp, 40 to 45 minutes. Use two large spatulas to carefully transfer the strudel to a rack to cool slightly. Transfer to a board or serving platter, then cut slices along the scored lines. Serve warm or at room temperature.

Fall Fruit Strudel **Tips**

- Scoring the top of the strudel is important because the top crust will shatter if it is cut without previously scored lines as a guide.
- Use a mix of at least 2 varieties of apples (Granny Smith and Golden Delicious are good choices) for the best and most complex flavor.
- To use up that extra phyllo, make more strudels—baked and even unbaked strudels freeze fine.

Fall Fruit Strudel **Variations**

- If you can find it, substitute one quince for one of the apples. Quince has a distinct, perfumed flavor that complements other fall fruits.
- Substitute 1 cup of quartered fresh figs for the pears.
- Substitute raisins or chopped dates for the cranberries.
- Make the strudel with only apples or only pears.

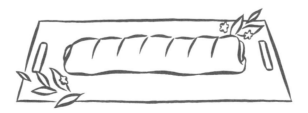

spiced baklava

Baklava, the most famous of all Greek pastries, is a favorite confection throughout the Middle East and eastern Mediterranean, where its ingredients, flavorings, syrups, and shapes vary from region to region and even within neighborhoods. Most versions use widely available walnuts, a slightly bitter nut that best balances the toothachingly sweet syrup that distinguishes baklava from all other phyllo pastries. In Connecticut, where there is a substantial Greek-American population, the best baklava I've tasted is very spicy and uses brown sugar as well as lemon and orange juices in the syrup to give a caramel and citrus edge to the confections.

4 cups (1 pound) chopped walnuts

$^1/_2$ cup granulated sugar

2 teaspoons ground cinnamon

$^1/_2$ teaspoon ground cloves

30 sheets (about 12 x 17 inches) phyllo dough, thawed in the box overnight in the refrigerator

16 tablespoons (2 sticks) unsalted butter, melted

HONEY SYRUP

1 cup honey, preferably orange flower honey

$^1/_2$ cup packed light brown sugar

$^1/_2$ cup orange juice

2 tablespoons lemon juice

2 teaspoons grated orange zest

1 teaspoon grated lemon zest

$^1/_2$ teaspoon ground cardamom

1 tablespoon orange flower water, optional

1   Preheat the oven to 350°F. In a mixing bowl, stir together the nuts, sugar, cinnamon, and cloves. Have ready a 9 x 13-inch baking dish or pan.

2   Unroll the phyllo onto a large tea towel, use a sharp knife to trim it to approximately 10 x 14 inches, then immediately cover the unwrapped phyllo with a large tea towel. Brush the baking

dish lightly with some of the melted butter, then place 1 sheet of phyllo in the pan. Brush it lightly but completely with butter. Repeat with 5 more sheets of phyllo, buttering each layer. Sprinkle the top layer with one-fourth of the nut mixture (about 1 cup). Repeat the layering of 6 buttered phyllo sheets and nuts to make 4 more layers, using all the nuts and ending with a layer of buttered phyllo.

3   Use a sharp knife to score the top layer of phyllo lengthwise into 4 strips, then score on the diagonal to make diamond shapes. (There will be extra corners—snacks for the cook.)

4   Bake for 45 minutes.

5   While the baklava is baking, prepare the syrup by combining the honey, brown sugar, orange and lemon juices, orange and lemon zests, and ground cardamom in a medium saucepan. Bring to a boil, stirring to dissolve the sugar. Simmer for 3 minutes, then remove from the heat and stir in the orange flower water, if using.

6   After the baklava has baked for 45 minutes, reduce the oven temperature to 325°F. Slowly pour the hot syrup evenly over the pastry, then return it to the oven to bake until glossy and rich golden brown, 5 to 10 minutes more.

7   Place the baking dish on a rack and cool completely before cutting along the score lines. Use a small spatula to transfer the baklava pieces to a serving plate.

Spiced Baklava **Tips**

- Baklava can be assembled ahead, covered, and refrigerated for up to 4 hours before baking, but it is much better to store it already baked.
- The phyllo is cut slightly larger than the baking dish, and it is okay if the pastry extends a bit on the edges, since this part is easier to cut.
- Be sure your nuts are fresh. Opened bags of nuts can lose flavor and become rancid after a few weeks.
- Baklava can be stored, covered, at room temperature for 3 days.

Spiced Baklava **Variations**

- For a less pronounced citrus and spice syrup, simmer two 1-inch strips of lemon and orange peel, and 3 lightly crushed cardamom pods in place of the lemon and orange zests and the ground cardamom. Discard the peels and pods before pouring over the baklava.
- Substitute 2 teaspoons pumpkin pie spice blend for the cinnamon and cloves in the nut mixture.
- Substitute any flavorful honey of your choice for the orange flower honey.

s'more phyllo flowers

America's favorite campfire treat gets all dressed up here in a whimsical phyllo flower pastry. The marshmallow center puffs up and toasts in the oven to cover the chocolate "seeds" underneath, while the phyllo flower petals are layered with graham cracker crumbs. The phyllo flowers are as versatile as flowers in nature, so be sure to check the variations.

> 3 tablespoons unsalted butter, melted
> 4 sheets (12 x 17 inches) phyllo dough, thawed according to
>   package directions
> 1/4 cup graham cracker crumbs
> 6 tablespoons miniature chocolate chips
> 6 full-size marshmallows, preferably colored marshmallows
> 1/2 cup high-quality hot fudge sauce, heated

1   Preheat the oven to 375°F. Have ready a standard-size muffin tin or six 4-ounce ovenproof custard cups. Lightly brush the tin or cups with melted butter.

2   Unroll the phyllo onto a large tea towel. Place 1 sheet on a work surface, then immediately cover the remaining sheets with another large tea towel.

3   Brush the phyllo with melted butter, then sprinkle with 1 heaping tablespoon of the graham cracker crumbs. Continue to layer, sprinkle, and brush to use all of the phyllo, butter, and crumbs, and ending with a layer of buttered phyllo. Use a small plate or large saucer as a template to cut six 5- to 6-inch circles from the phyllo stack. Place circles directly on top of the cups, then push and ease the circles into the tin or cups to contour the shape. The edge of the phyllo will rise above the cups by about 1/2 inch or so. Place 1 tablespoon miniature chocolate chips in the bottom of each cup, then place a marshmallow on top of the chips. Place the custard cups on a baking sheet.

4   Bake until the phyllo is rich golden brown and crisp and the marshmallow is puffed up and toasted, 25 to 30 minutes. Carefully transfer the hot phyllo flowers to a rack to cool for about 10 minutes, then serve warm with hot fudge sauce drizzled over and around.

S'more Phyllo Flowers **Tips**

- If your muffin tin has more than 6 cups, either make additional "flowers" or use every other cup for even baking.
- The dessert should be served warm, but not straight from the oven when the hot marshmallow will burn the roof of your mouth.
- It doesn't matter if the circles are exactly 5 or 6 inches, just as long as they don't extend more than 1 inch from the tops of the tins or cups, or the edges might burn.

S'More Phyllo Flowers **Variations**

- The phyllo flowers can be filled with 2 to 3 tablespoons applesauce; $1/4$ cup diced, sweetened fruit, such as apples or peaches or apricots; or 1 tablespoon each peanut butter and jelly.
- Replace the graham cracker crumbs with vanilla wafer crumbs, chocolate cookie crumbs, or plain dried bread crumbs, depending upon the filling of choice.
- The phyllo flowers can be baked unfilled, then cooled completely and later filled with small scoops of ice cream, sorbet, or pudding. Unfilled flowers can be baked a day ahead and stored, covered, at room temperature.

chocolate cherry phyllo turnovers

Like strudels, turnovers can contain a variety of fillings, and you can make them larger or smaller as well. Phyllo turnovers are fun and easy to make. Though the directions could sound complicated . . . just think back to your scouting days: It's like folding a flag. Dried cherries and chopped bittersweet chocolate make a most sophisticated turnover, but they are only one of many excellent fillings (see Variations).

$1/4$ cup halved dried cherries

2 tablespoons kirsch or cranberry juice

$1/4$ cup coarsely chopped bittersweet chocolate

4 tablespoons sugar

$1/4$ cup graham cracker crumbs

$1/4$ teaspoon ground cinnamon

**6 sheets (12 x 17 inches) phyllo dough, thawed according to
    package directions**

4 tablespoons unsalted butter, melted

8 small scoops vanilla ice cream, optional

1   In a small saucepan or microwave-safe dish, combine the cherries and kirsch or cranberry juice. Heat just to a simmer, then let cool to room temperature. Stir in the chocolate and 3 table-spoons of the sugar. In a small dish, combine the graham cracker crumbs and cinnamon.

2   Preheat the oven to 350°F. Have ready a large ungreased baking sheet. Unwrap the phyllo onto a large tea towel. Place 1 sheet on a work surface, then quickly cover the remaining sheets with another large tea towel.

3   Brush the phyllo sheet with melted butter, then sprinkle with 1 tablespoon of the crumbs. Repeat the layering, brushing, and sprinkling of crumbs with another phyllo sheet, then top with a third layer of phyllo, and brush the top with butter. Use a sharp knife to cut the layered phyllo crosswise into 4 strips, each approximately 4 inches wide.

4   Place about 2 tablespoons chocolate cherry filling in the top corner of one of the strips, then

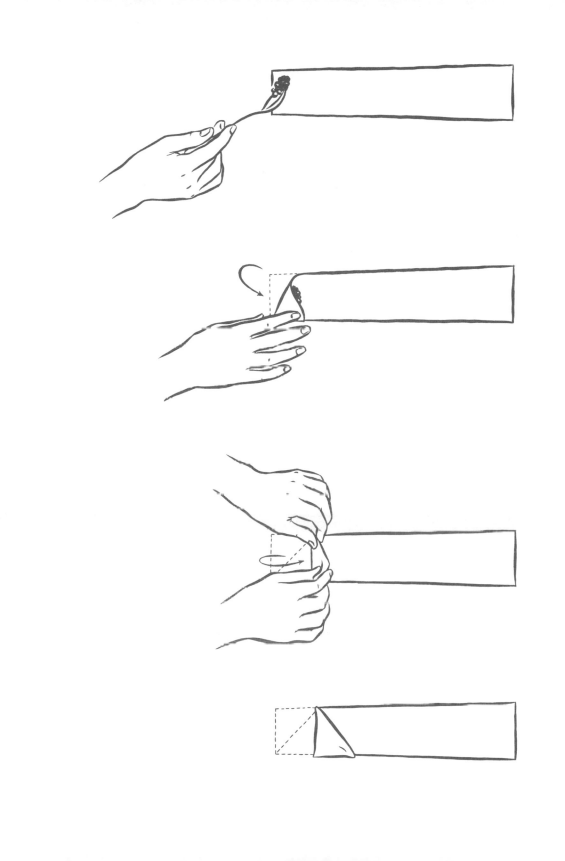

fold the filled corner diagonally to form a triangle. Continue to fold the length of the strip, as you would fold a flag. Place the folded triangle, seam side down, on the baking sheet. Brush with a little butter and sprinkle with about $1/4$ teaspoon of the remaining sugar. Continue to make 3 more turnovers in the same way. Finally, repeat the entire process to use the remaining 3 phyllo sheets, crumbs, filling, and butter to make a total of 8 turnovers. Place each turnover at least 1 inch apart on the baking sheet.

5 Bake until the phyllo is rich golden brown and crisp, 20 to 25 minutes. Carefully transfer to a rack to cool for at least 5 minutes before serving warm with a small scoop of ice cream, if desired.

Chocolate Cherry Phyllo Turnovers Tips

- The turnovers can be made smaller, with eight 2-inch pieces per stack, using 1 tablespoon filling. These can be eaten out of hand.
- Unbaked turnovers can be frozen for up to a week, then baked from the frozen state. Add a few minutes to the baking time.
- Turnovers can be baked several hours ahead of serving, then reheated for a few minutes in a 350°F oven just to warm the filling and melt the chocolate.

Chocolate Cherry Phyllo Turnovers Variations

- Use dried cranberries or chopped dried apricots and/or milk or hazelnut chocolate in place of the cherries and bittersweet chocolate.
- Sprinkle the phyllo layers with vanilla or chocolate wafer crumbs.
- Fill the turnovers with 2 tablespoons hazelnut-chocolate spread (Nutella) in place of the cherries and chocolate.
- For the filling, blend 8 ounces regular or light cream cheese with 3 tablespoons sugar, 2 tablespoons dried currants, and 1 tablespoon liqueur of choice. Fill each turnover with 2 tablespoons of the mixture.

cobblers, crisps, and more

Crisps, cobblers, crumbles, crunches, grunts, slumps, and pandowdies are the **oddball** names of some of the **best** of original American desserts. Most have their roots in Colonial hearth cooking, are fruit based, and take their names from their **looks**, their **sounds**, and their **textures**. Though a grunt or a slump or a pandowdie may not read a bit **appetizing**, overlook the title and go straight to the recipe. Most are variations on the familiar cobbler, though each recipe features its own dough, including biscuits, puff pastry, piecrust, and even cookie doughs as streusel. All have stood the **test of time**, and are as delicious today as they were hundreds of years ago baked in a beehive oven or simmered over an open fire.

plum hazelnut crumble

A crumble is a lot like a crisp, but according to the late Richard Sax, who knew more about old-fashioned desserts than anyone else, a crumble is usually made with oats. Crumbled oatmeal cookie dough, mixed with coarsely chopped nuts, makes a terrific crumble, and the cookie dough is also already spiced with cinnamon.

3 ounces (about $3/4$ cup) dried plums (prunes), quartered

$1/2$ cup orange juice

2 teaspoons grated orange zest

$1 1/2$ pounds firm fresh plums, preferably Italian prune plums, pitted and quartered

$1/2$ cup sugar

One-third 18-ounce package or tube refrigerated oatmeal or oatmeal raisin cookie dough

$1/2$ cup coarsely chopped hazelnuts

1   Preheat the oven to 400°F. In a small saucepan or microwave-safe bowl, heat the dried plums, orange juice, and zest just until the juice is nearly simmering. Let cool to room temperature.

2   In a 9-inch square baking dish or deep 9-inch pie plate, stir together the fresh plums, sugar, and dried plum mixture, including any juice. Spread the fruit evenly in the dish. In a small bowl, use your hands to crumble the cookie dough into approximately $1/2$-inch chunks. Stir in the nuts. Sprinkle the cookie dough and nut mixture over the plums.

3   Bake until the topping is browned and crisp and the plums are soft and bubbling, 30 to 40 minutes. Let the crumble cool slightly, then serve warm or at room temperature. The crumble is best served within 2 hours of baking, but can be reheated in a 350°F oven to recrisp the topping.

Plum Hazelnut Crumble **Tips**

- Depending upon the softness of the dried plums, they may absorb all of the juices.
- The nuts should just be coarsely chopped for the best "crumble."
- The crumble is best served on the day of baking, but can be recrisped for breakfast or dessert the next day by heating it in a 300°F oven just until warmed.

Plum Hazelnut Crumble **Variations**

- Substitute other dried fruits, such as cranberries or apricots or figs, for the dried plums.
- Substitute fresh apricots for the fresh plums.
- Substitute other nuts, such as walnuts or pecans, for the hazelnuts.

triple apple walnut crisp

Unlike some other old-fashioned American fruit desserts, a crisp is self-explanatory: The topping needs to be very crisp. Here, sugar cookie dough is crumbled finely, then mixed with lots of spices and chopped nuts.

3 ounces (about $^3/_4$ cup) dried apple slices

$^1/_4$ cup dates

$^1/_2$ cup apple cider or juice

2 teaspoons unsalted butter

1$^1/_2$ pounds (about 3 large) tart apples, peeled, cored, and sliced

$^1/_2$ cup packed light brown sugar

6 ounces refrigerated sugar cookie dough, well chilled

1 teaspoon apple pie spice blend

$^1/_2$ cup coarsely chopped walnuts

1   Preheat the oven to 400°F. In a small saucepan or microwave-safe bowl, heat the dried apples, dates, and cider just until the cider is nearly simmering. Let cool to room temperature. Smear a 9-inch square baking dish or deep 9-inch pie plate with the butter.

2   In the prepared baking dish, stir together the apples, brown sugar, and dried apple mixture and any juices. Spread the mixture evenly in the dish. In a small bowl, use your hands to finely crumble the cookie dough and spice blend into pieces about the size of peas. Stir in the nuts. Sprinkle the cookie dough evenly over the apples.

3   Bake until the topping is browned and the apples are soft and bubbling, 30 to 40 minutes. Let the crisp cool slightly, then serve warm or at room temperature.

Triple Apple Walnut Crisp **Tips**

- Depending upon the softness of the apples, they may absorb all of the juice. If the slices are large, cut them in half crosswise.
- If you don't have apple pie spice blend, use $1/2$ teaspoon ground cinnamon, $1/4$ teaspoon grated nutmeg, $1/8$ teaspoon ground ginger, and $1/8$ teaspoon ground allspice.
- The crisp is best served within 2 hours of baking, but can be recrisped and rewarmed in a 300°F oven for about 10 minutes.

Triple Apple Walnut Crisp **Variations**

- Substitute raisins, especially cinnamon-coated ones, for the dates.
- Make a triple pear crumble with fresh and dried pears and pear or apple cider.
- Substitute other nuts, such as pecans, for the walnuts.

cinnamon bun blackberry cobbler

Cobblers take on many guises, and can have myriad bread, pastry, or biscuit toppings, making them perfect for inclusion in your recipe repertoire, since virtually all cobbler variations are exceptionally simple to prepare and well loved by all. This version makes excellent use of sweet yeast bun dough. The little can of icing in the dough package can be drizzled over the finished cobbler or stirred into the fruit before baking for added sweetness, though neither is essential to the recipe. Blackberries, though a bit seedy, make a wonderful cobbler. You can use either fresh or frozen berries with good results.

1^1/$_2$ tablespoons unsalted butter

4 cups fresh or partially thawed frozen blackberries

^{3}/$_4$ cup sugar

1 tablespoon all-purpose flour

3 tablespoons orange juice

1 tablespoon lemon juice

1 teaspoon vanilla extract

1 teaspoon grated orange zest

One 12.4-ounce tube refrigerated cinnamon roll dough with icing

1   Preheat the oven to 375°F. Generously butter a 9-inch square baking dish or a deep 10-inch pie plate with ^{1}/$_2$ tablespoon of the butter.

2   In the prepared baking dish, toss together the berries, sugar, and flour. Add the orange and lemon juices, vanilla, and orange zest, and toss to mix. Spread evenly in the dish. Separate the rolls into 8 pieces and place them, cinnamon side down and evenly spaced, on top of the berry mixture.

3   Bake for 10 minutes, then reduce the oven temperature to 350°F and continue to bake until the buns are risen and golden and the berry filling is bubbling, 20 to 22 minutes more.

4 Cool the cobbler for a few minutes, then serve warm or at room temperature. The cobbler is best served within 2 hours of baking. If desired, the tops of the baked buns can be iced with the tub of icing provided with the roll dough.

Cinnamon Bun Blackberry Cobbler **Tips**

- Though the cobbler can be reheated, the buns are at their best served warm first time around.
- Be sure that the baking dish is deep enough to allow for bubbling up, or the cobbler may bubble over onto the oven floor.
- Placing the buns cinnamon side down flavors the fruit and keeps the tops of the buns from burning.

Cinnamon Bun Blackberry Cobbler **Variations**

- Replace blackberries with blueberries or use a combination of both.
- Use orange sweet roll dough in place of the cinnamon roll dough.
- Stir the icing provided with the roll dough into the unbaked berry mixture in place of $\frac{1}{4}$ cup of the sugar.

rhubarb cobbler

Rhubarb seems to have fallen from favor lately, and more's the pity. This wonderfully old-fashioned fruit is nicknamed "pie plant" because in pioneer days it was grown in nearly every garden expressly for pie (which in those days was often really a cobbler). Unlike many other fruits, rhubarb is inedible raw, and indeed only the stalks are edible even when cooked—the huge leaves are toxic.

A superhardy plant, rhubarb grows in the yard of my 250-year-old home, and I bet it's been there nearly that long. Every May, when the stalks are about two feet long and reddish all around, I cut them up and make this simple cobbler and serve it warm with a scoop of vanilla ice cream—my husband's favorite dessert. In case you don't have access to fresh rhubarb, or if it's out of season, frozen rhubarb works just fine.

1 tablespoon unsalted butter

1^1/$_2$ pounds fresh or frozen rhubarb stalks, cut crosswise into
^{1}/$_2$-inch slices

^{3}/$_4$ cup sugar

1 tablespoon all-purpose flour

1 teaspoon grated orange zest

1 teaspoon ground cinnamon

^{1}/$_4$ cup orange juice

One 7.5-ounce tube refrigerated biscuit dough

6 scoops vanilla ice cream

1   Preheat the oven to 400°F. Generously butter a 9-inch square or other deep 2-quart baking dish. In the baking dish, toss together the rhubarb, all but 1 tablespoon of the sugar, flour, orange zest, cinnamon, and orange juice. Bake for 10 minutes.

2   Separate the biscuit dough into 10 biscuits and place them, at least 1 inch apart, on top of the rhubarb. Sprinkle the biscuit tops with the remaining 1 tablespoon sugar.

3   Reduce the oven temperature to 375°F. Bake the cobbler until the biscuits are rich golden brown and the rhubarb is soft and bubbling, 20 to 25 minutes more.

4   Let the cobbler cool for a few minutes, then spoon out warm fruit and biscuits into shallow dessert bowls, and top with scoops of ice cream.

Rhubarb Cobbler Tips

- There are more biscuits than servings, so some people will want one and others two biscuits, or feel free to cut into them as well.
- Cobblers are best served shortly after baking, but the fruit mixture can be tossed together a couple of hours ahead of baking.
- Frozen rhubarb is already sliced or diced, and can be baked from the frozen state. Just add a few minutes to the initial baking time before placing the biscuits on top.

Rhubarb Cobbler Variations

- Strawberries and rhubarb are seasonal and flavor partners, so substitute 1 cup sliced strawberries for about 1 cup rhubarb, if you like.
- For a really contemporary version of an old-fashioned dessert, substitute orange liqueur for the orange juice.
- For richer, and more, biscuits, use a 12-ounce tube of buttermilk biscuits, which will nearly cover the top of the rhubarb. Baking time is about the same.

puff pastry peach and cherry pot pies

Pot pies are usually homespun savory casseroles with biscuit or piecrust toppings. This one breaks all those rules, and is a sophisticated sweet dessert with an elegant puff-pastry top crust fashioned and served in individual baking dishes. You can, of course, bake the pot pie in a single baking dish and spoon out the servings.

> 2 teaspoons unsalted butter
>
> 4 cups peeled and sliced peaches
>
> 1 cup pitted sweet red cherries
>
> $\frac{1}{2}$ cup sugar
>
> 1 tablespoon cornstarch
>
> 1 tablespoon kirsch
>
> 1 teaspoon lemon juice
>
> 1 sheet frozen puff pastry from a 17.3-ounce box, thawed but well chilled

1   Preheat the oven to 425°F. Position the oven rack in the center. Smear the butter in six $\frac{3}{4}$- to 1-cup individual baking dishes or a deep 9-inch pie plate.

2   In a mixing bowl, toss together the peaches, cherries, all but 1 tablespoon of the sugar, cornstarch, kirsch, and lemon juice. Divide the fruit mixture among the individual baking dishes or spoon it into the pie plate.

3   Unfold the puff pastry and use a rolling pin to press out the fold lines. Cut the pastry into pieces or a piece about $\frac{1}{4}$ inch smaller in diameter than the size of the baking dishes or pie plate. Place the pastry on top of the fruit, without sealing the edges to the dish in order to allow for maximum puff. Sprinkle the top of the pastry with the reserved 1 tablespoon sugar.

4   Bake for 10 minutes, then reduce the oven temperature to 400°F, and bake until the pastry is puffed, rich golden brown and crisp on the top, and the fruit is bubbling, 20 to 22 minutes more.

5   Let the pot pies or pie cool slightly, then serve warm or at room temperature.

Puff Pastry Peach and Cherry Pot Pies **Tips**

- To peel the peaches, drop whole peaches into a pan of boiling water for about 15 seconds, then remove with tongs, cool under running water, and slip off the skins with your fingers.
- Choose ripe peaches that yield to slight pressure for best flavor and easy peeling.
- Cutting the pastry slightly smaller than the baking dishes or dish ensures that it will not stick to the sides, which would inhibit puffing.

Puff Pastry Peach and Cherry Pot Pies **Variations**

- Other seasonal fruit combinations, such as rhubarb and strawberries (use $1/4$ cup more sugar), apples and cranberries (use $1/4$ cup more sugar), or peaches and blueberries (use the same amount of sugar), can be substituted for the peaches and cherries.
- Add $1/2$ teaspoon cinnamon or other sweet spice to the fruit.
- Substitute orange juice or peach nectar for the kirsch.

spiced cider applesauce grunt

It is said that this old-fashioned American dessert takes its name from the sound made by the simmering dumplings. It's not really a grunt, but instead a pleasantly fragrant bubbling, and the aroma and sound are most appealing on a cold, rainy autumn day. Usually made with a biscuit dough dumpling, here cinnamon yeast bun dough works beautifully and also flavors this dessert, which makes it a wonderful breakfast dish as well. This is one of the few recipes in this book that doesn't bake in the oven at all.

1 cup chunky applesauce

1 cup apple cider or apple juice

2 applesauce apples, such as McIntosh, peeled, cored, and cut into rough $1/2$-inch chunks

$1/4$ cup raisins or dried currants

$3/4$ teaspoon grated nutmeg, preferably freshly grated

One 7.3-ounce tube refrigerated cinnamon bun dough

$1/2$ cup heavy or light cream, warmed, optional

1   In a deep 9- or 10-inch skillet, stir together the applesauce, cider, apples, raisins, and nutmeg. Bring to a simmer, stirring over medium heat.

2   Meanwhile, separate the cinnamon buns into 5 rolls, and cut each into quarters. (Reserve the icing for other uses, such as spreading on cookies.) Drop the dough pieces onto the simmering applesauce mixture. Cover the pan and reduce the heat to medium-low. Simmer until the rolls are puffed, cooked through, and no longer doughy in the center, 15 to 20 minutes. Remove the skillet from the heat and let the grunt rest for about 10 minutes.

3   Serve warm with a pitcher of cream for pouring, if desired.

Spiced Cider Applesauce Grunt **Tips**

- Softer apples, like McIntoshes, are ideal for this recipe, since it is fine that they become mushy, but any cooking apple can be used.
- A skillet with a tight-fitting lid is essential so that the rolls can steam in the aromatic liquids.
- The grunt should be served soon after simmering, since the rolls will become soggy as they cool.

Spiced Cider Applesauce Grunt **Variations**

- Other spices, such as cloves, cardamom, or apple pie spice blend, can be substituted for the nutmeg.
- Substitute one pear for one of the apples.
- Substitute dried cranberries or dates for the raisins.

blueberry citrus slump

What's the difference between a slump and a grunt? It's a matter of semantics, tracing back to individual Colonial cooks and cookbooks. Some say the noisy grunt of the simmering biscuits is the defining factor, but others talk about the biscuits "slumping" into the simmering fruit. Call them what you will, these homely treats are amazingly easy to make, and are loved by everyone of every generation, from Colonial times to now.

5 cups fresh or frozen blueberries, picked over

$^3/_4$ cup sugar

$^1/_4$ cup orange juice

1 tablespoon lemon juice

1 teaspoon grated orange zest

1 teaspoon grated lemon zest

1 teaspoon ground cinnamon

One 7.5-ounce tube refrigerated buttermilk or other style biscuits

$^1/_2$ pint lemon or orange gelato

1   In a deep 9- or 10-inch skillet, stir together the blueberries, all but 1 tablespoon of the sugar, orange and lemon juices, orange and lemon zests, and $^1/_2$ teaspoon of the cinnamon. Bring to a simmer, stirring often, over medium heat.

2   Meanwhile, separate the biscuits into 5 pieces, and cut each into quarters. Drop the biscuit pieces onto the simmering blueberries. In a small dish, combine the remaining 1 tablespoon sugar and $^1/_2$ teaspoon cinnamon. Sprinkle over the biscuits. Cover the pan and reduce the heat to medium-low. Simmer until the biscuits are puffed, cooked through, and no longer doughy in the center, 15 to 20 minutes. Remove the skillet from the heat and let the dessert rest for about 10 minutes.

3   Serve warm with small scoops of lemon or orange gelato.

Blueberry Citrus Slump **Tips**

- This is a perfect use for frozen blueberries, so the slump makes a great wintertime dessert.
- Always grate citrus zest before squeezing the juice.
- Serve the slump soon after simmering, since the biscuits will become soggy upon standing.

Blueberry Citrus Slump **Variations**

- Substitute blackberries for half of the blueberries.
- Substitute coarsely diced peaches for half of the blueberries.
- Serve the dessert with sweetened whipped cream in place of the gelato.

cranberry crunch

Native American cranberries are an underused dessert fruit, and it's high time they got the recognition they deserve. Loaded with vitamin C, these brilliant garnet jewels are also the most spectacularly beautiful of all cooked fruits. Simmered in the oven with a topping of crumbled oatmeal raisin cookie dough, the richly flavored berries and spiced crunchy cookies make a homespun dessert worthy of the Thanksgiving table.

2 teaspoons unsalted butter

12 ounces (3 cups) fresh or frozen cranberries

$^3/_4$ cup sugar

$^1/_2$ cup orange juice

1 tablespoon cranberry liqueur, optional

**One-third 18-ounce package or tube refrigerated oatmeal raisin
    cookie dough**

$^1/_4$ cup chopped pecans

1 pint vanilla ice cream, optional

1   Preheat the oven to 350°F. Use the butter to generously grease a shallow 2-quart baking dish or deep 9-inch pie plate. Place the cranberries, sugar, orange juice, and cranberry liqueur, if using, in the prepared dish, and stir to mix well.

2   Place the cookie dough and nuts in a small bowl. Use your hand to coarsely crumble the dough and mix in the nuts. Crumble the mixture over the cranberries.

3   Bake until the cranberries have popped and are bubbling, and the cookie dough is browned and crunchy, 30 to 40 minutes.

4   Serve warm, accompanied by vanilla ice cream, if desired.

Cranberry Crunch Tips

- If you use frozen berries, partially thaw them before tossing with sugar and orange juice.
- Store unused cookie dough, well wrapped, for up to 3 days in the refrigerator, or freeze for up to 1 month.
- The dessert may be baked a few hours ahead and reheated, but you may need to use up to $1/4$ cup additional orange juice to keep the cranberries from getting too dry when reheated.

Cranberry Crunch Variations

- Substitute walnuts for the pecans.
- Add $1/4$ cup raisins to the cranberries.
- Substitute orange liqueur for the cranberry liqueur.

pear pandowdy

A pandowdy is related to a pie, as it uses the same type of pastry. But the baking method goes quite against the usual pie-baking rules. Instead of attempting to keep the pastry from "sogging" into the fruit, the baker actually pushes the partially baked crust right into the fruit, thus totally rendering the dessert "dowdied." The dessert is then returned to the oven, where the dowdied crust now miraculously becomes caramelized and not a bit soggy. Those Colonial bakers knew a thing or two about baking, it seems. Indeed, the dowdy was probably the result of needing to moisten up the rock-hard day-old crust of a fruit pie, which was then served (as most pandowdies were) for breakfast. Those Colonial bakers knew a thing or two about being thrifty as well.

3 ripe, firm pears (about $1^1/_2$ pounds), peeled, cored, and sliced

$^1/_2$ cup dried cranberries

$^1/_2$ cup sugar

$^1/_4$ cup pear nectar

1 tablespoon lemon juice

1 tablespoon brandy or pear liqueur

$^1/_4$ teaspoon ground cloves

1 tablespoon unsalted butter, cut into small pieces

One-half 15-ounce package refrigerated folded piecrusts

2 teaspoons milk

1   Preheat the oven to 425°F. In a mixing bowl, toss together the pears, cranberries, all but 2 teaspoons of the sugar, the nectar, lemon juice, brandy, and cloves. Transfer the mixture to a deep 9-inch pie plate. Dot the fruit with the butter.

2   Unfold the piecrust and use a sharp knife to cut it into rough 2-inch squares. Arrange the squares, approximating the original crust shape, on the fruit, fluting the squares at the edges of the pie plate. It is not important that the fruit be entirely covered. Brush the pastry with the milk and sprinkle with remaining 2 teaspoons sugar.

3 Bake for 30 minutes, then use the back of a spoon to push the pastry partially into the simmering fruit, but do not push fluted pastry at the edges. Reduce the oven temperature to 350°F and continue to bake until the pastry is rich golden brown and the fruit is bubbling, about 10 minutes more.

4 Use a wide spoon to serve the pandowdy in shallow bowls, either warm or at room temperature.

Pear Pandowdy **Tips**

- It doesn't matter how much of the pastry is "dowdied" or if it looks pretty. Remember that this is a dowdy dessert that tastes quite fashionable.
- Try not to disturb the crust that is fluted so that the fluting will remain intact.
- Slide the partially baked dessert out of the oven to "dowdy" it, so you don't risk getting your hand burned.

Pear Pandowdy **Variations**

- Substitute apples or plums for the pears.
- Substitute raisins or diced dried apricots for the cranberries.
- Substitute ½ teaspoon of another spice, such as allspice, for the cloves.

pineapple upside-down "cake"

The original pineapple upside-down cake uses canned pineapple and maraschino cherries. This is a contemporary version of same, using fresh pineapple and dried cherries, but I have to confess that I like the old recipe just as much . . . probably something to do with Mom and comfort food. However, I do like the slightly offbeat concept of making these individual cakes by using large-size biscuits for the cake and having a little extra syrup to sweeten the whole thing.

$2^1/_2$ tablespoons unsalted butter

1 cup unsweetened pineapple juice

$^1/_2$ cup packed light brown sugar

1 tablespoon lemon juice

1 tablespoon dark rum or orange juice

$^1/_2$ cup dried sweet red cherries

Eight $^1/_2$- to $^3/_4$-inch thick slices fresh pineapple

One 16.3-ounce tube refrigerated large-size Southern-style or
     cornmeal biscuits

1 pint mango gelato or vanilla ice cream

1   Preheat the oven to 375°F. Use $^1/_2$ tablespoon butter to generously grease a shallow 2-quart baking dish.

2   In a small saucepan, boil the pineapple juice until it is reduced to $^2/_3$ cup. Stir in the brown sugar and remaining butter until melted, then stir in the lemon juice and rum. Pour the mixture into the prepared baking dish. Sprinkle with the cherries. Arrange the pineapple slices, at least 1 inch apart, in the juice mixture. Set the biscuits atop the pineapple.

3   Bake for 20 minutes, then reduce the oven temperature to 350°F and bake until the biscuits are rich golden brown and the juices are bubbling and caramelized, about 10 minutes more.

4 Let the dessert stand at room temperature for about 5 minutes, then use a spatula to pick up the pineapple and biscuits, one at a time, and invert each onto a dessert plate. Spoon the juices and cherries in the pan onto the desserts. Serve warm accompanied by scoops of mango gelato or vanilla ice cream.

Pineapple Upside-Down "Cake" Tips

- If you buy presliced pineapple from the produce section, use the juice in the container for some or all of the pineapple juice in the recipe.
- If you peel and cut up your own pineapple, do so over a bowl to catch the juices as you cut.
- A shallow 2-quart baking dish is the same as a 9-inch square, a 7 x 11-inch rectangle, or a deep 10-inch round.

Pineapple Upside-Down "Cake" Variations

- Substitute a 20-ounce can of pineapple in juice for the fresh pineapple. You will have about 2 extra slices of pineapple, but enough juice for the recipe.
- Substitute 8 maraschino cherries for the dried cherries, placing each one in the center of the pineapple slice.
- Substitute dried cranberries or dried mixed tropical fruits for the dried cherries.

caramel apple dumplings

If you can get maple sugar, use it in place of the brown sugar for a pronounced maple flavor. No matter which you use, the richly caramelized syrup crisps the pastry on the bottom, while the spiced apple interior remains soft and moist. There are unlimited ways to prepare apple desserts, and this is one of my favorites. Folks in Vermont (where apple baking is practically a religion) would serve these dumplings, like apple pie, with a wedge of Vermont Cheddar cheese, which I really like. But a scoop of Vermont vanilla ice cream (think Ben & Jerry's) would be just as authentic and delicious.

3 cups (about $1\frac{1}{2}$ pounds) peeled, cored, and diced tart apples

7 tablespoons light brown or maple sugar

$\frac{1}{4}$ cup chopped walnuts

1 tablespoon all-purpose flour

2 teaspoons apple pie spice blend

One 15-ounce package refrigerated folded piecrusts

$1\frac{1}{4}$ cups apple cider

2 tablespoons butter

2 tablespoons maple syrup

8 small wedges Vermont Cheddar cheese, optional

1 pint vanilla ice cream, optional

1   Preheat the oven to 400°F. In a mixing bowl, toss together the apples, 6 tablespoons of the brown sugar, walnuts, flour, and 1 teaspoon of the spice blend.

2   Unwrap one piecrust, keeping the remaining one refrigerated until ready to use. Cut the crust into 4 pieces along the fold lines. On a lightly floured surface, roll each piece to a rough 6- to 7-inch circle. Place about $\frac{1}{3}$ cup apple mixture into the center of each circle. Fold up the piecrust to enclose the fruit, firmly pinching the edges together at the top to seal. Repeat the procedure with the remaining piecrust and apple filling. Place the filled dumplings, at least 1 inch apart, in a 9 by 14-inch or other shallow 3-quart baking dish. Sprinkle with the remaining 1 tablespoon sugar.

3 In a small saucepan, bring the cider, butter, and maple syrup to a simmer, stirring to melt the butter. Pour the sauce around the apple dumplings.

4 Bake for 20 minutes, then spoon some of the syrup over the dumplings to baste them. Continue to bake, basting 1 or 2 more times, until the pastry is a rich golden brown and flaky, and the syrup is reduced and caramelized, about 20 minutes more.

5 Let the dumplings rest in the baking dish for about 5 minutes, then use a spatula to transfer the dumplings carefully to dessert plates. Spoon the caramel sauce over the dumplings. Serve warm or at room temperature with wedges of Cheddar cheese or scoops of ice cream, if desired.

(continued)

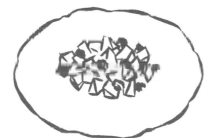

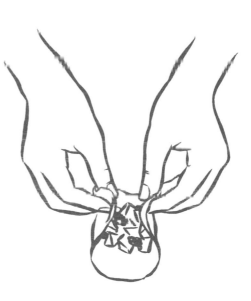

Caramel Apple Dumplings **Tips**

- Use the correct-size baking dish in order for the dumplings to bake in the syrup without soaking or drying out.
- Pour the sauce around, not over the dumplings in the beginning of baking.
- A bulb baster works beautifully to baste the apples, but a wide spoon is fine, too.

Caramel Apple Dumplings **Variations**

- Use pears or peaches in place of the apples.
- Use pecans in place of the walnuts.
- Use $\frac{1}{4}$ cup of prepared mincemeat in place of the apple mixture.

other desserts

Here is a collection of my **favorite** desserts that just don't seem to fit in any specific category other than they are just plain terrific, and are especially suited for **celebrations** large or small. All types of doughs play important roles in dessert making, from a cookie crust or base for a mousse cake or baked Alaska to **hot** shortcakes from the oven, hosting the best strawberries of the season. Brownie dough becomes a pudding cake or a **decadent** molten cake, and cookies turn into ice cream sandwiches. Each and every dessert is made so much **easier** with these doughs.

chocolate malted mousse cake

Malted milk powder and chocolate-covered malted milk balls give this cake the old-fashioned flavor of a chocolate malted milkshake, recalling the romance of an old-fashioned ice cream parlor. The brownie "cake" base is a perfect combination of crisp and chewy.

MALTED BROWNIE BASE

One 18-ounce package refrigerated brownie dough

$1/4$ cup malted milk powder

1 teaspoon vanilla extract

CHOCOLATE MALTED FILLING

6 ounces chocolate-covered malted milk balls

8 ounces milk chocolate, coarsely chopped

6 ounces bittersweet or semisweet chocolate, coarsely chopped

$2^1/2$ cups heavy cream, well chilled

$1/3$ cup malted milk powder

1 teaspoon vanilla extract

1   Preheat the oven to 350°F.

2   For the brownie base: Use a spoon or spatula to scrape the brownie batter into a mixing bowl, then stir in the malted milk powder and vanilla until blended. Spread evenly on the bottom of a 10-inch springform pan. Bake until the base is firm, about 25 minutes. Let cool completely in the pan on a rack.

3   For the filling: Set aside 12 of the malted milk balls for garnish. Finely chop the remainder in a food processor or place in a heavy plastic bag and crush with a rolling pin.

4   In a medium saucepan or microwave-safe bowl, gently melt together the milk and bittersweet chocolates. In another small bowl, stir together $1/2$ cup of the cream, the malted milk powder, and vanilla until the powder is dissolved. Stir into the chocolate until smooth. Let cool to room temperature.

5   In a large mixing bowl, whip the remaining 2 cups cream to firm peaks. Stir about 1 cup of the whipped cream into the chocolate mixture to lighten it, then fold the chocolate into the whipped cream until almost no streaks of white remain. Fold in the reserved crushed malted milk balls. Spoon the mousse onto the brownie base, smoothing the top. Refrigerate until firm, at least 2 hours or up to 12 hours. Arrange the 12 whole malted milk balls around the perimeter of the mousse.

6   To serve, run a metal spatula around the sides of the pan to separate the mousse from the pan, then remove the sides of the pan. Cut the mousse into wedges. Store any leftover mousse cake in the refrigerator.

Chocolate Malted Mousse Cake Tips

- Malted milk powder is found in the cocoa powder and flavored milk powder section of the market.
- The brownie "cake" base can be made a day ahead and stored at room temperature.
- The finished dessert can be frozen, tightly covered, for up to 2 weeks. Thaw in the refrigerator.

Chocolate Malted Mousse Cake Variations

- The recipe uses regular malted milk powder, but chocolate malted milk powder can also be used.
- The dessert can also be made in a 9 x 12-inch baking pan and cut into squares to serve.
- Malted milk balls are an old-fashioned boxed candy, but are even easier to find in candy stores or wherever candy is sold in big jars by the pound.

white chocolate raspberry chiffon torte

This very large, very beautiful torte is ideal for summer entertaining, since it can be made in the cool of the morning and served with great fanfare and no effort at dessert time on a warm summer evening. Frozen raspberries are used in the filling, with the more expensive fresh berries reserved as a garnish.

The cookie dough for the torte shell will be soft and puffed after baking, but it is easily flattened and shaped into a shell with the back of a spoon while still warm from the oven.

TORTE SHELL

One 18-ounce tube refrigerated sugar cookie dough

$1/2$ cup finely chopped almonds

1 teaspoon vanilla extract

$1/2$ teaspoon almond extract

3 ounces white chocolate baking bar, chopped

RASPBERRY CHIFFON FILLING

Two 10-ounce packages frozen sweetened raspberries, thawed

1 envelope unflavored gelatin

2 tablespoons Framboise or raspberry liqueur, or raspberry syrup

$1^{1}/2$ cups heavy cream, well chilled

1 pint fresh raspberries

2 ounces white chocolate, shaved or curls, optional

1   Preheat the oven to 350°F. In a large mixing bowl, use your hands to break up the cookie dough, then knead in the almonds and vanilla and almond extracts until well blended. Press the dough evenly into the bottom of a 9-inch springform pan.

2   Bake the crust until it is rich golden brown, 25 to 30 minutes. The center of the torte will be puffed. Remove the pan from the oven. Immediately, while still warm, use the back of a spoon to push down the center and press the dough toward the sides to build up the edges. Let the torte shell cool completely in the pan on a rack. In a small bowl set over hot water or in a microwave oven, melt the 3 ounces white chocolate and spread over the cooled base. Place in the refrigerator for at least 10 minutes to set the chocolate.

3   Puree the frozen raspberries with their syrup in a food processor, then press through a strainer into a saucepan, discarding the seeds in the strainer. Sprinkle the gelatin over the raspberries. Let stand for about 2 minutes to soften the gelatin. Place the pan over medium heat and stir until the mixture is lukewarm and the gelatin is dissolved, 2 to 3 minutes. Stir in the liqueur or syrup. Refrigerate the raspberry mixture, stirring occasionally, until the mixture mounds slightly, about $1^1/2$ hours.

4   In a medium bowl, whip the cream to firm peaks. Fold about one-fourth of the whipped cream into the raspberry mixture to lighten it, then fold the raspberry mixture and whipped cream together until no streaks of white remain. Spread the filling smoothly over the torte base. Refrigerate for 15 to 20 minutes to firm slightly, then arrange the fresh raspberries, stem side down, to cover the top. Refrigerate until ready to serve, at least 2 hours or up to 12 hours.

5   To serve, cut into wedges and sprinkle each slice with a few white chocolate shavings or curls, if desired. (continued)

White Chocolate Raspberry Chiffon Torte **Tips**

- Be sure to buy frozen raspberries in light or heavy syrup, not dry-packed raspberries, which are unsweetened.
- Use white chocolate in a bar, not chips, which do not melt as well.
- To shave or curl white chocolate, have a block or bar at cool room temperature, then carefully shave off curls, using a swivel vegetable peeler. Use a toothpick to transfer the delicate curls to a plate, and refrigerate until ready to use.
- To test if the gelatin is dissolved, rub a little of the mixture in your fingers—it should not feel grainy.

White Chocolate Raspberry Chiffon Torte **Variations**

- The torte can be made with fresh and frozen strawberries in the same manner.
- Substitute semisweet chocolate for the white chocolate.
- The torte can become a tart if you make it in an 11-inch tart pan with a removable bottom, or in two 8- or 9-inch tart pans with removable bottoms.

molten chocolate clementine brownie cakes

Inspired by the molten chocolate cakes on restaurant dessert menus, this is a sensational dessert worthy of your finest dinner party, and easy enough to make for Tuesday night supper for your finest guests—your family. If clementines are not in season, use small seedless oranges.

2 teaspoons unsalted butter, softened

2 teaspoons sugar

One 18-ounce package refrigerated brownie dough

2 eggs

2 tablespoons orange liqueur

2 teaspoons vanilla extract

1 pint orange gelato

4 clementines, peeled and sectioned

1 Preheat the oven to 350°F. Lightly butter eight 6-ounce custard cups or individual soufflé dishes, and sprinkle with sugar, shaking out the excess. Place the cups on a baking sheet.

2 In a mixing bowl, use a mixing spoon to break up the brownie dough. Add the eggs, liqueur, and vanilla. Beat until the batter is smooth. Divide the batter evenly among the custard cups or soufflé dishes.

3 Bake until the center of the batter is puffed and barely loses its wet shine, about 20 minutes. Do not overbake.

4 Remove the cups or dishes from the oven, let stand for 2 to 3 minutes, then use a knife to loosen the cakes from the sides of the cups. Invert the cakes onto individual serving plates. Garnish each with a small scoop of gelato and clementine wedges. Serve immediately.

(continued)

Molten Chocolate Clementine Brownie Cakes **Tips**

- Nestlé's brownie dough works best for this recipe.
- Don't overbake the cakes—it's better to underbake them by a couple of minutes than cook the center beyond the molten liquid stage. The tops should just lose the wet, shiny look.
- If the cakes cool completely or overbake, the centers will firm up, but the dessert will still taste great.

Molten Chocolate Clementine Brownie Cakes **Variations**

- Use another liqueur flavor in place of the orange liqueur, or substitute strong coffee or flavored syrups, such as almond or raspberry.
- Substitute raspberries or small whole strawberries for the clementines.
- Substitute vanilla ice cream or mango, passion fruit, or raspberry gelato for the orange gelato.

hot fudge brownie pudding cake

MAKES 8
SERVINGS

This recipe is the easiest and hands-down best version for this perennial favorite hot chocolate dessert. Serve it warm with ice cream, at room temperature with whipped cream, or from the refrigerator spooned out of the pan and into your mouth. The dessert thickens as it cools, and when cold is downright caramel-sticky, like solidified hot fudge sauce with a brownie on top. At every temperature, it is a chocoholic's delight. By the way, the coffee is present to deepen and enhance the chocolate flavor, which is a little known but excellent coffee quality.

One 18-ounce package refrigerated brownie dough
$1/3$ cup sugar
3 tablespoons unsweetened cocoa powder
2 tablespoons instant coffee granules
1 teaspoon vanilla extract
1 cup boiling water

1   Preheat the oven to 350°F. Lightly grease an 8 x 8-inch baking pan.

2   Separate the brownies and place them in the pan, according to the package directions. In a mixing bowl, whisk together the sugar, cocoa, and coffee. Add the vanilla and boiling water, stirring to dissolve the mixture.

3   Pour the hot liquid evenly over the brownies in the pan. Bake until the batter is very dark and bubbly all over, about 35 minutes. Cool the pudding cake in the pan for at least 15 minutes before scooping out and serving. When warm, the cake will be very soft with a liquid bottom; served at room temperature, it will be soft with a creamy thick bottom; chilled, it will have a sticky brownie top with a creamy dark chocolate saucy bottom.   *(continued)*

Hot Fudge Brownie Pudding Cake Tips

- This won't look a bit like brownies during baking, but instead like brownies in a bubbling chocolate liquid. That's just fine.
- When the cake is warm, you will have to use a serving spoon to scoop out portions, but served chilled, the pudding can be cut and served with a spatula.
- Nestlé's brownie dough works best for this recipe.

Hot Fudge Brownie Pudding Cake Variations

- If you don't like coffee, simply omit it from the recipe.
- One-half cup chopped nuts can be sprinkled over the unbaked brownies in the pan and pressed lightly into the dough before adding the hot liquid.
- Substitute 2 tablespoons almond or raspberry syrup for 2 tablespoons boiling water, if desired.

oatmeal raisin snack cake

This recipe came about in one of those what-if-I-mixed-these-together? moments. I wanted to make a bar cookie that was moist and would cut more like a cake, so I added cream cheese for richness and eggs for moisture. Then the batter looked a little plain, so I sprinkled it with nuts and cinnamon sugar. The result was eaten up so fast by my family that I hardly got to taste it for testing purposes. So I made it a few more times. Same thing every time. The snack cake is also a good "keeper," and is just as good a couple of days after baking as it is warm from the pan.

**One 18-ounce tube or package refrigerated oatmeal raisin cookie
dough**

8 ounces cream cheese, softened

2 eggs

1 teaspoon vanilla extract

3 teaspoons apple pie spice blend

$1/2$ cup chopped walnuts

2 tablespoons sugar

1 Preheat the oven to 350°F.

2 In a mixing bowl, use your hands to break up the cookie dough and the cream cheese. Add the eggs, vanilla, and 2 teaspoons of the spice blend. Use a spoon to mix the ingredients until blended and a thick batter forms. Spread the batter in an 8-inch square baking pan. Sprinkle with the nuts, sugar, and remaining 1 teaspoon spice blend.

3 Bake until a toothpick inserted into the center of the cake comes out with a few crumbs, about 45 minutes. Cool the cake in the pan on a rack. Cut into squares to serve. *(continued)*

Oatmeal Raisin Snack Cake **Tips**

- The cake will be done when a toothpick inserted in the center has a few crumbs attached, but the center looks set and no longer wet. It will continue to cook slightly as it cools.
- Store the cake, covered, at room temperature.
- If your brand of oatmeal raisin cookies doesn't have enough raisins for your taste, stir in up to $1/4$ cup more.

Oatmeal Raisin Snack Cake **Variations**

- Use pumpkin pie spice blend in place of apple pie spice; or if you really like cinnamon, use it only.
- Substitute pecans or almonds for the walnuts.
- Bake in 12 paper-lined cupcake tins to make individual snack cakes. Bake for about 25 minutes, or until a toothpick comes out with a few crumbs attached.

strawberry
shortcake

Strawberry shortcake is the simplest of all desserts, and is best in its original version. Some, like my children, consider it a whole meal—their defense is that it's dairy, grain, and fruit. I tend to agree, at least once during the short season in which our local strawberries come to market. You can, of course, embellish strawberry shortcake, but I don't approve. So, there are no variations to this recipe.

3 tablespoons unsalted butter, softened

$1/2$ cup sugar

One 17.3-ounce tube refrigerated buttermilk biscuit dough

2 pints strawberries, sliced

1 cup heavy cream, well chilled

1 Preheat the oven to 400°F. Melt 2 tablespoons of the butter and place in a shallow dish. Place 2 tablespoons of the sugar in another shallow dish. Dip the tops of the biscuits into the melted butter, then into the sugar to coat. Place the biscuits, at least 2 inches apart, on a large baking sheet.

2 Bake the biscuits until a rich golden brown, 14 to 16 minutes. Transfer the biscuits to a rack to cool slightly.

3 While the biscuits are baking, in a mixing bowl stir together the remaining 6 tablespoons sugar and the strawberries. Let stand at room temperature for at least 15 minutes. In another small bowl, whip the cream to soft peaks.

4 To assemble the shortcakes, split the warm biscuits and spread the cut sides with the remaining 1 tablespoon butter. Place the biscuit bottoms on 8 dessert plates. Spoon most of the strawberries and juices over the biscuit bottoms. Replace the lids, spoon the remaining strawberries and juices over the tops, and dollop with whipped cream. Serve immediately.

(continued)

Strawberry Shortcake **Tips**

- Buttermilk biscuit dough makes the flakiest shortcake biscuits.
- Dipping the biscuit dough into butter, then sugar produces a crackly, richly browned top crust.
- Use only really wonderful, fragrant strawberries. If they're not available, make another dessert.
- There are no wonderful, fragrant strawberries in December.
- Cream that is whipped to soft peaks is also known as Chantilly cream in classic cookbooks. This works even better if you use regular pasteurized heavy cream, not the ultrapasteurized variety.
- Always use heavy cream, not "whipping cream," which has a lower butterfat content.

red/white/blueberry cookie shortcakes

Adding a couple of eggs to sugar cookie dough results in a more cakelike, tender cookie that absorbs fruit juices really beautifully. Because you can make them ahead of time, these shortcakes can be as last minute as you like. They are also a particularly good (and relatively healthy) after-school snack. Vary the fruit according to the season.

COOKIE SHORTCAKES

One 18-ounce tube refrigerated sugar cookie dough

2 eggs

1 teaspoon grated orange zest

1 teaspoon vanilla extract

1/2 teaspoon grated nutmeg, preferably freshly grated

1 tablespoon sugar

FRUIT FILLING

2 pints strawberries

1 pint blueberries

1/2 cup sugar

1 teaspoon lemon juice

1 pint vanilla ice cream, softened

1   For the cookies: Preheat the oven to 350°F. Lightly grease two large baking sheets.

2   In a mixing bowl, use your hands to break up the cookie dough. Add the eggs, orange zest, vanilla, and nutmeg. Use your hands or a mixing spoon to mix or knead the dough until all the ingredients are incorporated and a soft dough forms. Drop the dough by heaping tablespoons, at least 3 inches apart, on the prepared baking sheets, forming about 24 cookies and sprinkle with sugar.

3   Bake until the cookies are pale gold with golden edges, 13 to 15 minutes. Use a spatula to transfer the cookies to a rack to cool completely.   *(continued)*

4   For the fruit filling: In a mixing bowl, crush half of the strawberries with the back of a spoon, then slice the remaining strawberries. Add the sliced strawberries to the crushed berries along with half of the blueberries. Place the remaining blueberries, sugar, and lemon juice in a small saucepan. Stir over medium heat, crushing the berries with the back of a spoon, and cook until the juices are released and a syrup forms. Let cool, then stir the blueberry syrup into the fruit mixture in the bowl. Let stand at room temperature for at least 15 minutes or refrigerate for up to 4 hours.

5   To assemble the shortcakes, place one cookie on a dessert plate. Spoon about $\frac{1}{3}$ cup of the fruit mixture over the cookie, then top with another cookie. Spoon about $\frac{1}{4}$ cup softened ice cream over the top cookie. Serve immediately.

Red/White/Blueberry Cookie Shortcakes Tips

- Use the best berries you can find, but this dessert is also perfectly good made with frozen strawberries in syrup and frozen blueberries. No need to cook them at all and no need to add extra sugar.
- The cookies can be made up to 3 days ahead and stored, tightly covered.
- Extra cookies are delicious on their own.

Red/White/Blueberry Cookie Shortcakes Variations

- Use sliced peaches in place of the strawberries.
- Substitute ground cinnamon for the nutmeg in the cookies.
- Substitute $\frac{1}{2}$ teaspoon ground cloves for the nutmeg in the cookies.

double peanut butter and concord grape shortcakes

MAKES 6 SERVINGS

While definitely not "the real thing," this nonstrawberry, nonbiscuit shortcake will have equal appeal, since it combines two of America's favorite native culinary concepts—shortcakes and peanut butter and jelly. Both an adult and a kid version are given here, though when it comes to PB&J, everyone is a kid. Any type of grapes will work, but a mixture, especially with some tiny champagne grapes, is especially nice. Growing up along the Lake Erie coastline, where Concord grapes are a major crop, I spent my youth popping grapes out of the skin right into the mouth. There are no more flavorful table grapes on earth!

One-half 18-ounce tube refrigerated peanut butter cookie dough

1 cup Concord grape jam (not jelly)

$1/3$ cup full-bodied red wine or Concord grape juice

1 tablespoon lemon juice

2 cups mixed small grapes, such as red or green seedless, champagne, or peeled and seeded Concords

$1/2$ cup crunchy peanut butter

1   Preheat the oven to 400°F. Position the oven rack in the center. Cut the cookie dough crosswise into 12 slices. Place the slices, at least 1 inch apart, on a baking sheet.

2   Place the baking sheet in the oven and immediately reduce the oven temperature to 375°F. Bake until the cookies are browned at the edges, and golden brown in the center, 10 to 12 minutes. Transfer the cookies to a rack to cool slightly.

3   While the cookies are baking, in a small saucepan simmer together the jam and wine until reduced by about one-third, about 5 minutes. Stir in the lemon juice and half of the grapes. Set aside but keep warm.

4   To assemble, spread one side of each cookie with about 2 teaspoons peanut butter. Place 1 cookie, peanut butter side up, on a dessert plate. Spoon about $1/4$ cup grape sauce over the cookie. Top with another cookie, peanut butter side down. Repeat to make 6 shortcakes. Spoon

the remaining grape sauce over the top cookies. Sprinkle the remaining grapes around the shortcakes.

Double Peanut Butter and Concord Grape Shortcakes Tips

- Any really flavorful grapes are delicious, but a mixture is especially pretty. Concords need to be skinned by just popping the skin off with your fingers.
- Grape jam and juice are almost always made largely from Concord grapes.
- Use your favorite brand of peanut butter—if you use the nonhomogenized kind, be sure to stir it first.
- The grape sauce can be prepared a day ahead and reheated. Add the grapes shortly before serving.

Double Peanut Butter and Concord Grape Shortcakes Variations

- You could use strawberry jam and berries—it tastes just as good—but not if you are a PB&J aficionado. Only grape jam is acceptable then.
- Use sugar cookie dough in place of the peanut butter cookie dough.
- Use smooth peanut butter in place of the crunchy.
- Use cinnamon-spiced peanut butter and applesauce in place of the grape sauce and grapes.

Quick Cookies-and-Ice-Cream Desserts

Here are some ideas for using prepared doughs to make quick but wonderful and delicious ice cream desserts based on prepared doughs.

ice cream
sandwiches

Use premium-quality ice cream, which will soften more evenly without melting than low-fat ice cream or frozen yogurt. The flavor combinations are limited only by your imagination.

> One 18-ounce tube or package refrigerated cookie dough, any
>   flavor or type
> 1 pint premium-quality ice cream, barely softened
> Hot fudge sauce, finely chopped nuts, or miniature chocolate
>   chips, optional

1   For round sandwiches, preheat the oven to 375°F. Cut the cookie dough into 24 slices or 36 slices for smaller sandwiches. Place on baking sheets, at least 2 inches apart, then press down to lightly flatten the dough. Bake until golden and firm, 10 to 14 minutes, depending upon the size of the cookies.

2   For square sandwiches, preheat the oven to 350°F. Divide the dough in half and press each half into an 8-inch square pan. Bake until golden and firm, 20 to 23 minutes. Let cool in the pan for 10 minutes, then cut the dough in each pan into 16 squares. Let the squares cool in the pan for another 10 minutes, then use a spatula to transfer them to a rack to cool completely.

3   To assemble, spoon about 2 tablespoons ice cream onto the flat side of half of the cookies or bars, then sandwich with the flat sides of the remaining bars. If desired, dip half of each bar cookie into hot fudge sauce, or roll in nuts or miniature chocolate chips.

4   Immediately place the sandwiches on a baking sheet and freeze until firm, at least 1 hour. Then, wrap the sandwiches individually in plastic wrap and store in the freezer until ready to use, up to 3 days.

cookie or
brownie sundaes

When you want a really big, really gooey dessert in no time and with no effort, this is the answer. Since the big dessert urge might present itself with little warning, it's worth it to have the three major ingredients—cookie dough, ice cream, and sauce—on hand. My favorite combination is peanut butter cookies with butter pecan ice cream, caramel sauce, and crushed peanut brittle sprinkled over the top. On chocolate days, the choice is brownies with coffee ice cream, hot fudge sauce, and a sprinkle of chocolate-covered coffee beans. In summer, a fruit sundae of sugar cookies, peach ice cream, sliced sweetened strawberries, and whipped cream can't be beat.

One 18-ounce tube or package refrigerated cookie or brownie
   dough, any flavor
$1/2$ gallon ice cream, gelato, or frozen yogurt
2 cups hot fudge or caramel sauce
Chopped nuts, fresh berries, sliced banans, whipped cream,
   and/or sprinkles, optional

1   Bake the cookies according to the package directions, but bake at 375°F until golden and crisp. Or press the cookie dough into two 8-inch square baking pans. Bake at 350°F until the dough is lightly browned and set, 20 to 23 minutes. Bake the brownies according to the package directions. Cut bar cookies or brownies into 12 to 16 large bars.

2   Assemble the sundaes by placing 1 or 2 cookies or a large bar in a shallow dessert bowl. Ladle each sundae with sauce, then garnish as desired.

cookie or brownie baked alaska

Baked Alaska is a most impressive dessert, but also one of the easiest to make. It can be largely assembled well ahead of time, with just the meringue, brief baking, and spectacular presentation left to the last minute.

One-half tube or package refrigerated cookie or brownie dough
2 pints premium-quality ice cream
6 egg whites
$^1/_4$ teaspoon cream of tartar
$^3/_4$ cup sugar

1   Preheat the oven to 350°F. Press the cookie or brownie dough into a 9-inch tart pan with a removable bottom. Bake until the base is just set and lightly browned, 20 to 23 minutes. Cool completely in the pan on a rack, then carefully remove the sides of the pan and slide the cookie, still on the base of the pan, onto a small baking sheet.

2   Slightly soften the ice cream, then spread evenly over the top of the cookie base. Place in the freezer until the ice cream is frozen hard again, at least 2 hours or up to 12 hours, covering with plastic wrap or aluminum foil after 2 hours.

3   Preheat the oven to 450°F. In a large mixing bowl, use an electric mixer to beat the egg whites until frothy. Add the cream of tartar and continue to beat to soft peaks. Add the sugar, 1 table-spoon at a time, beating until firm, shiny, and moist peaks form. Remove the ice cream base from the freezer, and immediately spread the meringue to completely cover the ice cream and cookie base. Mound and swirl the meringue in the center.

4   Immediately bake the dessert until the meringue is pale golden and browned at the swirl tips, 4 to 5 minutes.

5   Use a large spatula to quickly transfer the baked Alaska from the baking sheet to a serving plat-ter. Serve immediately, cut into wedges.   *(continued)*

Cookie or Brownie Baked Alaska **Tips**

- The cookie or brownie base can be made a day ahead and stored at room temperature.
- Egg whites beat higher when they are at room temperature in a grease-free bowl.
- Premium-quality ice cream is key for a baked Alaska, since lower-butterfat ice cream or frozen yogurt may melt in the oven.
- The egg whites in this recipe will not be fully cooked; so if this poses a problem for you, use pasteurized egg whites or meringue powder, following the directions for a 6-egg meringue.

Cookie or Brownie Baked Alaska **Variations**

- Make individual baked Alaskas by baking the cookie or brownie dough in eight 4$\frac{1}{2}$-inch tart pans or in an 8-inch square pan and cutting into 8 squares. Increase the meringue ingredients by half in order to cover all the individual Alaskas.
- Make a brown sugar meringue by substituting $\frac{1}{2}$ cup packed light brown sugar for $\frac{1}{2}$ cup of the granulated sugar.
- Serve the baked Alaskas with hot fudge sauce or sweetened berries or sliced peaches.

cookies

Probably the most **fun** I've had in writing this book is translating favorite American cookies into prepared dough recipes. In most cases, the transformation was **astoundingly simple**, with only a very few ingredients added, notably pure vanilla to counter the artificial stuff that is the standard in most nationally branded cookie doughs. Increasingly, smaller companies and **regional** bakeries are marketing their own doughs, and these often feature **pure** flavoring **extracts** and require no additional vanilla at all. In developing these recipes, my final exam was baking two or three dozen Christmas cookie varieties (which took about 10 percent of my usual time) and asking **family and friends** what they thought. Everyone wanted the recipes.

sugar cookie cutouts

There is a cookie cutter for every occasion and holiday. But even if you don't own a single cutter, fanciful cookies can be made by simply using different sizes of glasses or jars to cut circles. Then decorate the unbaked cookies with a shower of colored sugar, or ice baked cookies with confectioners' sugar icing (see page 133), tinted with food coloring to suit the occasion. You can get as elaborate as you wish with cookies, and they are the perfect project for little hands learning to bake.

One 18-ounce tube refrigerated sugar cookie dough
$1/2$ cup all-purpose flour
1 teaspoon vanilla extract
$1/2$ teaspoon grated nutmeg
1 tablespoon granulated sugar

1   In a mixing bowl, use your hands to break up the cookie dough. Sprinkle with the flour, vanilla, and nutmeg. Use your hands to knead the dough until the ingredients are fully incorporated and the dough is stiff. Divide the dough into 4 parts, wrap in plastic wrap, and refrigerate for at least 30 minutes or up to 8 hours.

2   Preheat the oven to 375°F. Lightly grease a large baking sheet.

3   Working with one part of the dough at a time and keeping the remainder refrigerated, roll the dough on a lightly floured surface to slightly less than $1/4$-inch thickness. Cut with lightly floured cookie cutters to desired shapes. Use a spatula to transfer the cookies, at least 1 inch apart, to the prepared baking sheet. Sprinkle the cookies with the granulated sugar.

4   Bake until the cookies are firm to the touch, pale golden with rich golden brown edges, 10 to 12 minutes. Use a spatula to transfer the cookies to a rack to cool.

Sugar Cookie Cutouts Tips

- The dough needs to be chilled before rolling, so plan a bit ahead of time to bake the cookies.
- A cold rolling pin and rolling surface help to keep the dough from sticking, thus you need a minimum of flour. Place the rolling pin in the freezer for about 15 minutes, and cool the rolling surface by placing a bag of ice cubes or a freezer pack on it for a few minutes just before using it.
- If you can find coarse "sanding" sugar in your market with the cake decorating supplies, use it in place of granulated sugar for a prettier effect.

Sugar Cookie Cutouts Variations

- Sprinkle unbaked cookie cutouts with colored sugar, or press raisins, dried cranberries, or miniature chocolate chips into the cutout dough before baking.
- Frost baked cookies with confectioners' sugar icing made by mixing 2 cups confectioners' sugar with about 2 tablespoons milk and a few drops of food coloring, if desired, until a spreading consistency is achieved. You may need a little more or less sugar or milk.
- Glaze baked cookies with 1 cup confectioners' sugar mixed with 1 to 2 tablespoons water to form a clear glaze that will harden as it dries. The cookies will have a crackly sheen.

MAKES
ABOUT 36
COOKIES

orange gingerbread persons

Gingerbread cutout cookies are a classic during the Christmas season, partly for their taste but equally as much for the wonderful aromas they deliver during baking. Refrigerated gingerbread cookie dough is pleasant enough, but doesn't deliver nearly enough ginger for my taste. So, I go straight to the source and knead grated fresh ginger into the dough, along with a little grated orange zest whose sweetness offsets the sharp ginger. Though the scent says Christmas, gingerbread cookies at other times of the year are known as gingersnaps, and loved just as much.

One 18-ounce tube refrigerated gingerbread cookie dough
1/2 cup all-purpose flour
1 tablespoon grated or finely chopped fresh ginger
1 tablespoon grated orange zest
1 teaspoon vanilla extract
Raisins, candied ginger, cinnamon red-hot candies, or other decorations of your choice

1 In a mixing bowl, use your hands to break up the cookie dough. Sprinkle with the flour, ginger, orange zest, and vanilla. Use your hands to knead the dough until the ingredients are fully incorporated and the dough is stiff. Divide the dough into 4 parts, wrap in plastic wrap, and refrigerate for at least 30 minutes or up to 8 hours.

2 Preheat the oven to 375°F. Lightly grease a large baking sheet.

3 Working with one part of the dough at a time and keeping the remainder refrigerated, roll the dough on a lightly floured surface to slightly less than 1/4-inch thickness. Cut with lightly floured cookie cutters to desired shapes. Use a spatula to transfer the cookies, at least 1 inch apart, to the prepared baking sheet. Decorate with raisins, candied ginger, red-hots, or other decorations as desired.

4 Bake until the cookies are firm to the touch and darker brown around the edges, 10 to 12 minutes. Use a spatula to transfer the cookies to a rack to cool.

Orange Gingerbread Persons **Tips**

- Use a coarse citrus grater to grate fresh ginger, or finely chop the pieces with a knife.
- Thick, rough-skinned oranges tend to have the most flavorful peel.
- Grate only the colored part of the orange peel, avoiding the bitter white pithy layer.

Orange Gingerbread Persons **Variations**

- To make gingersnaps, pinch off pieces of dough and roll into 1- or $1^{1}/_{2}$-inch balls. Roll the balls in granulated sugar, then place on the cookie sheets. Using the bottom of a glass, flatten the balls to about $^{1}/_{2}$ inch thick. Bake until firm and darker around the edges, 12 to 14 minutes. Cool on racks.

whoopie pies

For some of us who grew up in a certain generation, whoopie pies are not just a cookie, they are a mini-meal. Indeed, these semisoft chocolate cookies, sandwiched with snowy white fluffy crème (not cream), are more filling than a traditional cookie. When we were young, and all our fifties moms baked cookies at home, no one made whoopie pies from scratch. Instead, they represented the new, highly cool, and slightly forbidden genre of "bought" cookies. Today, it's hard to find a real whoopie pie in the bakery, and it's easy to make them at home. Note: Don't try to get too upscale and use all butter in the filling. It won't be right for a whoopie pie.

COOKIES

Two 18-ounce tubes refrigerated sugar cookie dough

$^1/_2$ cup unsweetened cocoa powder

2 teaspoons vanilla extract

FILLING

$^1/_3$ cup unsalted butter, softened

$^1/_3$ cup vegetable shortening (Crisco)

1 cup confectioners' sugar

$1^1/_2$ tablespoons light corn syrup

2 teaspoons vanilla extract

One 7-ounce jar ($1^1/_3$ cups) marshmallow fluff

1   **For the cookies: Preheat the oven to 350°F.**

2   **In a large mixing bowl, use your hands to break up both rolls of cookie dough. Sprinkle with the cocoa and vanilla. Knead the dough until the cocoa is fully incorporated. Pinch off tablespoon-size pieces of dough and roll into balls. Place on cookie sheets, about 2 inches apart, and flatten each cookie with the bottom of a glass to about $^1/_4$ inch thickness.**

3   **Bake until the cookies are set and just firm, about 10 minutes. Use a spatula to transfer the cookies to a rack to cool completely.**

4   For the filling: In a mixing bowl, use an electric hand mixer or a whisk to whip the butter, shortening, confectioners' sugar, corn syrup, and vanilla until light and fluffy. Beat or whisk in the marshmallow fluff until fluffy.

5   To assemble the whoopie pies, spread about 1 tablespoon of the filling on the flat side of half of the cookies. Sandwich with the remaining cookies, flat side down.

Whoopie Pies Tips

- The filled cookies can be eaten immediately, but if they are allowed to stand for at least an hour, the filling will slightly soften the cookies, which will make them more like the traditional whoopie pies.
- You can make half a recipe of cookies using 1 tube of dough, but it's easiest to make the full recipe of filling. Extra filling can be refrigerated for several days; just whisk it again to make it fluffy before using. Use the extra filling to frost cupcakes, if you wish
- To store the cookies for up to 2 days, wrap each in plastic wrap.

Whoopie Pies Variations

- Make double chocolate whoopie pies by adding 3 tablespoons unsweetened cocoa powder to the filling.
- Make molasses-spice whoopie pies by substituting molasses for the corn syrup in the filling, using gingerbread cookie dough with 2 teaspoons ground ginger added, and deleting cocoa from the cookie dough.
- Make maple-walnut whoopie pies by kneading $1/2$ cup finely chopped walnuts into the dough and substituting maple syrup for the corn syrup in the filling.

sandy pecan cookies

There are very few commercial cookies that have had a long and well-loved shelf life. Oreos are one, and Pecan Sandies are another. Though either one is impossible to duplicate (the recipe is a closely guarded secret at both companies), a fine facsimile of the latter is easy to make at home. After many batches and tastings, it seems that the secrets lie in a touch of cinnamon and maple extract added to the dough along with really good-quality pecans. The maple extract approximates the brown sugar in the original cookie, and the higher baking temperature caramelizes the cookies.

One 18-ounce tube refrigerated sugar cookie dough
1 teaspoon vanilla extract
$^1/_2$ teaspoon maple extract
$^1/_2$ teaspoon ground cinnamon
$^1/_2$ cup finely chopped toasted pecans

1   Preheat the oven to 375°F.

2   In a mixing bowl, use your hands to break up the cookie dough. Sprinkle with the vanilla and maple extracts, cinnamon, and pecans. Use your hands to knead the dough until all the ingredients are fully incorporated. Pinch off tablespoon-size pieces of dough and form into balls. Place the balls on a baking sheet, about $1^1/_2$ inches apart. Use the palm of your hand to flatten each to about $^1/_2$-inch thickness.

3   Bake until the edges of the cookies are browned and the tops are golden, 12 to 14 minutes. Transfer the cookies to a rack to cool completely.

Sandy Pecan Cookies **Tips**

- Buy the freshest pecans. Check the "sell by" or "use by" date on the bags.
- To toast the nuts, spread them on a baking sheet in a preheating oven. Toast, stirring once or twice, until they are fragrant and a shade darker, about 5 minutes. Let the toasted nuts cool completely before using them in recipes.

Sandy Pecan Cookies **Variations**

- Substitute walnuts or other nuts for the pecans.
- For a crisp-edged cookie with a soft interior, don't flatten the cookie balls before baking.
- For a completely crisp wafer cookie, flatten the cookie balls to $1/4$ inch before baking.

hazelnut
biscotti

Real biscotti from Italy often contain no shortening at all, but most American versions are variations on sugar cookie dough. It's the double-baking method that turns the cookies into biscotti. The dough is first shaped into a log and baked until just firm. The log is cooled slightly, then sliced on the diagonal. The slices are then baked again until very crisp. Variations on biscotti are endless, though most traditional versions have some nuts. Because they are very crisp and sturdy, these cookies are good keepers and are also good for mailing.

One 18-ounce tube refrigerated sugar cookie dough
$^1/_2$ cup all-purpose flour
$^1/_2$ cup chopped toasted hazelnuts
1 teaspoon vanilla extract
$^1/_2$ teaspoon almond extract

1   Preheat the oven to 350°F. Lightly grease a large cookie sheet.

2   In a mixing bowl, use your hands to break up the cookie dough. Sprinkle with the flour, nuts, and vanilla and almond extracts. Use your hands to knead the dough until all the ingredients are fully incorporated.

3   Divide the dough into two parts. Place each part on the prepared baking sheet and form each into a 12-inch log that is about 1 inch thick. Bake until the dough is pale golden and the top is just firm, 20 to 25 minutes.

4   Let the logs cool on the baking sheet for about 5 minutes, then use a sharp knife to cut each log into 12 diagonal slices, each about 1 inch thick. Place the slices, cut side up and about 1 inch apart, on the same baking sheet. Continue to bake the cookies until they are rich golden brown and quite firm, 10 to 15 minutes. Transfer the cookies to a rack to cool completely. The cookies can be stored, tightly covered, for up to 1 week.

Hazelnut Biscotti Tips

- Don't underbake the cookies. They should be quite crisp.
- To pack the cookies for shipping, wrap each in plastic wrap, then box with bubble wrap or air-popped popcorn.
- To cut the slightly warm cookie rolls, use a sharp knife and a gentle downward, not sawing, motion.

Hazelnut Biscotti Variations

- Substitute toasted pine nuts or chopped almonds for the hazelnuts.
- For chocolate biscotti, substitute $1/4$ cup unsweetened cocoa powder for $1/4$ cup of the flour, and use toasted walnuts in place of the hazelnuts.
- Substitute $1/4$ cup dried cranberries for $1/4$ cup of the hazelnuts.

malted milk "balls"

Malted milk powder was first marketed many years ago as a "health food," then it became quite popular as the signature ingredient in soda-parlor chocolate malteds. Today, it's making a comeback in all sorts of new uses, from cheesecakes and dessert sauces to this outstanding cookie. The addition of the malted milk powder not only flavors the cookies, it makes them ultracrispy and crackly. Be sure to try the variation in which the cookie dough is rolled around or topped with malted milk candy balls—it's a double malt treat.

One 18-ounce tube refrigerated sugar cookie dough
$1/2$ cup malted milk powder
$1/4$ cup all-purpose flour
$1/2$ teaspoon vanilla extract

1   Preheat the oven to 350°F. Position the oven rack in the center. Lightly grease a large cookie sheet.

2   In a mixing bowl, use your hands to break up the cookie dough. Sprinkle with the malted milk powder, flour, and vanilla. Use your hands to knead the dough until the ingredients are fully incorporated.

3   Drop the dough by tablespoons onto the prepared baking sheet, spacing at least 2 inches apart. Bake until the cookies are browned on the edges and golden in the center. Use a spatula to transfer the cookies to a rack to cool completely.

Malted Milk "Balls" Tips

- The cookies will spread quite a bit during baking, so be sure to leave enough space in between each cookie.
- Look for malted milk powder in the chocolate syrup or canned milk section of the supermarket.

Malted Milk "Balls" Variations

- Use chocolate-flavored malted milk powder, if you wish.
- Knead in an additional 2 tablespoons flour, then form the dough into balls, pressing a whole malted milk candy ball into the center of each before baking.
- Knead in $\frac{1}{4}$ cup chopped malted milk candy balls.

double peanut butter cookies

Nothing beats the flavor of real peanuts and peanut butter. You can make a triple peanut version if you start with peanut butter cookie dough, though sugar cookie dough is easier to find and works just as well. There are several variations on this theme, including turning the cookies into jelly "sandwiches" or pressing a chocolate "kiss" into the center of each. All are decadent and delicious.

One 18-ounce tube refrigerated sugar cookie dough
$1/3$ cup all-purpose flour
$1/3$ cup peanut butter, smooth or crunchy
$1/2$ cup coarsely chopped roasted peanuts
$1/2$ teaspoon vanilla extract

1   Preheat the oven to 350°F.

2   In a mixing bowl, use your hands to break up the cookie dough. Add the flour, peanut butter, peanuts, and vanilla. Use your hands to knead the dough until the ingredients are fully incorporated. Drop the dough by tablespoons onto a baking sheet, at least $1^1/2$ inches apart. Dip the tines of a fork into flour, then press the cookies twice, in a crisscross design, to flatten them to about $1/2$-inch thickness.

3   Bake until the cookies are golden and the edges are lightly browned, 12 to 14 minutes. Use a spatula to transfer the cookies to a rack to cool completely.

Double Peanut Butter Cookies **Tips**

- Do not use natural or nonhomogenized peanut butter for this recipe.
- The crisscross top is the traditional decoration for homemade peanut butter cookies.
- If the finished dough seems too soft to shape, refrigerate it for about 15 minutes first.

Double Peanut Butter Cookies **Variations**

- Use peanut butter cookie dough in place of the sugar cookie dough.
- Add $\frac{1}{4}$ cup all-purpose flour to the dough. Shape tablespoons of dough around unwrapped chocolate kisses or bite-size chocolate peanut butter cups, then place on the baking sheet.
- Flatten the cookies to about $\frac{1}{4}$-inch thickness before baking. Sandwich 2 flat sides of the cookies together with about 2 teaspoons grape or other flavor jam.

mocha latte pinwheels

Pinwheel cookies are simple to make, and the flavor and/or color variations are limited only by your imagination. Try cinnamon red and green for Christmas, pink peppermint and vanilla for Valentine's Day, green mint for St. Patrick's Day . . . you get the idea. But for everyday, this mocha latte version can't be beat.

One 18-ounce tube refrigerated sugar cookie dough

6 tablespoons all-purpose flour

1 teaspoon vanilla extract

2 tablespoons unsweetened cocoa powder

$1/4$ teaspoon ground cinnamon

1 tablespoon instant coffee or espresso powder

1   In a mixing bowl, use your hands to break up the cookie dough. Sprinkle with the flour and vanilla. Use your hands to knead the dough until all the ingredients are thoroughly blended. Divide the dough in half and place one half in another bowl. Add the cocoa and cinnamon to one part of the dough and the coffee powder to the other part. Knead each part of the dough until the additions are thoroughly incorporated. Wrap each part of the dough in plastic wrap and refrigerate for at least 30 minutes or up to 8 hours.

2   Preheat the oven to 375°F.

3   On a lightly floured surface, roll the cocoa-flavored dough and the coffee-flavored dough separately to a rough 4 x 14-inch rectangle. Use a spatula to lift the cocoa dough onto the coffee dough, patching and pushing to seal any breaks or tears. Use a spatula to assist in rolling the dough from the long side into a pinwheel, rolling up as for a jelly roll. Press the edges to seal the doughs together.

4   Use a sharp knife to cut the rolls into $1/4$- to $1/2$-inch slices. Place each slice on a cookie sheet, at least 1 inch apart. Bake until the dough is firm on top and the edges are rich golden brown, 10 to 12 minutes. Use a spatula to transfer the cookies to a rack to cool.

Mocha Latte Pinwheels **Tips**

- It's not necessary for the rectangle to be perfect. You can use your fingers to push it into shape. Similarly, if the cocoa dough breaks or tears during the transfer to the coffee dough, use your fingers to patch and seal it.
- Use coffee or espresso powder, not granules, since granules will not dissolve as easily into the dough.
- Be sure the doughs are chilled before rolling, so that you can shape and transfer them more easily.

Mocha Latte Pinwheels **Variations**

- Flavor one dough with cinnamon and tint it pink, or flavor it with peppermint and tint it green, or flavor the doughs with almond extract and tint each part a different pastel color.
- Knead $1/4$ cup finely chopped nuts (any kind) into one part of the dough and flavor it with almond or maple extract.
- Knead $1/4$ cup chopped dried cherries into one part of the dough and tint it pink.

snickerdoodles

Snickerdoodles are a very simple cookie with a very funny name. Though definitely American, there is however a great deal of regional competition about who claims the snickerdoodle's invention. Nearly every community cookbook from Maine to California has a similar version: extra large, lightly spiced, rolled in cinnamon sugar, and baked to a crisp edge and chewy-soft interior. Here is undoubtedly the easiest version of all.

3 tablespoons sugar

1 teaspoon ground cinnamon

One 18-ounce tube refrigerated sugar cookie dough

$^1/_3$ cup all-purpose flour

2 teaspoons vanilla extract

$^1/_2$ teaspoon grated nutmeg

1 egg

1   Preheat the oven to 375°F. Lightly grease a large cookie sheet. In a small dish, stir together the sugar and cinnamon.

2   In a mixing bowl, use your hands to break up the cookie dough. Add the flour, vanilla, nutmeg, and egg. Use your hands to knead the dough until the ingredients are thoroughly incorporated. The dough will be slightly sticky.

3   With lightly floured hands, pinch off heaping tablespoon-size pieces of dough. Roll the dough into balls, then roll the balls in the cinnamon sugar to coat completely. Place the cookies, at least 1$^1/_2$ inches apart, on the prepared cookie sheet. Flatten the cookies with your hands to about $^1/_2$ inch thick.

4   Bake until the edges are rich golden brown and the tops are pale golden with browned edges, 12 to 14 minutes. Use a spatula to transfer the cookies to a rack to cool completely.

Snickerdoodles Tips

- The egg makes the cookies crisp-edged and tender in the center.
- Be sure your spices are "fresh." Ground spices keep no more than about a year on the shelf before beginning to lose potency.
- For maximum flavor, store vanilla and other extracts, tightly covered in the original bottle, in a cool, dark cupboard.

Snickerdoodles Variations

- Roll the cookies in other spiced sugar and vary the spices in the dough. They won't be snickerdoodles, but they will still be great-tasting.
- Snickerdoodles can be sandwiched with peanut butter for maximum kid appeal.
- Use snickerdoodles as a base for a peach cookie shortcake by spooning sliced sweetened peaches over one cookie, then topping with a second cookie, and ending with a dollop of whipped cream.

maple walnut spice drops

If you can get granulated maple sugar, sprinkle the tops of the cookies with it before baking. The addition of a little maple syrup gives the cookies a rather chewy texture as well as a more pronounced maple flavor.

One 18-ounce tube refrigerated gingerbread cookie dough

$^1/_2$ cup chopped toasted walnuts

1 tablespoon all-purpose flour

1 tablespoon maple syrup

1 teaspoon vanilla extract

1 teaspoon maple extract

1 teaspoon pumpkin pie spice blend

1 tablespoon maple sugar, optional

1   Preheat the oven to 375°F. Lightly grease a large cookie sheet.

2   In a mixing bowl, use your hands to break up the cookie dough. Sprinkle with the walnuts, flour, maple syrup, vanilla and maple extracts, and spice blend. Use your hands to knead the dough until the ingredients are fully incorporated.

3   Drop the dough by heaping tablespoons onto the prepared cookie sheet. Sprinkle with the maple sugar, if using. Bake until the edges are crisp and rich golden brown, and the cookies are set in the center, 10 to 12 minutes. Transfer to a rack to cool.

Maple Walnut Spice Drops Tips

- Toast nuts by spreading on a small baking sheet, then place in the pre-heating oven. Toast, stirring often, until nuts are a shade darker and fragrant, 6 to 8 minutes.
- Use good-quality maple extract for maximum true flavor.
- If you can find it, use grade B maple syrup, which is darker but has a stronger maple flavor.

Maple Walnut Spice Drops Variations

- Use pecans in place of the walnuts.
- Use molasses or dark corn syrup in place of the maple syrup.
- Sprinkle the tops of the cookies with granulated brown sugar if you don't have maple sugar.

jam thumbprints

This cookie is a favorite on many homemade Christmas cookie platter assortments, probably because it is so versatile and colorful. Any color and flavor of jam and marmalade can be used, and all sorts of nuts can be used in which to roll the cookie dough. This "fancy" cookie, however, is so easy to make that it need not be reserved for holidays only.

One 18-ounce tube refrigerated sugar cookie dough
$^1/_4$ cup all-purpose flour
1 teaspoon vanilla extract
$^1/_2$ teaspoon almond extract
$^3/_4$ cup finely chopped almonds
$^1/_4$ cup apricot preserves
$^1/_4$ cup seedless raspberry jam

1   Preheat the oven to 350°F.

2   In a mixing bowl, use your hands to break up the cookie dough. Sprinkle with the flour, and vanilla and almond extracts. Use your hands to knead the dough until all the ingredients are thoroughly incorporated.

3   With lightly floured hands, pinch off tablespoon-size pieces of dough and form into balls. Roll the dough in the nuts to coat, then place the balls at least 1$^1/_2$ inches apart on a large baking sheet. Use your thumb to make an indentation in the center of each cookie.

4   Bake until the cookies are pale golden and still barely soft in the center, about 10 minutes. Use the back of a small spoon or your thumb to again press an indentation in the dough. Bake until the cookies are just set and golden, about 3 minutes more. Spoon a scant teaspoonful of apricot jam into the center of half of the cookies and the raspberry jam into the other half. Return to the oven to bake for 2 minutes more. Transfer the cookies to a rack to cool.

Jam Thumbprints **Tips**

- The thumbprints must be pressed in twice, since the dough will rise during the initial baking.
- If the dough is too hot to make the second indentations with your thumb, use the back of a small spoon, such as a $1/2$-teaspoon measuring spoon.
- No need to toast the nuts ahead of time for this recipe, since they will toast in the oven during the baking.
- Be sure the nuts are finely chopped for the best coverage of the cookies.

Jam Thumbprints **Variations**

- Any flavor and color of jam, preserves, or marmalade can be used in the thumbprints.
- The cookies can be baked without any jam at all, and when cooled, they can be filled instead with colored powdered sugar icing or chocolate icing.
- The cookies can be baked with a candied cherry or whole nut inserted into the dough before baking.
- Other nuts, such as walnuts, hazelnuts, or pecans, can be used in place of the almonds.

cocoa pretzel cookies

Coarse sugar is the "salt" for these dark chocolate pretzel-shaped cookies, but you can use this as a starting point for myriad variations limited only by your imagination. Easy to shape, these crisp cookies are also good keepers, and perfect for dunking into a glass of cold milk as an after-school snack or at bedtime.

> **One 18-ounce tube refrigerated sugar cookie dough**
> **$1/4$ cup unsweetened cocoa powder, plus additional for rolling**
> **$1/4$ cup all-purpose flour**
> **1 teaspoon vanilla extract**
> **2 tablespoons coarse sugar, such as amber sugar crystals**

1   Preheat the oven to 375°F. Lightly grease a large baking sheet.

2   In a mixing bowl, use your hands to break up the cookie dough. Sprinkle with the cocoa, flour, and vanilla. Use your hands to knead the dough until all the ingredients are incorporated. Divide the dough into 24 pieces. Lightly dust a work surface with cocoa. One at a time, roll each piece of dough on the work surface to a 9-inch rope. Twist the rope into a pretzel shape and place on a large baking sheet, leaving at least $1^1/2$ inches between each cookie. Sprinkle the tops of the cookies with the coarse sugar, pressing it in lightly to adhere.

3   Bake until the dough is firm and a shade darker, 12 to 14 minutes. Transfer the cookies to a rack to cool.

Cocoa Pretzel Cookies Tips

- Coarse sugar is found in the baking section of the grocery store.
- Lightly dust your hands with cocoa to keep the dough from sticking while you form the pretzels, but use as little cocoa for rolling as possible to keep the cookies tender.
- For the most mellow flavor, use European-style (Dutch process) unsweetened cocoa.

Cocoa Pretzel Cookies **Variations**

- For vanilla cookies, increase the flour to $^1/_2$ cup, the vanilla to 2 teaspoons, and omit the cocoa. Shape and bake as directed.
- In place of coarse sugar, top the cookies with chopped nuts, shredded coconut, or colored sugar.
- For almond pretzel cookies, add $^1/_2$ teaspoon almond extract to either the cocoa dough or vanilla dough, or top the cookies with chopped almonds.

black and whites

New Yorkers have loved them for years, but until they became the focus of a famous *Seinfeld* episode, black and whites were virtually unknown in the rest of the country. To everyone else, they might just be sugar cookies iced in both chocolate and vanilla frostings. To a New Yorker, however, they have to be a little cakey, slightly eggy, a touch lemony, and the icings have to be very shiny and just thick enough to coat the cookies. I tried a lot of homemade cookie recipes, but this very easy version is closest to the original. The icing is inspired by Nancy Baggett in her terrific *The All-American Cookie Book.*

COOKIES

One 18-ounce tube refrigerated sugar cookie dough

2 eggs

1 teaspoon vanilla extract

2 drops lemon oil or $^1/_4$ teaspoon lemon extract

BLACK AND WHITE ICINGS

$^1/_2$ cup water, plus additional if needed

$^1/_4$ cup light corn syrup

5 cups confectioners' sugar

1 teaspoon vanilla extract

2 ounces finely chopped unsweetened chocolate

1   **Preheat the oven to 350°F. Lightly grease two large baking sheets.**

2   **In a mixing bowl, use your hands to break up the cookie dough. Add the eggs, vanilla, and lemon oil or extract. Use your hands or a mixing spoon to knead or beat the dough until all the ingredients are incorporated and a soft dough forms. Drop the dough by heaping tablespoons, at least 3 inches apart, on the prepared baking sheets.**

3   **Bake until the cookies are pale gold with golden edges, 13 to 15 minutes. Use a spatula to transfer the cookies to a rack to cool completely before icing.**

4   **For the icings: In a saucepan, bring the water and corn syrup to a boil. Remove from the heat**

and whisk in the confectioners' sugar and the vanilla until the icing is smooth. Place the chocolate in a small bowl and pour half (about 1 cup) of the icing over it. Stir until smooth and the chocolate is melted. If necessary, stir about 1 tablespoon hot water into the chocolate icing to thin to a fluid consistency. Allow both icings to cool for about 5 minutes before using.

5 To frost the cookies, place them on a rack over a sheet of wax paper. Use a small spatula to frost half of each cookie with the vanilla icing, then the other half with the chocolate icing. If the icing becomes too thick to spread, warm it slightly in a microwave oven. Let the cookies stand on the rack until the icing is set, at least 2 hours.

Black and Whites Tips

- The cookies will spread during baking, so be sure to leave enough room in between each.
- For the prettiest presentation, frost with the vanilla icing first, using a table knife to draw an edge down the center, then frost with the chocolate icing right up to the edge.
- Lemon oil gives the truest flavor, but a high quality lemon extract is fine and more readily available.

Black and Whites Variations

- For lemon cake cookies, increase the lemon oil to 4 drops or lemon extract to $1/2$ teaspoon and add 1 teaspoon grated lemon zest to the dough. Frost with vanilla icing only, with 2 teaspoons grated lemon zest added and thinned with 2 teaspoons lemon juice.
- For orange cake cookies, follow the directions for the lemon variation above, but substitute orange extract, zest, and juice.
- For cookie strawberry shortcakes, leave the cookies unfrosted. Place one cookie in a shallow dessert bowl, spoon sweetened sliced strawberries over, then top with another cookie and some whipped cream.

molasses tuiles

Tuiles are very thin, delicate French cookies shaped like roof tiles (*tuiles*) by draping the hot, still soft cookies over a rolling pin. Of course, they are just as good flat, but the rolled version is very pretty alongside a cup of tea, or served with ice cream or sorbet. As they cool, the cookies become very crisp with a slightly chewy interior—a cross between a candy and a cookie. It is one of the easiest and most dramatic cookies in this book. And one of my favorites.

One 18-ounce tube refrigerated sugar cookie dough
1/4 cup molasses
1 teaspoon vanilla extract

1   **Preheat the oven to 350°F. Lightly grease two large baking sheets. If planning to make tuiles, lightly grease a rolling pin.**

2   **In a mixing bowl, use your hands to break up the cookie dough. Add the molasses and vanilla. Use a mixing spoon to beat until all the ingredients are incorporated and a soft dough forms. Drop the dough by tablespoons, at least 3 inches apart, on the prepared baking sheets.**

3   **Bake, one sheet at a time, until the cookies are flattened, thin, and just firm in the center, 13 to 15 minutes. As soon as the cookies are taken from the oven, work quickly to transfer them to drape over the rolling pin if making tuiles. Otherwise, transfer them to racks to cool. The cookies on the rolling pin will firm and cool within a minute or so and should be then slid off and transferred to the rack to cool completely.**

Molasses Tuiles **Tips**

- Work quickly, since the baked cookies tend to stick to the baking sheet as they cool.
- If the cookies are hard to take off the baking sheet and drape over the rolling pin, return the baking sheet to the oven for about a minute to soften the cookies again.
- Let the cookies cool completely before storing to ensure their crispness.

Molasses Tuiles **Variations**

- Add 2 teaspoons grated orange or lemon zest to the dough.
- Add $\frac{1}{2}$ cup finely chopped walnuts or pecans to the dough. Do not drape over a rolling pin.
- Add 1 teaspoon instant coffee powder to the dough.

cookie variations

Here are some ideas for quick drop or cookie ball variations. To one 18-ounce tube refrigerator sugar cookie dough, knead in 1 teaspoon vanilla extract in addition to any of the following, then form into 1-inch balls or drop by heaping teaspoonfuls onto greased baking sheets. Bake in a 375°F oven until the cookies are golden and browned at the edges, 10 to 13 minutes.

- 1/3 cup chopped almonds or other nuts and 1/2 teaspoon almond extract
- 1/3 cup chopped candied or dried fruits or mixture of fruits and nuts
- 1/3 cup shredded coconut and 1/4 teaspoon almond extract
- 1/4 cup unsweetened cocoa powder
- 1/3 cup unsweetened cocoa powder, 1/4 cup finely chopped almonds, and 1/2 teaspoon ground cinnamon
- 2 to 3 teaspoons instant coffee powder and 1/2 teaspoon ground cinnamon
- 2 tablespoons chopped fresh rosemary and 2 tablespoons grated orange zest
- 1 tablespoon grated lemon zest and 4 drops lemon oil or 1/2 teaspoon lemon extract
- 1/3 cup crushed peppermint or other hard candies
- Roll any of the cookies around small chocolate kisses, whole nuts, or lemon drop candies
- Roll any of the cookies in a mixture of 3 tablespoons sugar and 1 teaspoon ground cinnamon or grated nutmeg or 1/2 teaspoon ground cloves
- Roll any of the cookies, while warm, into confectioners' sugar or unsweetened cocoa powder

bars

Bars are the **easiest and quickest** of all cookies to bake and serve. The dough is simply spread or patted into a pan, then baked, cooled, and cut. Brownies are the best-known bars, and these homely **chocolate** cookies are easily elevated into truffles, baked fudge, and **souffléd** petit fours. Lemon bars, cheesecake bars, hermits, and shortbreads are brownies' nonchocolate cousins, all part of the **great** heritage of **American** cookie baking.

almond hazelnut shortbreads

The simple kneading together of almond paste, sugar cookie dough, and chopped nuts produces a sophisticated, versatile shortbread cookie that is one of my favorites. Shortbreads are technically a rich, unleavened butter cookie, and this is a variation on the theme.

Although terrific as soon as they cool from the oven, these shortbreads mellow and become even richer the next day, making them a perfect do-ahead recipe to serve alone with a cup of espresso or as a formal dessert with sweetened sliced peaches spooned over.

1 cup coarsely chopped hazelnuts
One 18-ounce tube refrigerated sugar cookie dough
One 7-ounce tube almond paste

1   Preheat the oven to 350°F. Spread the hazelnuts out on a small baking sheet and bake, stirring once or twice, until fragrant and lightly toasted, 5 to 7 minutes. Let the nuts cool completely. Keep the oven on.

2   In a mixing bowl, use your hands to break up the cookie dough and almond paste. Knead the two mixtures together until well blended, then knead in the nuts. Press and pat the dough into an 11-inch tart pan with a removable bottom. Use a knife to score the dough into 16 wedges.

3   Bake the shortbreads until golden and firm, 30 to 35 minutes. Let the shortbreads cool in the pan on a rack before cutting them into wedges along the scored lines.

Almond Hazelnut Shortbreads Tips

- For this recipe, use almond paste in a tube, not the canned paste, which is more firm and crumbly.
- The shortbreads will keep, covered at room temperature, for a week, and the flavor actually deepens the day after baking.
- Don't be tempted to mix the dough in a food processor or mixer. It is better, quicker, and easier to do it by hand.

Almond Hazelnut Shortbreads Variations

- For a double almond shortbread, substitute coarsely chopped skin-on almonds for the hazelnuts.
- For shortbread squares, bake in a 9 x 12-inch baking pan, cool, and cut into 16 or more squares.
- Coarsely chopped hazelnuts are available in bags. If you plan to chop your own, toast the whole nuts with the skins, then place the nuts in a dish-towel and rub to remove most of the skin before chopping the nuts.
- The baked shortbread can also be a base for a fresh fruit tart—just brush it with preserves or jam, top with sliced peaches or strawberries, then brush the fruit with more preserves.

italian fig-filled bars

Fig Newtons are famous American-made cookies, but they have origins in an equally famous (at least in my Sicilian family) Italian bar cookie. This very streamlined version relies on fig preserves, a wonderful sweet that is now available in most well-stocked supermarkets in the jam and jelly section. This is one cookie in which the dough needs to be chilled for easy rolling.

COOKIE DOUGH

One 18-ounce tube refrigerated sugar cookie dough

$1/2$ cup all-purpose flour

1 teaspoon vanilla extract

FIG FILLING

$1/2$ cup fig preserves

$1/4$ cup chopped dried figs

1 teaspoon lemon juice

$1/2$ teaspoon grated lemon zest

$1/2$ teaspoon ground cinnamon

1   Preheat the oven to 350°F. Position the oven rack in the center. Lightly grease a large baking sheet.

2   In a mixing bowl, use your hands to break up the cookie dough. Sprinkle with the flour and vanilla. Use your hands to knead the dough until all the ingredients are thoroughly incorporated. Form the dough into a 4 x 6-inch rectangle, wrap in plastic wrap, and refrigerate for at least 15 minutes or up to 4 hours.

3   While the dough is chilling, make the filling. In a small bowl, stir together the preserves, figs, lemon juice and zest, and the cinnamon.

4 On a lightly floured surface, roll the dough to a rough 4 x 16-inch rectangle. Spread the filling down the center of the dough. Use a small spatula to fold and roll both sides of the dough over the filling to form a filled roll. Pinch the dough edges together to seal the filling in the roll. Use a small, sharp knife to cut the roll into 3/4-inch diagonal slices. Use a spatula to transfer the slices, dough side up, to the baking sheet, at least 1 inch apart.

5 Bake until the dough is lightly browned and set, 15 to 17 minutes. The cookies will spread a bit, but the filling should remain contained. Let the cookies cool for about 1 minute on the baking sheet, then use a spatula to transfer the cookies to a rack to cool completely.

Italian Fig-Filled Bars Tips

- The cookies will be soft and are best eaten on the day of baking.
- Any type of dried figs can be used in the filling.
- Cut the filled cookie dough rolls with a firm downward motion.

Italian Fig-Filled Bars Variations

- The bars can also be filled with prepared mincemeat. Drain first if it is very juicy.
- The bars can also be filled with other thick preserves or marmalades.
- The bars can be drizzled with confectioners' sugar icing (mix 2 cups confectioners' sugar, $1/2$ teaspoon vanilla, and just enough orange juice to make a drizzling consistency) and sprinkled with colored sugars. This is typical in Italy.

panforte

In Italy, panforte is so rich with fruit and nuts and chocolate that it is as much a confection as it is a cookie. Excellent with a cup of dark espresso, these cookies (and their variations) are ideal on a holiday party tray as well. Don't be put off by the fruits and nuts—this is definitely not a fruitcake.

One 18-ounce tube refrigerated sugar cookie dough
$1/4$ cup all-purpose flour
$1/4$ cup unsweetened cocoa powder
1 teaspoon ground cinnamon
1 teaspoon vanilla extract
$1/2$ teaspoon almond extract
$1/4$ teaspoon ground cloves
$1/3$ cup chopped mixed dried fruits
$1/4$ cup chopped toasted almonds
$1/4$ cup miniature chocolate chips

1   Preheat the oven to 350°F. Lightly grease a 12-inch pizza pan or a 10- to 12-inch tart or springform pan with a removable bottom.

2   In a mixing bowl, use your hands to break up the cookie dough. Sprinkle with the flour, cocoa, cinnamon, vanilla and almond extracts, cloves, dried fruits, almonds, and chocolate chips. Knead the dough until all the ingredients are fully incorporated. Pat the dough evenly into the prepared pan.

3   Bake until the dough is firm, 15 to 17 minutes in the 12-inch pan and 17 to 20 minutes in the 10-inch pan. Let the panforte cool in the pan on a rack for 5 to 8 minutes, then use a sharp knife to cut into wedges, but do not remove the cookies. Allow the bars to cool completely before serving.

Panforte Tips

- The bars cut best while still warm, but need to cool and firm up before removing from the pan.
- The bars can also be baked in a 9- or 10-inch square pan, and cut into squares.
- Any type of unsweetened cocoa powder will work, but Dutch-process or European-style cocoa gives a mellower flavor.

Panforte Variations

- Other flavorings, such as anise extract, can be used in place of the almond extract.
- Substitute hazelnuts or walnuts for the almonds.
- Other dried fruits, such as cranberries or cherries, can be used in place of the mixed fruits.
- For panforte drop cookies, omit the flour and drop the dough by tablespoons onto baking sheets, at least 1 inch apart. Bake until firm, 12 to 14 minutes.

hermit bars

Hermits are an old-fashioned American bar cookie that probably dates back to Colonial New England. Cookie lore holds that they are so named because they taste even better a day or so after baking, having been stored away like hermits. Usually rather soft and chewy, hermits are often sweetened with molasses or brown sugar, and almost always contain dried fruits, usually raisins. Pressing the gingerbread cookie dough into a pan to bake as a bar cookie gives them a chewy and moist texture, and the candied ginger adds a contemporary kick to this timeless favorite.

One-half 18-ounce tube refrigerated gingerbread cookie dough
$^{1}/_{2}$ cup raisins
$^{1}/_{4}$ cup all-purpose flour
3 tablespoons chopped candied ginger
1 teaspoon pumpkin pie spice blend
2 teaspoons vanilla extract
1 cup confectioners' sugar
2 tablespoons orange juice

1   Preheat the oven to 350°F. Lightly grease an 8-inch square baking pan.

2   In a mixing bowl, use your hands to break up the cookie dough. Sprinkle with the raisins, flour, candied ginger, spice blend, and vanilla. Use your hands to knead the dough until all the ingredients are incorporated. Press the dough evenly into the bottom of the prepared pan.

3   Bake until the dough is set but still soft to the touch, 15 to 17 minutes. Let cool in the pan on a rack.

4   In a mixing bowl, whisk together the confectioners' sugar and orange juice to make a thin icing. Drizzle the icing over the cooled bars. Let stand until the icing is set, at least 1 hour.

Hermit Bars **Tips**

- The bars can be enjoyed right after baking, but are even better the next day when the flavors have had a chance to blend. Store, tightly covered, in the baking pan.
- It's easiest to chop candied ginger with a lightly floured or sugared knife, or by snipping with kitchen shears.
- Pumpkin pie spice, found in the spice section of the market, is a blend of cinnamon, ginger, nutmeg, and allspice.

Hermit Bars **Variations**

- The dough can be formed into 1-inch balls and baked as individual cookies on a baking sheet for 12 to 14 minutes. They will be more cakey and firm, and less chewy.
- Substitute dried currants or cranberries for the raisins, or use a mixture of dried fruits
- For more orange flavor, add 2 teaspoons grated orange zest to the cookie dough.

pecan gingerbread cheesecake bars

Cut these bars a bit bigger and you have a real dessert, not just a snack cookie. However you serve them, they are sure to please cheesecake lovers, and there are legions of these. They are also sure to please the gingersnap crowd. The rich simplicity of cheesecake and the hot spiciness of gingerbread are a natural pairing.

COOKIE BASE

One-half 18-ounce tube refrigerated gingerbread cookie dough

$1/3$ cup finely chopped pecans

2 tablespoons all-purpose flour

1 teaspoon pumpkin pie spice blend

$1/2$ teaspoon vanilla extract

CHEESECAKE TOPPING

8 ounces cream cheese, softened

6 tablespoons sugar

1 teaspoon vanilla extract

1 egg

$1/4$ cup sour cream

1   Preheat the oven to 375°F. Lightly grease an 8-inch square baking pan.

2   In a mixing bowl, use your hands to break up the cookie dough. Sprinkle on the pecans, flour, spice blend, and vanilla. Use your hands to knead the dough until all the ingredients are incorporated. Pat the mixture evenly into the prepared baking pan.

3   Bake the base until lightly colored and just firm, 11 to 13 minutes. Remove from the oven and reduce the oven temperature to 325°F.

4   While the base is baking, beat the cream cheese, sugar, vanilla, and egg with a spoon or whisk or hand-held electric mixer until smooth. Stir in the sour cream until well blended. Pour and spread the mixture over the partially baked base.

5   Bake until the edges of the cheesecake are pale golden and the center is just set, 45 to 50 minutes. Transfer the pan to a rack to cool completely before cutting into bars. Store extra bars in the refrigerator up to 3 days.

Pecan Gingerbread Cheesecake Bars **Tips**

- Use cream cheese, regular or reduced fat (but not nonfat) in a brick, not the whipped type in a tub.
- The cheesecake topping can be mixed by hand with a spoon and whisked if the cream cheese is well softened. Use an electric mixer if you have one.
- Cheesecakes bake best at lower temperatures (the base needs the higher temperature), but it is fine to put the cheesecake in the oven before the temperature is completely reduced to 325°F.

Pecan Gingerbread Cheesecake Bars **Variations**

- Use a different spice or spice blend, such as apple pie spice, or $1/2$ teaspoon each of nutmeg and cinnamon. Go light on ground cloves, as they are very strong.
- Use chopped walnuts or hazelnuts in place of the pecans.
- Use chopped macadamias in place of the pecans, and sprinkle the top of the cheesecake batter with $1/4$ cup shredded coconut before baking.

lemon bars

This updated version of the perennial American favorite, lemon bars, has the extra dimension of lemon zest in the sugar cookie base. This is the cookie that lemon meringue pie lovers choose every time, and it's a lot easier to make than pie.

COOKIE BASE

One-half 18-ounce tube refrigerated sugar cookie dough

$1/4$ cup all-purpose flour

2 teaspoons grated lemon zest

$1/2$ teaspoon vanilla extract

LEMON CUSTARD TOPPING

$3/4$ cup sugar

2 tablespoons all-purpose flour

$1/4$ teaspoon baking powder

2 eggs, beaten

$1/4$ cup fresh lemon juice

1 tablespoon grated lemon zest

Confectioners' sugar, optional

1   Preheat the oven to 350°F. Lightly grease an 8 x 8-inch baking pan.

2   For the cookie base: In a mixing bowl, use your hands to break up the cookie dough. Sprinkle on the flour, lemon zest, and vanilla. Use your hands to knead the dough until all the ingredients are incorporated. Pat the dough evenly onto the bottom of the prepared baking pan. Bake until golden, 15 to 18 minutes. Remove the pan from the oven and let cool for 5 minutes.

3   For the filling: In a mixing bowl, whisk together the sugar, flour, and baking powder to blend. Whisk in the eggs, lemon juice, and lemon zest. Pour the filling over the cookie base. Return the pan to the oven and bake until the filling is set in the center and golden at the edges, about 20 minutes.

4   Let cool completely in the pan on a rack before cutting into bars. Just before serving, dust the bars lightly with confectioners' sugar, if desired.

Lemon Bars Tips

- Be sure to use fresh lemon juice. It makes all the difference in the taste.
- Store the bars in the refrigerator, but return to cool room temperature to serve.
- Don't dust with confectioners' sugar until just before serving or it will "melt" and be absorbed into the bars.

Lemon Bars Variations

- For Lemon-Lime Citrus Bars: Substitute lime juice for about one-third of the lemon juice and zest in both the cookie base and filling.
- For Spiced Lemon Bars: Substitute gingerbread cookie dough for the sugar cookie dough as the base.
- For Lemon-Orange Citrus Bars: Add 2 teaspoons grated orange zest to both the cookie base and the filling.

oatmeal pb&j streusel bars

There are many outstanding jams and preserves on the market today, so try several variations when making these bars, which have a lunchbox name, but are definitely not just for kids. The bars are rich, so cut them as large or as small as you wish.

1 cup confectioners' sugar

1 cup smooth or crunchy peanut butter

2 teaspoons vanilla extract

One 18-ounce tube or package refrigerated oatmeal or oatmeal raisin cookie dough

$1/3$ cup red fruit jam or preserves, such as Morello cherry or strawberry

$1/2$ cup chopped peanuts

1   Preheat the oven to 350°F. In a small mixing bowl, stir together the confectioners' sugar, peanut butter, and vanilla until well blended. Set aside.

2   Cut the cookie dough in half crosswise. Press and pat half of the dough evenly onto the bottom of an ungreased 8 x 8-inch baking pan. Press the peanut butter mixture evenly over the dough. Spread the jam on top of the peanut butter. Use your hands to crumble the remaining cookie dough into a bowl and toss with the peanuts. Sprinkle the dough crumbles evenly over the jam.

3   Bake until the topping is golden brown and firm, 33 to 38 minutes. Cool completely in the pan before cutting into bars.

Oatmeal PB&J Streusel Bars **Tips**

- Use thick, good-quality jam or preserves.
- Be sure that all toppings and dough are spread evenly for even baking.
- Let the bars cool completely or even refrigerate them for about 30 minutes for easy cutting.

Oatmeal PB&J Streusel Bars **Variations**

- Use chocolate chip or sugar cookie dough, but knead in $1/4$ cup flour and 1 teaspoon vanilla before patting it in the pan and making the streusel.
- Substitute other jams, such as raspberry. Red jam looks the prettiest.
- Substitute other nuts, such as hazelnuts or pecans, for the peanuts.

spiced chocolate hazelnut bars

Sugar cookies are lovely in this sophisticated bar cookie, but chocolate chip dough would up the chocolate ante even more, especially if you belong to the "never enough chocolate" club, of which I am a charter member.

1$^{1}/_{4}$ cups chocolate-hazelnut spread (Nutella)

1 cup confectioners' sugar

1 teaspoon vanilla extract

$^{3}/_{4}$ teaspoon ground cinnamon

$^{1}/_{2}$ cup chopped hazelnuts

One 18-ounce tube refrigerated sugar cookie dough

1 Preheat the oven to 350°F. Lightly grease an 8 x 8-inch baking pan.

2 In a mixing bowl, use a spoon to combine the Nutella, confectioners' sugar, vanilla, and $^{1}/_{4}$ teaspoon of the cinnamon. Set aside.

3 Cut the cookie dough in half crosswise. Press and pat half of the dough onto the bottom of the prepared pan. Press the chocolate mixture evenly over the dough. Crumble the remaining cookie dough into a bowl and toss with the hazelnuts and remaining $^{1}/_{2}$ teaspoon cinnamon. Sprinkle the dough crumbles and nuts evenly over the chocolate mixture in the pan.

4 Bake until the topping is golden and firm, 33 to 38 minutes. Cool completely in the pan before cutting into bars.

Spiced Chocolate Hazelnut Bars **Tips**

- Have the Nutella at room temperature for easiest mixing.
- Chill the cookie dough well for crumbling with the nuts.
- Chopped hazelnuts are available in bags in the nut and baking section of the market.

Spiced Chocolate Hazelnut Bars **Variations**

- Substitute chocolate chip cookie dough for the sugar cookie dough.
- Add 1 tablespoon hazelnut liqueur to the filling.
- Add $\frac{1}{4}$ teaspoon ground cloves to the cookie dough.

mocha walnut baked fudge

The trick here is to underbake this extra-chocolate, coffee-laced walnut brownie batter. Some people (i.e., everyone who tested this) like it better than fudge candy. You decide.

> **One 18-ounce package refrigerated brownie dough**
> **3 ounces ($^1/_2$ cup) finely chopped semisweet or bittersweet chocolate**
> **$^1/_4$ cup finely chopped walnuts**
> **2 teaspoons instant coffee powder**
> **2 teaspoons vanilla extract**

1   Preheat the oven to 350°F. Lightly grease an 8 x 8-inch baking pan.

2   In a mixing bowl, use your hands or a spoon to break up the brownie dough. Knead or stir in the chopped chocolate, nuts, coffee powder, and vanilla until all the ingredients are incorporated. Spread and pat the dough into the prepared pan.

3   Bake until the dough is still soft, but no longer liquid and shiny in the center, 18 to 20 minutes. Let the pan cool completely on a rack, then refrigerate for at least 30 minutes until chilled before cutting into small bars. Serve at room temperature.

Mocha Walnut Baked Fudge **Tips**

- It's easiest to cut the bars when they are cold, but they have the best flavor when served at room temperature.
- Watch carefully so that the dough stays soft and doesn't overbake. However, if it does bake a bit more, you will still have wonderfully rich brownies.
- Use a premium-quality chocolate for the richest flavor.
- Of the national brands, Nestlé's brownie dough works best here. If your brand does not have chocolate chips sprinkled on top, add an additional 2 tablespoons chopped chocolate to the dough.

Mocha Walnut Baked Fudge **Variations**

- Use hazelnuts, almonds, or pecans in place of the walnuts.
- For black and white chocolate baked fudge, use $1/2$ cup (3 ounces) chopped white chocolate in place of the dark chocolate.
- For mint chocolate baked fudge, omit the coffee powder and add $1/2$ teaspoon mint extract. Use chopped mint-flavored or raspberry-flavored semisweet or bittersweet chocolate.
- For butter-brickle baked fudge, substitute $1/4$ cup butter brickle chips (such as Skor or Heath bar) for $1/4$ cup of the chopped chocolate.

chocolate chip brownie custard bars

For those who can't decide between a brownie and a chocolate chip cookie, this bar makes the choosing easy. Since the usual 8 x 8-inch pan requires half a package of both chocolate chip and brownie dough, make double the amount in two pans. Don't worry—they will be gone in no time.

One 18-ounce tube refrigerated chocolate chip cookie dough
2 tablespoons all-purpose flour
2 teaspoons vanilla extract
One 18-ounce package refrigerated brownie dough
2 eggs

1   Preheat the oven to 350°F. Lightly grease two 8 x 8-inch baking pans.

2   In a mixing bowl, use your hands to break up the chocolate chip cookie dough. Sprinkle on the flour and 1 teaspoon of the vanilla. Use your hands to knead the dough until all the ingredients are incorporated. Spread and pat half of the dough into each of the baking pans. Bake for 15 minutes.

3   Meanwhile, in a mixing bowl, use your hands or a spoon to break up the brownie dough. Beat in the eggs and remaining 1 teaspoon vanilla until all the ingredients are incorporated.

4   Spread the brownie mixture over the partially baked chocolate chip cookie dough, dividing equally between the two pans. Return the pans to the oven and bake until the brownie dough is puffed and just set on top, 14 to 16 minutes more.

5   Let the pans cool completely on a rack before cutting into 36 bars.

Chocolate Chip Brownie Custard Bars **Tips**

- Any brand of chocolate chip cookie dough that you like works well.
- Of the national brands, Nestlé's brownie dough is preferred for the custard layer. If your brand does not have chocolate chips sprinkled on top, stir 2 tablespoons miniature chocolate chips into the dough with the eggs.
- Take care not to overbake the brownie custard layer. It should be just set on top.

Chocolate Chip Brownie Custard Bars **Variations**

- Use gingerbread cookie dough in place of the chocolate chip cookie dough.
- Use sugar cookie dough with $1/2$ cup chopped nuts added in place of the chocolate chip cookie dough.
- Bake in two 8- or 9-inch heart-shaped cake pans for a Valentine's Day treat.

brownie truffles

There are almost unlimited variations on this delicious chocolate theme. Use liqueur or extract as you desire. Roll some of the "truffles" in several different coatings for a superb gift. Put each in a miniature paper muffin or candy cup and arrange them in a pretty box. Or just eat them all yourself. You deserve a gift once in a while.

> One 18-ounce package refrigerated brownie dough
> 3 ounces (about $^1/_2$ cup) finely chopped semisweet or bittersweet
>   chocolate
> 1 tablespoon liqueur or $^1/_2$ teaspoon extract of choice, such as
>   almond, rum, anise, or mint
> 2 teaspoons vanilla extract
> $^1/_4$ cup finely chopped nuts, coconut, confectioners' sugar, or
>   unsweetened cocoa powder for coating

1   Preheat the oven to 350°F. Lightly grease an 8 x 8-inch baking pan.

2   In a mixing bowl, use your hands or a spoon to break up the brownie dough. Knead or stir in the chopped chocolate, liqueur or extract, and vanilla until all the ingredients are incorporated. Spread and pat the dough evenly into the prepared pan.

3   Bake until the dough is still soft, but no longer liquid and shiny in the center, 18 to 20 minutes. Let the pan cool for at least 15 minutes, then use a spoon to scoop up tablespoons of the soft "truffles." Roll each truffle into a ball.

4   Place the coating of choice in a small dish or zipper-style plastic bag. Roll or shake the truffles in the coating to cover completely. Place the truffles on a rack for at least 15 minutes to set the coating.

Brownie Truffles Tips

- If the truffles stick to your hands while rolling into balls, lightly dust your hands with unsweetened cocoa powder or confectioners' sugar.
- Be sure not to overbake the truffle dough, but let it cool enough so that it is firm enough to roll into balls.
- Of the national brands, Nestlé's brownie dough works best here. If your brand does not have chocolate chips sprinkled on top, add 2 additional tablespoons chopped chocolate to the dough.

Brownie Truffles Variations

- Add $1/4$ cup finely chopped nuts to the dough.
- Dip the truffles into a coating of warm ganache made by melting 4 ounces semisweet chocolate with $1/3$ cup heavy cream and stirring until smooth. Let the ganache cool enough to coat the truffles.
- Form the truffle dough around a dried cherry or whole almond, then roll in the coating of choice.

brownie soufflé petit fours

Use half of the dough for the cookie base and the other half for the souffléd topping. This sophisticated little bar cookie is amazingly simple to make. Flavor the soufflé any way you wish. The smaller size is perfect as part of a petit fours plate with tea, and the larger size can be served as dessert with coffee.

One 18-ounce package refrigerated brownie dough

$1/2$ teaspoon vanilla extract

$1/4$ teaspoon ground cinnamon

1 egg

1 tablespoon dark rum, orange liqueur, amaretto, or Kahlua

1   Preheat the oven to 350°F. Lightly grease an 8 x 8-inch baking pan. Divide the brownie dough in half.

2   In a mixing bowl, use your hands or a mixing spoon to break up half of the brownie dough. Knead or beat in the vanilla and cinnamon until all the ingredients are incorporated. Spread and pat into the prepared pan. Bake for 12 minutes.

3   Meanwhile, in a mixing bowl, use your hands or a mixing spoon to break up the remaining half of the brownie dough. Beat in the egg and liqueur until smooth.

4   Spread the brownie topping over the partially baked dough in the pan, using a spatula to spread evenly. Continue to bake until the topping is puffed and just set on top, 12 to 14 minutes more.

5   Cool the pan on a rack completely before cutting into desired size bars.

Brownie Soufflé Petit Fours **Tips**

- You can use your hands to break up the brownie dough, but since it is softer than regular cookie dough, it is easier and less messy to use a mixing spoon.
- Don't overbake the bars once the souffléd topping is spread—the top should be just set and no longer look shiny and wet on top.
- These will cut most neatly if completely cooled or even slightly chilled, but serve at room temperature.

Brownie Soufflé Petit Fours **Variations**

- If you don't want to use liqueur, use 1 tablespoon prepared coffee or orange juice.
- For a pretty presentation, dust the tops of the petit fours with confectioners' sugar just before serving.
- The petit fours can be decorated with dots of melted white chocolate (like dominoes) for a more elaborate presentation.

bar cookie variations

To one-half of an 18-ounce tube or package of refrigerated cookie or brownie dough, knead in the following, then press the dough into a lightly greased 8-inch square baking pan. Bake until the top cookie dough is golden and the edges are browned, 20 to 25 minutes, or until the brownies are just set, 22 to 25 minutes.

- **Sugar cookie dough, 1 cup flaked coconut, and $1/2$ teaspoon each vanilla and almond or coconut extract. Spread 3 ounces melted bittersweet chocolate over the baked sugar cookies in the pan. Let stand to set the chocolate. Serve plain or as a base for an ice cream sundae.**
- **Oatmeal or oatmeal raisin cookie dough, $1/2$ cup chopped walnuts, $1/2$ cup snipped dried apples, 1 teaspoon apple pie spice blend, and $1/2$ teaspoon vanilla extract. Cut into squares and serve plain or with applesauce, or top with ginger or banana ice cream.**
- **Peanut butter cookie dough, $1/2$ cup chopped dried banana chips, $1/4$ cup chopped peanuts, 2 tablespoons all-purpose flour, and 1 teaspoon vanilla extract. Cut into squares and serve plain or frosted with marshmallow fluff, or as a base for an ice cream sundae.**
- **Brownie dough, 1 cup crumbled cinnamon graham crackers, and 1 teaspoon vanilla extract. Sprinkle the top of the baked brownies with $1^1/2$ cups miniature marshmallows, then run under the broiler for about a minute until the marshmallows are toasted.**
- **Brownie dough, $1/4$ cup each chopped dried cherries and toasted almonds, $1/2$ teaspoon vanilla extract, and $1/2$ teaspoon almond extract. Bake for 12 minutes, then spread the top of the baked brownies with $1/2$ cup cherry preserves or jam and bake another 10 minutes.**

sweet breads

Baking **homemade** coffee cakes and rolls was fast becoming a lost **art** for time-crunched home bakers until prepared doughs came into existence. Though most of these doughs start out as savory **ideas**, their treatment as a basic yeast dough produces doughnuts and Danish, sticky buns and stollens that take **less than an hour's** preparation for even the most novice baker. Biscuit dough is just as **versatile**, serving as a terrific base for baked and fried cake doughnuts and pull-apart coffee cakes. Nothing gets the **family** up earlier in the morning than the promise of a sweet bread **fresh** from the oven.

sugared cake doughnuts

Cake doughnuts are leavened with baking powder instead of yeast. They are usually rolled in sugar or frosted with a chocolate or vanilla icing, and often sport colorful "sprinkles." Though they can be made with any size, brand, or type of biscuit dough, I prefer the smaller-size regular biscuits that come 10 to a 7$^1/_2$-or 12-ounce can, depending upon how big you like your doughnuts. The biscuits labeled "flaky" are richer with shortening, which makes a denser doughnut. However, if you are a real fan of all things "supersize," feel free to try the recipe with oversized "grand" biscuits of any style. However you make them, homemade doughnuts are the ultimate breakfast treat.

$^1/_4$ **cup granulated sugar**

2 teaspoons ground cinnamon

Canola oil for deep-frying

One 7$^1/_2$-ounce, 10-ounce, or 12-ounce tube refrigerated biscuit dough

1   In a small bowl, stir together the sugar and cinnamon. In a wide, deep, 3-quart saucepan or deep fryer, heat at least 3 inches of oil to 360°F.

2   Separate the biscuits and use a 1-inch canapé cutter to cut out the centers of the biscuits to form 10 doughnuts and 10 holes. Fry the doughnuts, a few at a time, until rich golden on one side, 2 to 3 minutes. With a slotted spoon, carefully turn the doughnuts and fry until rich golden on the other side, 2 to 3 minutes more. Use the slotted spoon to transfer the doughnuts to drain in a single layer on paper towels.

3   Let the doughnuts drain for 1 minute, then toss or dredge them in the cinnamon sugar.

4   Repeat the procedure to fry all of the doughnuts, then fry and dredge the doughnut holes in the same manner, though the holes will take the minimum frying time.

5   Serve the doughnuts and holes immediately, if possible.

Sugared Cake Doughnuts **Tips**

- It's really helpful to have a candy thermometer to measure the oil temperature, but if you do not have one, test the oil by pinching off a piece of dough from one biscuit and dropping in the oil. It should float to the surface immediately and turn golden within 2 minutes. You will sacrifice a doughnut this way, but will have an accurate oil temperature.
- Wait 2 or 3 minutes between frying batches of doughnuts to allow the oil to return to the proper temperature.
- Use canola or another plain vegetable oil for frying.

Sugared Cake Doughnuts **Variations**

- Substitute grated nutmeg or pumpkin or apple pie spice blend for the cinnamon.
- Roll the doughnuts in confectioners' sugar instead of the cinnamon sugar.
- Substitute maple or brown sugar for the granulated sugar.
- For jelly-filled cake doughnuts, use the 7$\frac{1}{2}$-ounce-size biscuit dough and do not cut out doughnut holes. Fry the whole biscuit, then use a small knife to cut a deep slit into the fried and drained doughnut. Spoon or pipe in about 1 teaspoon jelly or jam. Roll the doughnuts in confectioners' sugar.
- For frosted cake doughnuts, omit the cinnamon sugar and frost the warm doughnuts with any chocolate icing or vanilla icing of your choice, then sprinkle with cake or cookie decorating sprinkles.

glazed doughnuts and crullers

These are as good as the designer doughnuts that people drive miles and stand hours in line to buy. The secret, of course, is enjoying the doughnut hot from the oil. Indeed, the shelf life of a yeast doughnut is measured in minutes, not days or even hours. So if you want the real thing, and don't live next door to Krispy Kreme, you will have to make them yourself. The good news is that these take no longer than walking next door.

1 cup confectioners' sugar

2 tablespoons water

$1/4$ teaspoon vanilla extract

Canola oil for deep-frying

One 11.3-ounce tube refrigerated dinner roll dough or 11-ounce
   tube refrigerated breadstick dough

1   In a small bowl, stir together the confectioners' sugar, water, and vanilla until smooth and the consistency of a thin glaze. Cover and set aside.

2   In a wide 3-quart saucepan or a deep fryer, heat 3 inches of oil to 360°F.

3   Separate the dinner rolls and flatten lightly with your hands. Use a 1-inch canapé cutter to cut holes from the center of each dinner roll. If using breadsticks to make crullers, separate the dough into 12 rectangles. Pull and twist each to a 4- to 5-inch twist. Fry the doughnuts or crullers, a few at a time, until rich golden brown on one side, 2 to 3 minutes. Use a slotted spoon to turn the doughnuts carefully in the oil and fry until the other side is rich golden brown, 2 to 3 minutes more. Use a slotted spoon to transfer the doughnuts and/or crullers to paper towels to drain. Fry the doughnut holes in the same manner, using the minimum frying time.

4   To glaze the doughnuts, either dip them into the glaze to coat, or place the doughnuts on a rack over a piece of wax paper and spoon the glaze over, turning to coat and scooping up excess glaze to reuse. Let the glazed doughnuts stand on the rack for at least 3 minutes for the glaze to set and the doughnuts to cool slightly. Serve immediately, if possible.

Glazed Doughnuts and Crullers **Tips**

- Yeast doughnuts puff up a great deal during frying, so be sure to leave enough space in between each so that they don't touch each other.
- Avoid crowding the frying oil with dough, which will lower the temperature and cause the doughnuts to absorb oil.
- Glaze the doughnuts while still very warm but not hot from the fryer.

Glazed Doughnuts and Crullers **Variations**

- Flavor the glaze with orange or lemon juice or rum in place of the water.
- Make sopaipillas by flattening dinner roll dough to about $1/2$ inch thick without cutting holes, then fry the dough as directed. Glaze the sopaipillas in warm honey or coat heavily with confectioners' sugar.
- For Chocolate Crème–Filled Doughnuts: Using dinner roll dough, separate each in half, then place a marshmallow on the bottom half and replace the tops, pinching together to seal. Fry as directed, then frost with a glaze made by stirring 4 ounces chopped bittersweet chocolate, 2 tablespoons light corn syrup, $1/4$ cup heavy cream, and $1/2$ teaspoon vanilla together in a small saucepan over medium-low heat until smooth.
- For Jelly-Filled Doughnuts: Using dinner roll dough, separate each in half, then place 2 teaspoons thick jam on the bottom half and replace the tops, pinching together to seal. Fry as directed, then dust heavily with confectioners' sugar.

filled and frosted yeast doughnuts

Cake doughnuts are great for dunking into hot chocolate, and glazed doughnuts are perfect with a cup of strong coffee. But a fluffy, creamy filled doughnut frosted in dark shiny chocolate is an edible work of art on its own. They were my favorites as a kid, and still are. If chocolate is not your passion, see the jelly doughnut variation (page 193).

CHOCOLATE GLAZE

  4 ounces (about $2/3$ cup) chopped bittersweet or semisweet
    chocolate

  2 tablespoons light corn syrup

  $1/4$ cup heavy cream

  $1/2$ teaspoon vanilla extract

DOUGHNUTS

  Canola oil for deep-frying

  One 11.3-ounce tube refrigerated dinner roll dough

  8 regular size or 24 miniature marshmallows

1 For the glaze: In a small saucepan or in a microwave oven, heat the chocolate, corn syrup, and cream over medium-low heat, stirring until smooth. Stir in the vanilla. Set aside until ready to use. If the icing becomes too thick, warm slightly to spreading consistency.

2 For the doughnuts: In a wide 3-quart saucepan or in a deep fryer, heat 3 inches of oil to 360°F.

3 While the oil is heating, separate each roll into 2 pieces. Place one marshmallow (or 3 miniature marshmallows) in the center of the bottom halves of the rolls. Replace the tops, pressing the edges together to seal them.

4 Fry the doughnuts, a few at a time, until rich golden brown on one side, 2 to 3 minutes. Use a slotted spoon to turn the doughnuts carefully and fry until rich golden brown on the other side, 2 to 3 minutes. Use a slotted spoon to transfer the doughnuts to paper towels to drain for 1 to 2 minutes.

5 Frost the warm doughnuts with the chocolate glaze. Serve warm within an hour of frying, if possible.

Filled and Frosted Yeast Doughnuts Tips

- Be sure to seal the dough edges securely after filling the doughnuts, so that the marshmallows don't leak out during frying.
- Use fresh, soft marshmallows.
- If you don't have marshmallows, use 2 teaspoons marshmallow fluff to fill the doughnuts.

Filled and Frosted Yeast Doughnuts Variations

- Fill the doughnuts with 1 miniature chocolate bar or chocolate kiss, then substitute white chocolate for the bittersweet chocolate in the icing.
- Fill the doughnuts with 2 teaspoons thick jam or jelly and roll the warm doughnuts in confectioners' sugar instead of frosting them.
- The icing can also be used to frost cake doughnuts.

baked jelly doughnuts

Some types of biscuit dough separate into flaky layers more easily than others, but it is also easy to use a small knife to make a pocket in the dough for filling with jelly or other ingredients. The important thing is to try to pinch and seal the pocket or layers together to retain the filling during baking. Large-size cornmeal biscuits make jumbo jelly doughnuts, but the flavor of cornmeal and strawberry jelly is incomparable. It's also a breeze to bake traditional "cake" doughnuts and doughnut holes (see Variations).

> One 17.3-ounce tube large-size refrigerated cornmeal or butter-
> milk biscuits, or one 12-ounce tube refrigerated buttermilk
> biscuit dough
> 1/3 cup strawberry or other flavor jelly
> 1/4 cup sugar

1   Preheat the oven to 375°F.

2   Separate the biscuit dough into 8 or 10 pieces, depending upon the directions on the tube. Use your fingers to separate flaky buttermilk biscuit dough in half. Place about 2 teaspoons jelly in the center of one half, then replace the other half, pressing the edges to seal. Use a small, sharp knife to make a pocket in the center of the cornmeal biscuits and insert about 2 teaspoons jelly into each pocket. Pinch the pocket to reseal. Place the sugar in a small, shallow dish. Dip the filled doughnuts into the sugar to coat. Place, at least 2 inches apart, on a baking sheet.

3   Bake until the doughnuts are risen and rich golden brown, 15 to 17 minutes, depending upon the size of the doughnut. Transfer to a rack to cool slightly, then serve warm. The doughnuts are best served within an hour of baking.

Baked Jelly Doughnuts **Tips**

- Don't be tempted to overfill the doughnuts or the jelly will seep out and burn on the baking sheet.
- Try to pinch the edges together to seal in the jelly, but don't worry if the seal isn't perfect.

Baked Jelly Doughnuts **Variations**

- Use any flavor jelly or preserves that you like.
- Fill the doughnuts with marshmallow fluff instead of jelly.
- Fill the doughnuts with apple butter instead of jelly and roll in sugar mixed with apple pie spice blend.
- Use any style refrigerated biscuits that you like, then drizzle the hot doughnuts with chocolate sauce and serve as dessert.
- Fill the doughnuts with chocolate peanut butter spread or chocolate hazelnut spread (Nutella).
- For Cinnamon Sugar Doughnuts and Holes: Use a 1-inch round cookie or canapé cutter to cut out the center of each biscuit. Dip both doughnuts and holes into a mixture of $1/4$ cup sugar and 1 teaspoon ground cinnamon, then place, at least 2 inches apart, on a baking sheet. Bake as directed.
- For Secret Center Doughnut Balls. Use one 12-ounce tube refrigerated buttermilk biscuits, separating into 10 biscuits. Use your hands to flatten each to about $1/4$-inch thickness, then fold and roll around a small chocolate truffle, chocolate kiss, or miniature candy bar. Roll in $1/4$ cup sugar. Bake as directed.

lemon cheese danish twist

Danish pastry is made from a rich dough that is a cross between bread and puff pastry. Crescent roll dough closely resembles it, and it has myriad uses for making Danish. Easy to shape, it is particularly pretty presented as a crisscross "braid" or twist. Like all coffeecakes, this one is best served within a few hours of baking. Because it is so easy to make, it's no problem to bake one up before breakfast, thus calling your family to the table with fresh oven aromas. If you really want to sleep in, make the filling the night before.

1 egg
¼ cup granulated sugar
2 teaspoons grated lemon zest
4 ounces cream cheese, softened
½ teaspoon vanilla extract
One 8-ounce tube refrigerated
   crescent roll dough

1   Preheat the oven to 350°F. Lightly grease a baking sheet.

2   Separate the egg, placing the yolk in a mixing bowl and placing the white in a small dish. Whisk the egg white with 1 teaspoon water until it is frothy. Set aside. In a small dish, whisk together the sugar and lemon zest. Remove and set aside 2 teaspoons of the flavored sugar. Add the remaining sugar, cream cheese, and vanilla to the yolk in the mixing bowl. Whisk or beat with a spoon until smooth.

3   Unroll the crescent roll dough into 2 rectangles. Place them together on the baking sheet to make 1 long rectangle, pressing the edges and perforations to seal them. Roll or press to a 6 x 14-inch

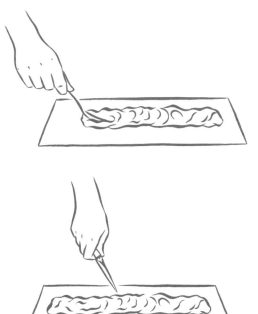

rectangle. Brush some of the egg white down the center of the dough in a 2-inch-wide strip. Spread the cream cheese mixture over the egg white. Use a small, sharp knife to cut diagonal strips of dough on both sides of the filling from the edges to within $1/2$ inch of the filling. Overlap and crisscross the strips on an angle to make the twist or braid. Brush the top of the braid with some of the remaining egg white, then sprinkle with the reserved sugar.

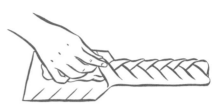

4   Bake until the dough is rich golden brown, 30 to 35 minutes. Use a spatula to transfer the braid to a rack to cool. Cut into slices to serve warm or at room temperature within a few hours of baking.

Lemon Cheese Danish Twist Tips
- Because it has a cream cheese filling, store leftover Danish in the refrigerator.
- Use regular or reduced-fat cream cheese in a brick, not cream cheese in a tub.
- Use freshly grated lemon zest, yellow part only.

Lemon Cheese Danish Twist Variations
- Substitute 1 tablespoon grated orange zest for the lemon zest.
- Add $1/4$ cup dried currants to the cheese filling.
- Substitute light brown sugar for the granulated sugar for a caramel flavor.
- Instead of the cream cheese filling, pat one 7-ounce tube of almond paste onto the dough rectangle, then cover with 1 large apple, thinly sliced, and sprinkle with 2 teaspoons lemon juice, then with 2 tablespoons sugar mixed with $1/2$ teaspoon ground cinnamon.

chocolate "croissants"

Chocolate croissants are a favorite after-school pastry for French children. Excellent with a tall glass of cold milk, they could become a favorite of children everywhere. Crescent roll dough is not exactly like croissant dough, but still makes a great wrapper for chocolate. Depending upon the size of the crescent rolls (regular or supersize), you can have small or large "croissants." For maximum flavor, be sure to use the best chocolate available. But don't be afraid to experiment with our favorite candy bars (see Variations).

6 ounces excellent-quality bittersweet or semisweet chocolate

One 8-ounce tube refrigerated crescent roll dough

2 teaspoons sugar

1 Preheat the oven to 375°F. Lightly grease a large baking sheet. Break 4 ounces of the chocolate into 8 pieces. In a small saucepan or in a microwave oven, melt the remaining 2 ounces chocolate. Set aside.

2 Unroll the crescent rolls, separating into 8 triangles along the perforated edges. Place piece of chocolate at the shortest side of each triangle. Roll up from the short side. Place, point side down, on the prepared baking sheet, at least 2 inches apart. Curve the rolls to form a crescent shape. Sprinkle the tops of the rolls with the sugar.

3 Bake until the rolls are risen and rich golden brown, 13 to 15 minutes. Transfer to a rack, drizzle with the melted chocolate, and let cool slightly, but serve warm.

Chocolate "Croissants" Tips

- The crescent roll dough is easiest to work with if it is well chilled.
- In warm weather, refrigerate the shaped pastries on the baking sheet for 15 minutes before baking.
- Excellent-quality chocolate is available in 4-ounce bars, which can easily be broken into 8 pieces.

Chocolate "Croissants" Variations

- Fill each "croissant" with 1 miniature candy bar, such as peanut butter cups, chocolate-covered toffee bars, nougat-filled bars, or coconut-filled chocolate bars.

- Fill each "croissant" with 1 tablespoon finely chopped peanut brittle or nuts tossed with cinnamon sugar.

- For 6 giant "croissants," use a 15.5-ounce tube of oversize crescent roll dough and double the amount of chocolate to fill the rolls. The amount of melted chocolate to drizzle remains the same. Increase the baking time to 15 to 20 minutes.

- For fruit-filled pastries, or Czechoslovakian kolachy, fill each triangle with 2 teaspoons thick jam or preserves or lekvar (prune butter). Sprinkle the shaped crescents with a streusel made by crumbling together 2 tablespoons flour, 1 tablespoon unsalted butter, 1 tablespoon sugar, and $1/4$ teaspoon ground cinnamon. Bake as directed.

- For nut "croissants," fill each triangle with 2 teaspoons peanut butter or 1 tablespoon chopped peanut brittle. Sprinkle the tops of each shaped croissant with about $1/4$ teaspoon sugar.

spiced cranberry pull-apart coffee cake

This is probably the most versatile of all coffee cakes. It can be made with any type and size of refrigerated biscuit dough, any dried fruit, and any sweet spice mixture. You can even add or substitute chopped nuts. The basic formula remains the same for all variations. The other real advantage is that the coffee cake goes together in minutes and serves a crowd. For fewer guests, jut cut the recipe in half and bake in a smaller tube pan or a 9-inch cake pan.

$1/2$ cup sugar

1 tablespoon apple pie spice blend

24 ounces (approximately) refrigerated biscuit dough

6 tablespoons unsalted butter, melted

$3/4$ cup dried cranberries

1 Preheat the oven to 350°F. Lightly grease a 9-inch tube pan, preferably one with a removable bottom, such as an angel food cake pan.

2 In a small dish or zipper-style plastic bag, combine the sugar and spice blend. Cut each biscuit into 2 to 6 pieces, depending upon the size biscuits you are using—each piece should be about 1 inch in diameter. Toss the biscuit pieces, a few at a time, in the melted butter, then toss in the sugar to coat. Place the biscuits randomly in the prepared pan, tossing the cranberries in with the biscuits.

3 Bake until the coffee cake is well risen and rich golden brown, 40 to 45 minutes. Let the coffee cake cool in the pan for 1 minute, then use a knife to loosen the sides. Invert onto a rack or a serving plate and let cool slightly. Serve warm.

Spiced Cranberry Pull-Apart Coffee Cake **Tips**

- Avoid dark metal baking pans, which tend to promote overbrowning during baking.
- To avoid sticking, be sure to loosen the sides of the coffee cake before unmolding.
- The coffee cake should be served within a few hours of baking and can be reheated in a 300°F oven for a few minutes.

Spiced Cranberry Pull-Apart Coffee Cake **Variations**

- Use any flavor and size biscuit dough that you prefer. Just be sure the total weight is about 24 ounces.
- Substitute raisins, chopped dried apricots or peaches, and/or chopped nuts for the dried cranberries.
- Substitute pumpkin pie spice blend or 2 teaspoons cinnamon plus $\frac{1}{2}$ teaspoon each of nutmeg and allspice for the apple pie spice blend.
- Cut the recipe in half and bake in a 9-inch cake pan for 25 to 30 minutes.

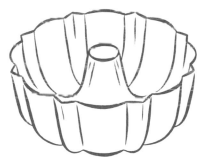

yeasted
walnut braids

If you are having just one or two friends over for coffee, serve them this coffee cake, since it isn't too big or sweet and looks so pretty. If you like, you can freeze the second coffee cake or serve it to your family for a snack or dessert with sliced fruit.

2 tablespoons sugar

1 teaspoon grated nutmeg

One 11-ounce tube refrigerated breadstick dough

2 tablespoons unsalted butter, melted

$^1/_4$ cup finely chopped walnuts

1   Preheat the oven to 350°F. Lightly grease a large baking sheet. In a small dish, combine the sugar and nutmeg.

2   Unroll the breadsticks into 6 long strips, pinching the perforations to seal. Place 3 strips side by side on a work surface. Brush lightly with the butter. Sprinkle with about $1^1/_2$ teaspoons of the sugar, then sprinkle half of the nuts down the center. Starting in the middle, braid by bringing the left strip over the center strip. Next bring the right strip over the new center strip. Repeat braiding to the end. Pinch both ends of the braid together to seal. Transfer to the prepared baking sheet. Repeat the process with the other 3 strips to make another braid. Brush the tops of both braids with the remaining melted butter and sprinkle with the remaining sugar.

3   Bake until rich golden brown, 25 to 28 minutes. Transfer to a rack to cool. Serve warm or at room temperature, cut into crosswise slices.   *(continued)*

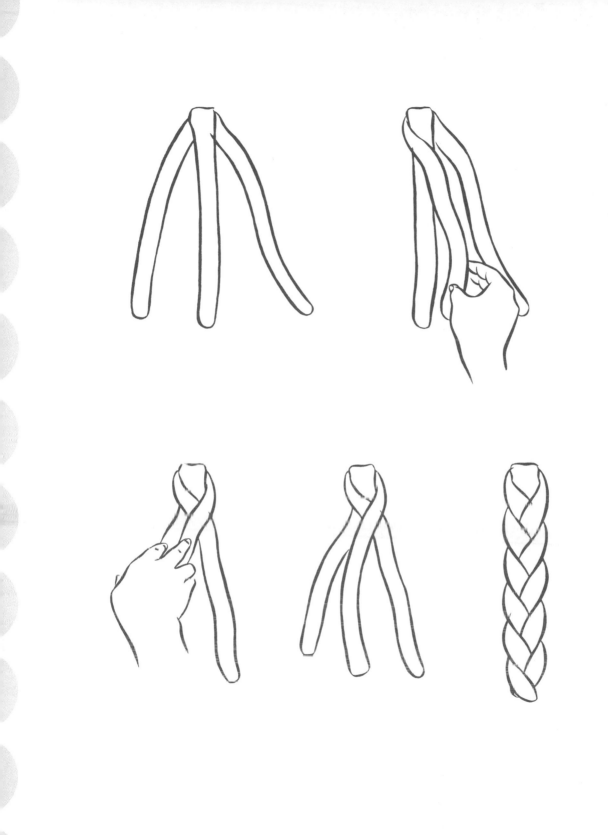

Yeasted Walnut Braids Tips

- Don't worry if your braids are not perfect, since they will puff and look great during baking.
- The second braid can be frozen for up to 1 week after baking. Reheat in a 300°F oven.
- Freshly grated nutmeg makes all the difference. Invest in a nutmeg grater.

Yeasted Walnut Braids Variations

- Substitute other nuts, such as pecans, pine nuts, hazelnuts, or even peanuts for the walnuts.
- Substitute other spices—cinnamon or a sweet spice blend, such as apple or pumpkin pie or Chinese five-spice—for the nutmeg.
- Fill the braid by spreading with lekvar (prune butter) or Nutella (hazelnut butter) or peanut butter in place of the nuts.

stollen

Stollen is a dried fruit and nut–filled yeast coffee cake that is traditional throughout Scandinavia. Like fruitcake, its success depends entirely on the quality of fruits used. Here, the usual candied cherries and pineapple are replaced by less sweet and more flavorful dried mixed fruits. Packaged as "fruit tidbits," the commercial mixture often contains apricots, peaches, apples, raisins, and prunes—a great combination for stollen (as well as eating out of hand). Almonds are most commonly used, and cardamom is the traditional spice for stollen.

$1/2$ cup mixed chopped dried fruits

3 tablespoons chopped almonds

3 tablespoons sugar

$3/4$ teaspoon ground cardamom

$1/2$ teaspoon ground mace

One 11-ounce tube refrigerated French bread dough

1 tablespoon unsalted butter, melted

Confectioners' sugar for dusting

1   Preheat the oven to 350°F. Lightly grease a baking sheet. In a small bowl, stir together the fruits, almonds, sugar, cardamom, and mace.

2   Place the bread dough on a lightly floured surface, and use your hands to flatten it to about 1 inch thick. Sprinkle with the fruit-and-nut mixture. With lightly floured hands, knead the fruits and nuts into the dough until incorporated. Pat or roll the dough to a 6 x 12-inch rectangle and place on the prepared baking sheet. Brush the top of the dough with some of the melted butter, then fold one long side over the other side, pressing to seal almost to the edge. You will now have a rough 3 x 12-inch rectangle. Brush the top with the remaining melted butter.

3   Bake until the bread is rich golden brown, 28 to 32 minutes. Transfer to a rack to cool. Just before serving, liberally dust the stollen with confectioners' sugar. Serve warm or at room temperature, cut into crosswise slices.

(continued)

Stollen **Tips**

- Knead the dough as gently as possible to avoid toughening it. It's fine if some of the fruits and nuts have to be patted on top.
- The fold-over shape is traditional and will look like a pocket.
- Wait until serving time to dust with the confectioners' sugar or it will be absorbed into the bread.

Stollen **Variations**

- Any combination of dried fruits and nuts can be used.
- Other sweet spices, such as cinnamon, cloves, or nutmeg, can be added to or substituted for the cardamom and mace.
- The stollen is best served on the day of baking.

greek easter bread

My friend Alice Hasapis gave me a wonderful, authentic recipe for Greek Easter bread that I made for years at Easter. It was time consuming, but we loved it. Now I make this easy variation about once a month all year round. While I only decorate it with hard-cooked eggs at Easter, I think of Alice every time for the inspiration.

3 tablespoons sugar

2 teaspoons grated lemon zest

1¹/2 teaspoons lightly crushed anise or fennel seeds

One 11-ounce tube refrigerated French bread dough

2 tablespoons unsalted butter, melted

3 hard-cooked eggs in the shell, preferably colored red, optional

1   Preheat the oven to 350°F. Lightly grease a large baking sheet. In a small dish, combine the sugar, lemon zest, and anise seeds.

2   Place the bread dough on the prepared baking sheet and press to flatten it to about 3 inches by 14 inches. Brush liberally with about half of the melted butter. Sprinkle with the sugar mixture. Use a sharp knife to cut the dough lengthwise into 6 equal strips. Starting in the middle, braid by bringing the left strip over the center strip. Next, bring the right strip over the new center strip. Repeat braiding to the end. Shape the braid into a circle, pinching the ends together to seal. Brush with the remaining melted butter. If using, push the eggs into the braid at even intervals, pushing down about 1 inch.

3   Bake until well risen and rich golden brown, 33 to 38 minutes. Carefully transfer to a rack to cool, then serve warm or at room temperature. *(continued)*

Greek Easter Bread **Tips**

- If you wish, the eggs need not be hard-cooked; in either case, they are not edible after baking, but are just for decoration.
- To crush anise seeds, place in a small plastic bag and roll with a rolling pin.
- To color eggs red, use beet juice or food color in a jar or tube, since liquid food color will make them pink, which is fine, too.

Greek Easter Bread **Variations**

- For a sweeter bread, drizzle the baked bread with an icing made by mixing 1 cup confectioners' sugar with 1 tablespoon water and 1 tablespoon anise liqueur or syrup.
- The eggs can be omitted and 2 tablespoons finely chopped pistachios added to the sugar mixture for the filling.
- The bread may be shaped like a crescent or simply left in a long braid, but pinch the ends together to seal them.

cinnamon raisin swirl bread

Hardly anything smells better in the kitchen (and will bring the kids home faster) than the aroma of homemade cinnamon raisin bread coming from the oven. Enough said.

2 teaspoons yellow cornmeal

2 tablespoons light brown sugar

1 teaspoon ground cinnamon

One 11-ounce tube refrigerated French bread dough

2 tablespoons unsalted butter, melted

$^1/_3$ cup raisins

1 egg white, beaten with 2 teaspoons water

1 Preheat the oven to 450°F. Lightly grease a large baking sheet. Sprinkle with the cornmeal. In a small dish, combine the brown sugar and cinnamon.

2 Unroll the bread dough onto the prepared baking sheet. Brush with the melted butter. Sprinkle with the cinnamon sugar, then sprinkle with the raisins. Reroll the bread into a long loaf, placing, seam side down, in the center of the baking sheet. Brush with some of the egg white.

3 Bake for 5 minutes, then reduce the oven temperature to 400°F and bake for an additional 5 minutes. Reduce the oven temperature to 350°F and continue to bake until the bread is rich golden brown and the top sounds hollow when tapped, about 18 to 22 minutes more. Transfer to a rack to cool before slicing.

(continued)

Cinnamon Raisin Swirl Bread Tips

- Placing the bread on a light dusting of cornmeal adds a little texture to the dough and the crust.
- Use moist, plump raisins.
- Brown sugar has a more caramel flavor than granulated sugar and adds a nice color to the bread, too.

Cinnamon Raisin Bread Variations

- Substitute dried cranberries for the raisins.
- For a softer top crust, brush with a little melted butter instead of beaten egg white.
- Add $1/2$ teaspoon grated nutmeg to the cinnamon sugar.

orange pecan sticky buns

Sticky buns are an American tradition, and in New England they are often served as part of the dinner roll basket. For breakfast, they are an incomparable treat and are definitely best straight from the oven, when they are at their stickiest.

$^2/_3$ cup packed light brown sugar

3 tablespoons unsalted butter

2 tablespoons maple syrup

1 tablespoon grated orange zest

1 tablespoon orange juice

$^1/_3$ cup chopped pecans

1 teaspoon ground cinnamon

1 8-ounce tube refrigerated crescent roll dough

1   Preheat the oven to 350°F.

2   In a small saucepan, combine $^1/_3$ cup of the brown sugar, 2 tablespoons of the butter, maple syrup, orange zest, and juice. Bring to a boil over medium heat, stirring to dissolve the sugar. Reduce the heat to medium-low and simmer for 1 minutes. Pour the hot syrup into an 8-inch round cake pan or pie plate. Sprinkle with the pecans.

3   Melt the remaining 1 tablespoon butter in a small saucepan or in a microwave oven. In a small dish, combine the remaining $^1/_3$ cup brown sugar and the cinnamon.

4   Unroll the crescent roll dough into 2 long rectangles. Overlap the long sides and press the perforations to seal. Brush the dough with the melted butter, then sprinkle with the cinnamon sugar. Roll up from the long side, then use a sharp knife to cut straight down into 8 rolls. Place the rolls, cut side up, over the syrup and nuts in the prepared pan. They will not be touching but will rise in the oven.

5   Bake until well risen and rich golden brown, 20 to 25 minutes. Let the rolls stand in the pan for 1 to 2 minutes, then invert onto a serving plate, holding the pan over the plate for a few sec-

onds so that all the topping flows onto the rolls. If there is topping left in the pan, scrape out and spoon onto the rolls.

6 Let the rolls cool, then serve warm or at room temperature.

Orange Pecan Sticky Buns **Tips**

- Be careful when inverting the rolls onto the plate, since the syrup is very, very hot.
- Don't worry if some of the topping sticks to the pan; just scrape it onto the rolls.
- Avoid using dark metal baking pans, since they promote overbrowning.

Orange Pecan Sticky Buns **Variations**

- Make giant sticky buns by increasing all the ingredients by half and using a 16.3-ounce tube of giant crescent roll dough, baking in a 10-inch cake pan or pie plate.
- Add $1/4$ cup raisins to the cinnamon sugar mixture.
- Use walnuts or hazelnuts in place of the pecans.
- For individual buns, divide the syrup and nuts among 8 muffin tins, then place each cut roll in a muffin tin. Bake for about 20 minutes. Invert onto a plate as soon as the rolls come from the oven.

savory breads

Bread baking is a grandma's **greatest secret**. Mothers are too busy driving to soccer games and rushing to work or school to bake bread, but grandmas have lots of time, or so it seems. Today's **savvy** (and busy) grandmas, however, are the ones who understand that **making dough** is nothing more than mixing flour, water, salt, and yeast, and that **someone else** can do that time-consuming part for them. Beginning with refrigerated French bread dough (which actually doesn't make a great loaf of French bread, but is **wonderful** for American bread) or breadstick, dinner roll, or pizza dough, the **modern** grandma assures a visit every time she calls to say that bread is cooling on the counter.

grandma's homemade slicing bread

It was my great good fortune to have two grandmas, both excellent bread bakers, and both from very different backgrounds. Nana was from Sicily and made the most wonderful, crusty bread with semolina flour. Grandma was of Pennsylvania Dutch heritage and made tall, golden, tender loaves. I loved them both, Nana and Grandma, and their breads. The picture on the bread dough tube looks a lot like Nana's Italian bread, but refrigerated French bread dough actually is far closer to Grandma's slicing loaf. Here is how I bake my quick and modern version of her homemade bread.

One 11-ounce tube refrigerated French bread dough
1 tablespoon unsalted butter, melted

1   Preheat the oven to 400°F. Lightly grease an 8 x 4-inch loaf pan. Unroll the bread dough onto a work surface. Then reroll it, starting from the short side. Place the new, shorter, and plumper loaf into the prepared loaf pan, seam side down. Brush with the melted butter.

2   Place the pan in the oven and immediately reduce the oven temperature to 375°F. Bake until the loaf is rich golden brown and the top sounds hollow when tapped, 30 to 35 minutes. Invert the bread onto a rack, then turn upright and cool.

Grandma's Homemade Slicing Bread **Tips**

- Let the bread cool completely before slicing with a serrated knife.
- Slice with a gentle sawing motion.
- Be sure the oven is properly preheated before baking the bread.

Grandma's Homemade Slicing Bread **Variations**

- The bread can be rerolled from the long side and baked free form on a greased baking sheet. Bake for 10 minutes at 400°F, then reduce the oven temperature to 375°F and bake an additional 15 to 20 minutes.
- The loaf can be brushed with beaten egg rather than butter, which gives a shinier and slightly crisper finish.
- The loaf can be baked in 4 mini-pans. Roll as directed, then cut into 4 pieces and fit into greased and cornmeal-dusted pans. Bake as directed, but reduce the baking time to about 20 minutes.

ham and swiss spiral bread

This is a great, hearty bread to serve with tomato soup or almost any other soup or main dish salad. Ham and Swiss cheese are just one possible combination. See the variations on page 217, but use your imagination and whatever you have on hand in the refrigerator to come up with even more ideas.

1 tablespoon olive oil

1 tablespoon yellow cornmeal

One 11-ounce loaf refrigerated French bread dough

2 tablespoons Dijon mustard

2 ounces very thinly sliced smoked ham

2 ounces very thinly sliced Swiss cheese

1   Preheat the oven to 400°F. Brush a baking sheet with about 2 teaspoons of the olive oil. Sprinkle with the cornmeal.

2   On the baking sheet, carefully unroll the French bread dough. Brush the dough rectangle with the mustard, then place the ham in a single layer over the dough. Top with a layer of the cheese. Reroll the bread dough from the long side. Turn the loaf so that the seam side is down. Brush the top with the remaining olive oil. Use a sharp knife to make 3 or 4 diagonal slashes in the top of the loaf.

3   Place the baking sheet in the oven and immediately reduce the temperature to 375°F. Bake until the loaf is rich golden brown and crusty, 20 to 25 minutes. Transfer the loaf to a rack to cool for at least 5 minutes. Use a serrated knife to gently cut the loaf into diagonal slices.

Ham and Swiss Spiral Bread **Tips**

- Slicing the ham and cheese thinly makes it easier to roll the loaf into a spiral.
- Serve the bread warm, but wait at least 5 minutes to slice it after baking so that the loaf can firm up a bit.
- The bread can be reheated, loosely wrapped in aluminum foil, in a 300°F oven for about 10 minutes.

Ham and Swiss Spiral Bread **Variations**

- Omit the ham and mustard, and layer the dough with thinly sliced salami and mozzarella cheese.
- Omit the ham and cheese, and spread the dough with $1/3$ cup basil or sun-dried tomato pesto.
- Omit the ham and cheese, and layer the mustard-spread dough with 3 ounces thinly sliced smoked salmon.

MAKES
1 LOAF;
SERVES 4
FOR DINNER
AND 8 AS A
SNACK

stromboli

When I was growing up in a largely Italian-American community, stromboli was sold in every corner grocery, and there was a grocery on practically every corner in town. It was related to pepperoni bread, a spiral Italian bread filled with thinly sliced pepperoni and sometimes a little cheese. Stromboli, however, had an egg-custard filling that turned ordinary crusty Italian bread into a sort of bread pudding in a loaf. Sliced in big hunks and served with a salad, stromboli was a meal. Cut in thinner slices, it made a hearty snack, which usually turned into supper. It's still a favorite in my hometown, and at my home table.

1 tablespoon olive oil

1 tablespoon yellow cornmeal

2 eggs, beaten

1 cup (4 ounces) shredded mozzarella cheese

1 cup (4 ounces) thinly sliced or diced pepperoni

1/4 cup grated Parmesan cheese

2 tablespoons chopped fresh basil

One 10-ounce tube refrigerated pizza dough

1   Preheat the oven to 400°F. Brush a baking sheet with 2 teaspoons of the olive oil. Sprinkle with the cornmeal. Stir 1 tablespoon beaten egg into the remaining 1 teaspoon olive oil. Set aside. In a mixing bowl, stir together the remaining egg, mozzarella, pepperoni, Parmesan, and basil.

2   Unroll the pizza dough onto the baking sheet. Spread the filling to within 1 inch of the edges of the dough. Roll the dough up from the long side like a jelly roll. Turn the dough, seam side down, on the baking sheet. Brush the top of the loaf with the reserved oil and egg mixture. Use a small, sharp knife to cut 4 or 5 diagonal slashes in the top of the loaf.

3   Bake until the loaf is rich golden brown, 28 to 32 minutes. Transfer the loaf to a rack to cool for about 5 minutes, then slice into the desired thickness.

Stromboli **Tips**

- A little of the cheese filling might seep out of the top slashes during baking, but that's fine.
- The loaf will be dense and slice easily without a serrated knife.
- Stromboli can be reheated, loosely wrapped in aluminum foil, in a 300°F oven for about 10 minutes.

Stromboli **Variations**

- Cooked Italian sausage can be substituted for the pepperoni.
- Grated Asiago or Romano cheese can be substituted for the Parmesan.
- Shredded provolone or Italian Fontina can be substituted for the mozzarella.

homemade bagels

If you live in New York City, home of real bagels, you will probably make this recipe just for fun, since New Yorkers know that the only real bagel comes right from the shop on the corner. If you live anywhere else, it's hard to find the real thing. What differentiates a bagel from an ordinary roll shaped like a doughnut is the cooking process. Bagels are first boiled in water with sugar and baking soda added, then baked. The boiling gives the traditional chewy texture and hard crust. It's easy to do at home, and the next best thing to living in New York.

2 quarts water

1 tablespoon baking soda

1 tablespoon sugar

One 11.3-ounce tube refrigerated dinner roll dough

1 egg white beaten with 1 teaspoon water

1 teaspoon poppy or sesame seeds

1   Preheat the oven to 400°F. Lightly grease a large baking sheet. In a 3-quart saucepan, bring the water, baking soda, and sugar to a boil.

2   Separate the dough into 8 rolls. Use your finger to poke a hole in the center of each roll, stretching the hole to about 1 inch. Drop the dough into the water, a few at a time. Boil gently for about 20 seconds until puffed and spongy. Use a slotted spoon to gently turn the bagels and boil on the other side for about 10 seconds. Use a slotted spoon to drain the bagels, then place them on the prepared baking sheet, at least 2 inches apart. Brush with the beaten egg white, taking care that it does not drip onto the baking sheet. Sprinkle with the seeds.

3   Bake until rich golden brown and the crust is crisp, 20 to 25 minutes. Transfer to a rack to cool. Serve warm or at room temperature.

Homemade Bagels **Tips**

- Don't crowd the pan of water during boiling or the bagels will stick to each other.
- Drain the boiled bagels before placing them on the baking sheet; however, don't pat them dry.
- If the egg wash drips down from the bagel to the baking sheet, it will solidify and inhibit rising.

Homemade Bagel **Variations**

- Substitute coarse salt for the seeds, or leave the bagels plain.
- Make bialys by poking a hole in the center of the roll, but not stretching it. The hole will close to a depression during boiling. Fill the depression with about 2 teaspoons finely chopped onion sautéed in a little butter until softened.
- For a more golden "egg" bagel, brush with a whole egg beaten with 1 teaspoon water in place of the egg white.

hot pretzels

Hot pretzels have long been sold from street carts all over Manhattan, and they are fast becoming a fixture at airports and malls across the country. There is something quite special about a hot, chewy, salty, golden brown hunk of bread that just isn't the same as a hard pretzel from a box. The characteristic texture of a hot pretzel comes from boiling it in water, similar to making a bagel, and the pretzel flavor comes largely from a generous amount of baking soda added to the water. Making hot pretzels is easy and fun to do at home, and will make your house the snack place of the neighborhood.

2 quarts water

$1/4$ cup baking soda

One 11-ounce tube refrigerated breadstick dough

1 egg white, beaten with 1 teaspoon water

2 teaspoons coarse kosher salt or sea salt

1   **Preheat the oven to 400°F. Lightly grease a large baking sheet. In a 3-quart saucepan, bring the water and baking soda to a boil.**

2   **Separate the dough into 6 long strips, pinching the perforated edges to seal if making large pretzels, or separate into 12 shorter strips for small pretzels. Pull the strips to about 12 inches for large pretzels and about 6 inches for small ones. Twist into a pretzel shape, pinching the ends of the loops to seal the shape together.**

3   **Drop the pretzels, a few at a time, into the boiling water. Boil gently for about 20 seconds until puffed and spongy. Use a slotted spoon to gently turn the pretzels and boil on the other side for about 10 seconds for small pretzels and 20 to 30 seconds for large pretzels. Use a slotted spoon to drain the pretzels, then place them on the prepared baking sheet, at least 2 inches apart. Brush with the beaten egg white, taking care that it does not drip onto the baking sheet. Sprinkle with the salt.**

4   **Bake until rich golden brown and the crust is crisp, 20 to 25 minutes. Transfer to a rack to cool, then serve warm or at room temperature within a few hours of baking.**

Hot Pretzels **Tips**

- The pretzels are best warm from the oven, but can be reheated a few hours later in a 300°F oven for a few minutes.
- The coarse kosher salt is important because it does not dissolve onto the crust, but stays crunchy.
- Don't crowd the pan of water during boiling or the pretzels will stick to each other.

Hot Pretzels **Variations**

- For a more richly browned crust, brush with a whole egg beaten with 1 teaspoon water.
- Shape the dough into "sticks" by omitting the shaping into a pretzel and instead boiling the 12 breadsticks according to step 3.
- For "unsalted" pretzels, omit the kosher salt, though the pretzels will still taste a bit salty from the baking soda in the water.

santa fe pull-apart corn bread

Cornmeal biscuit dough is terrific for this recipe, but the variations on this theme are numerous and any other type of biscuit can easily be substituted. The corn bread makes a great appetizer or snack, but can practically become a meal with side dips of salsa, guacamole, and sour cream.

4 tablespoons olive oil

1 teaspoon cumin seeds

2 large garlic cloves, finely chopped

1 tablespoon chili powder

$1/2$ cup thinly sliced green onion

$1/4$ cup chopped good-quality black olives

$1/4$ cup drained and chopped pimiento

$1/4$ cup shredded Monterey Jack or Cheddar cheese

One 17.3-ounce tube refrigerated cornmeal biscuit dough

1   Preheat the oven to 400°F. Brush a 9- or 10-inch round cake pan with about 2 teaspoons of the oil.

2   In a medium skillet, heat the remaining oil and stir the cumin seeds, garlic, and chili powder over medium heat for 30 seconds. Remove the pan from the heat, stir in the green onion, olives, and pimiento. Let cool, then stir in the cheese.

3   Separate the dough into 8 biscuits, then cut each into 6 pieces. Toss the biscuit pieces, a few at a time, in the oil mixture. Arrange the biscuits randomly in the prepared pan. Sprinkle with any remaining oil mixture.

4   Bake until the biscuits are rich golden brown and form a "pull-apart" loaf, 18 to 20 minutes. Use a sharp knife to loosen the biscuits from the side of the pan, then invert onto a rack. Let cool for a few minutes, then invert onto a serving plate, and serve warm.

Santa Fe Pull-Apart Corn Bread Tips

- The corn bread is best served warm soon after baking, but can be loosely wrapped in aluminum foil and reheated in a 300°F oven to serve on the same day.
- The baked corn bread can also be frozen for up to 1 week, thawed, and reheated.
- Use good olives and pimientos from the deli.

Santa Fe Pull-Apart Corn Bread Variations

- For an Italian flavor, substitute 3 tablespoons chopped mixed herbs, such as basil, marjoram, oregano, and/or rosemary for the chili powder; roasted red pepper for the pimiento; and grated mozzarella for the Jack cheese.
- For a French flavor, use buttermilk biscuits and substitute 1 tablespoon each chopped fresh tarragon and thyme for the chili powder; pitted and chopped Niçoise olives for the black olives; and crumbled blue or goat cheese for the Jack cheese.
- Use any flavor biscuits of your choice in any of the variations.
- For a Yeast Parmesan Garlic Pull-Apart bread: Use two 11-ounce tubes of refrigerated breadstick dough, cut into 1-inch pieces. Brush the pan with oil as directed, then sprinkle the pan with 1 tablespoon yellow cornmeal. Cook about 2 tablespoons finely chopped garlic in 6 tablespoons olive oil for about 30 seconds, then toss the dough pieces in the oil, then in a mixture of about $1/3$ cup grated Parmesan mixed with about 3 tablespoons chopped fresh oregano or other herbs. Place in the pan as directed and bake at 350°F until the bread is rich golden with a crusty top, 40 to 45 minutes. Loosen and remove from the pan as directed.
- Both the biscuit and yeast quantities can be halved (one 8- to 12-ounce tube biscuit dough) and baked in a 4 x 8-inch loaf pan for 30 to 35 minutes.

provençal puff pastry twist

Inspired by the Provençal version of pizza, called a pissaladière, which is often made with puff pastry, this twist can be served in thin slices atop a bed of arugula for a first course, as an accompaniment to a light soup supper, or as a stand-alone snack anytime. Many variations on the theme add even more serving options. Caponata and tapenade are available in tins in good markets, as well as freshly prepared in many delis.

1 sheet frozen puff pastry from a 17.3-ounce box, thawed but well chilled

1/4 cup prepared caponata or olive tapenade

2 tablespoons finely chopped green onion

2 teaspoons chopped fresh thyme

1 egg white, beaten with 1 teaspoon water

2 teaspoons sesame seeds

1   Lightly grease a large cookie sheet. On the cookie sheet, roll the pastry to a 9 x 12-inch rectangle. Spread the caponata or tapenade down the center of the long side in a 3-inch strip. Sprinkle the green onion and thyme over the caponata or tapenade. With a sharp knife, cut diagonal strips 1 inch apart on either side to within 1/2 inch of the filling. Fold the strips at an angle across the filling, alternating from side to side. Brush the top with some of the egg white. Refrigerate or freeze the cookie sheet for 15 minutes.

2   Preheat the oven to 400°F. Place the cold cookie sheet in the oven and immediately reduce the temperature to 375°F. Bake until the pastry is rich golden brown and puffed, 30 to 35 minutes. Use a spatula to transfer the pastry carefully to a rack to cool. Serve warm or at room temperature, cut in slices.

Provençal Puff Pastry Twist Tips

- Chilling the pastry before baking helps to create maximum puff and flakiness.
- Buy only good-quality caponata or tapenade. Italian delis often make it fresh.
- Even if your twist crisscross technique isn't perfect, the pastry will puff to a beautiful finish.

Provençal Puff Pastry Twist Variations

- Substitute basil or roasted red pepper or sun-dried tomato pesto for the caponata.
- Substitute mascarpone for the caponata and sprinkle the herbs with $1/4$ cup grated Parmesan. Sprinkle the top of the egg-brushed pastry with another tablespoon of grated cheese.
- Make a layer of 2 ounces thinly sliced pepperoni, $1/4$ cup chopped sun-dried tomatoes, and $1/3$ cup grated mozzarella in place of the caponata filling.

hush puppies

Hush puppies, a favorite in the American South, are a cross between corn bread and dough-nuts. Served as savory rolls with everything from sausage to fried chicken, they are often sweetened by dipping in honey or molasses, another Southern favorite. Sweetened hush puppies are a great accompaniment to fruit salad for dessert, but Southerners also serve fruit salad as a supper side dish. I like the way the South thinks about food.

Canola oil for deep frying

One 16.3-ounce tube refrigerated large-size cornmeal biscuits

3 tablespoons yellow cornmeal

Cayenne pepper or warm honey or molasses, optional

1   In a wide 3-quart saucepan, heat 3 inches of oil to 360°F. Use a 1-or 1½-inch canapé cutter to cut the biscuits into 3 pieces each. Place the cornmeal in a small zipper-style bag. Shake the biscuit rounds in the cornmeal to coat lightly.

2   Fry the biscuit rounds, a few at a time, until rich golden brown on one side, 2 to 3 minutes. Use a slotted spoon to turn the biscuits and fry until rich golden brown on the other side, 2 to 3 min-utes. Use a slotted spoon to transfer the hush puppies to paper towels to drain for a few min-utes. Sprinkle the hush puppies with cayenne pepper or dip in warm honey or molasses, if desired. Serve immediately, if possible.

Hush Puppies Tips

- If you don't have canapé cutters, cut each biscuit into 3 or 4 pieces and fry as directed.
- Be forewarned: Hush puppies become hockey pucks when cold.
- A candy thermometer is really useful for measuring oil temperature. If you don't have a thermometer, drop a scrap from the biscuit cuttings into the hot oil as a test case to fry it in the prescribed time.

aromatic asian steamed buns

MAKES
8 BUNS

Steamed buns, or mantou, are a traditional accompaniment to Peking duck and other Chinese duck dishes. Adding herbs and spices to the steaming water infuses the snowy, puffed yeast buns with exotic aromas. If your steamer is not big enough, you may need to steam the buns in two batches. Though not a bit Asian, see page 230 for American steamed breakfast buns with maple syrup.

2 tablespoons vegetable oil

1/4 cup fresh cilantro sprigs

1/2 teaspoon crushed hot red pepper flakes

2 tablespoons soy sauce

2 tablespoons dry sherry

1 tablespoon rice wine vinegar

2 tablespoons finely chopped green onions

One 11.3-ounce tube refrigerated dinner roll dough

1 Brush a steamer rack with about 1 teaspoon of the vegetable oil. Fill the bottom of a steamer or wide saucepan with water to come just below the steamer rack. Add all but 1 or 2 sprigs of the cilantro, and all but a pinch of the red pepper flakes. Place the remaining cilantro, red pepper flakes, and 1 tablespoon of the oil in a small bowl. Add the soy sauce, sherry, vinegar, and green onions. Let this sauce stand while you steam the buns.

2 Place the steamer rack in the steamer or pan, cover, and bring to a simmer. Meanwhile, separate the dough into 8 rolls. Brush the rolls with the remaining oil. Place the rolls, without touching each other, in the steamer basket. Cover tightly and steam over simmering water until the buns are puffed and firm when depressed with your fingers, 15 to 17 minutes.

3 Serve the buns hot with the sauce for dipping. *(continued)*

SAVORY BREADS   231

Aromatic Asian Steamed Buns **Tips**

- If you don't have a steamer, make one by placing a rack in a large pan, elevated at least 1 inch from the bottom so that water can be poured in.
- Don't let the steamer basket touch the water or the buns will simmer instead of steam.
- If you have an electric vegetable steamer, it will work beautifully for these buns.

Aromatic Asian Steamed Buns **Variations**

- Other non-Asian herbs, such as tarragon or rosemary, can be placed in the steamer, and the buns can be brushed with olive oil.
- Place cinnamon sticks and whole cloves in the steaming water, then serve the buns for breakfast, drizzled with maple syrup.
- Stuff the buns with seasoned cooked ground pork sausage or other meats or minced cooked vegetables. Use a small knife to make a pocket in each unsteamed roll, then insert about 2 teaspoons filling. Pinch the dough back together to seal. Steam as directed.

flaky parmesan crackers

These are unbelievably easy, and the perfect accompaniment to a mug of hot soup or heaped in a basket for a cocktail snack. Variations are unlimited.

One 15-ounce package refrigerated folded piecrusts
6 tablespoons grated Parmesan cheese
$1/2$ teaspoon coarsely ground black pepper

1   Preheat the oven to 450°F. Unfold the piecrusts onto an ungreased large baking sheet. Sprinkle the crusts evenly with the cheese. Use a sharp knife to cut each piecrust into quarters along the fold lines, then cut each quarter into 3 wedges.

2   Bake until the pastry is golden and crisp, 9 to 10 minutes. Serve warm or at room temperature.

Flaky Parmesan Crackers Tips
- The crackers can be made a day in advance, cooled completely, then stored in a covered container.
- Avoid baking on a dark metal baking sheet, which will cause the piecrust to burn.
- For best results, bake in the center of the oven.

Flaky Parmesan Crackers Variations
- Omit the cheese and sprinkle the piecrusts with a total of 1 tablespoon fennel or sesame or poppy seeds, or 2 teaspoons coarse kosher or sea salt, or 2 tablespoons chopped fresh rosemary, or 2 teaspoons paprika.
- Make sweet crackers by sprinkling the piecrusts with a total of 2 tablespoons sugar mixed with 1 teaspoon ground cinnamon.
- Spread baked crackers with about $1/2$ teaspoon caponata or olive spread or pesto and serve as an hors d'oeuvre.

traditional american dinner roll shapes

Dinner roll dough produces rolls that have a light crust and a soft interior, which is typical of American dinner rolls.

One 11.3-ounce tube refrigerated dinner roll dough
2 tablespoons unsalted butter, melted

Preheat the oven to 375°F. Bake all of the rolls until rich golden brown, 10 to 15 minutes. Serve warm.

- **For cloverleaf rolls, grease 8 muffin tins. Pull each roll into 3 pieces and shape into 3 balls. Place 3 balls in each muffin tin. Brush the tops with melted butter.**
- **For Parker House rolls, grease a baking sheet. Use your hand to flatten each roll to a $3^{1}/_{2}$-inch round. Brush the dough with melted butter, then fold over, pressing to help the fold to be secured. Place, at least 2 inches apart, on the prepared baking sheet.**
- **For poppy seed rolls, form the rolls into rounds, then brush with melted butter and sprinkle each roll with about $^{1}/_{8}$ teaspoon poppy seeds. Place on a baking sheet.**

breadstick variations

MAKES 6 LARGE OR 12 SMALL BREAD-STICKS

Breadstick dough can be twisted, rolled, twirled into an S-shape or other alphabet shape, or just left long. They can be sprinkled, filled, and brushed with butter or egg. Brushing with butter gives them a rich, soft crust, whole egg a golden, slightly crisp crust, and egg white a shiny, very crisp crust. The following variations are just suggestions. You can think of more, I'm sure.

> One 11-ounce tube refrigerated breadstick dough, regular or corn bread
>
> 2 tablespoons unsalted butter, melted; *or* 1 egg, beaten; *or* 1 egg white, beaten with 1 teaspoon water

Preheat the oven to 400°F. Grease a large baking sheet. Unroll the breadstick dough onto a work surface, breaking into 12 lengths for small breadsticks and 6 lengths for large breadsticks.

- For traditional flat or shaped breadsticks, separate into 6 or 12 breadsticks and place each at least 1 inch apart on the prepared baking sheet, leaving them long or shaping them into alphabet shapes, such as a C or an O. Brush with melted butter, beaten whole egg or egg white, and sprinkle with a total of 2 tablespoons grated Parmesan cheese, chili powder, sesame or other seeds, or chopped fresh herbs. Bake until rich golden brown, 12 to 15 minutes.

- For twists, twist the rolls to form a spiral. Bake until rich golden brown, 12 to 15 minutes.

- For double twists, stretch each small breadstick about 1 inch longer, then place 2 side by side on the baking sheet. Twist the sticks together to form a double roll, pinching the ends to seal together. Place in the oven and immediately reduce the temperature to 375°F. Bake until rich golden brown, 14 to 18 minutes.

- For savory swirl rolls, separate the dough into two sections of 6 breadsticks each. Spread the sections with a mixture of $1/2$ cup finely chopped onion, cooked until tender in 1 tablespoon butter, then seasoned with 1 tablespoon chopped fresh herbs. Roll up from the long side, then cut each roll along the perforated breadstick lines into 6 rolls. Place, cut side up, on a greased baking sheet. The savory breadstick sections can also be spread with a total of $1/2$ cup basil or sundried tomato pesto or spreadable herb cheese, such as Boursin or Rondelé, then rolled and cut as directed. Place in the oven and immediately reduce the oven temperature to 375°F. Bake until rich golden brown, 14 to 18 minutes.

- For grissini, the Italian pencil-thin breadsticks, separate the dough into 12 breadsticks, then carefully stretch each to 18 inches long. Place, at least 1 inch apart, on lightly greased large baking sheets. If desired, brush with beaten egg or egg white, then sprinkle with seeds or coarse salt. Bake until rich golden brown and crisp, 13 to 15 minutes.

biscuit variations

Biscuit dough can be cut, split, filled, and/or rolled in various coatings. Each size and type of dough has its own special qualities. Each should be baked on an ungreased baking sheet, at least 2 inches apart, in a preheated 375°F oven.

- **Use a small, sharp knife to make a pocket in each of 8 biscuits from a 17.3-ounce tube of refrigerated cornmeal biscuits. Fill each with about 1 tablespoon chopped smoked ham and 1 tablespoon shredded or sliced Swiss cheese. Pinch to seal the pockets. Brush the top of each biscuit with about 1 teaspoon Dijon mustard. Bake until rich golden brown, 15 to 17 minutes.**

- **Brush the tops of biscuits from a 7.5-ounce or 12-ounce tube with melted butter, then dip the tops into coarse salt or grated Parmesan, and bake until rich golden brown, 12 to 16 minutes.**

- **Brush the tops of biscuits from a 7.5-ounce or 12-ounce tube with one egg beaten with 2 teaspoons water, then sprinkle with chopped fresh or dried herbs or seeds, such as fennel, poppy, or sesame. Bake until rich golden brown, 12 to 16 minutes.**

- **Separate buttermilk or flaky biscuits from any size tube into 2 or 4 layers each. Brush each layer with melted butter and sprinkle lightly with grated Parmesan. Bake until rich golden brown and crisp, 10 to 12 minutes.**

pizza and flatbread

Pizza is as American as apple pie these days. Since World War II veterans brought home a taste for this **simple**, **savory** flatbread and newly minted Italian Americans responded to the call, there is hardly a village in the United States that doesn't have at least one pizza parlor. Wolfgang Puck took California pizza to new and **outrageously delicious** non-Italian frontiers, and today's pizzas are topped with **every-thing** from prosciutto to pineapple (I draw the line at pineapple). Nonetheless, you can have **whatever you want** in the privacy of your home pizza parlor with these recipes. Indeed, flatbreads of every kind are important in many **cuisines**, and are **easy** to make at home, so try your hand at Tandoor-style and German bacon and onion flatbreads, too.

pizza margherita

This is the simplest and perhaps most classic of all Italian pizzas (extra cheese and pepperoni are definitely American). It is dependent upon a few very fresh, very summery ingredients—ripe tomatoes, slivered basil, garlic, freshly grated Parmesan cheese, and the best olive oil. A splash of good balsamic vinegar is the secret ingredient that brings out the best flavor and marries all the ingredients together.

The basic baking instructions for pizza apply to all the variations. A really fun birthday party or family supper idea is to put out an array of toppings, then let people assemble their own pizza portions. Or, if they are really picky, cut the dough into 2 or 3 pieces, and allow them to have their own personal pizzas.

1 tablespoon yellow cornmeal

One 10-ounce tube refrigerated pizza dough

3 tablespoons extra virgin olive oil

3 large garlic cloves, finely chopped

12 ounces ripe, meaty tomatoes, seeded and thinly sliced

Salt and pepper

1/2 cup thinly sliced fresh basil

1 cup shredded mozzarella cheese

1/4 cup grated Parmesan cheese

2 teaspoons balsamic vinegar

1   Preheat the oven to 450°F. Sprinkle a large baking sheet with the cornmeal. Unroll the dough onto the baking sheet, pressing and stretching to a rough 12-inch square. In a small dish, stir together the oil and garlic.

2   Brush the top of the dough with about half of the garlic oil. Top evenly with the tomatoes, then sprinkle lightly with salt and generously with freshly ground pepper. Sprinkle with all but about 2 tablespoons of the basil, and all of the mozzarella and Parmesan.

3 Place in the oven and immediately reduce the temperature to 425°F. Bake until the crust is rich golden brown and crisp on the bottom, and the cheese is bubbly, about 12 minutes. Sprinkle with the vinegar and remaining basil.

4 Use a pizza cutter or sharp knife to cut the pizza into squares.

Pizza Margherita Tips

- Stretch or pat the dough as evenly as possible to avoid thin spots that will brown too much.
- The tomatoes should be seeded to squeeze out excess liquid so that the pizza will not be soggy.
- To seed tomatoes, cut in half crosswise, then gently squeeze out the seeds and excess watery liquid.

Pizza Margherita Variations

- Add $1/4$ cup slivered prosciutto, smoked ham, or cooked pancetta to the toppings.
- In place of the listed toppings, layer one $14^1/2$-ounce can "pasta-ready" diced tomatoes, 1 cup thinly sliced pepperoni, 1 tablespoon bottled Italian seasoning, and 2 cups shredded mozzarella.
- In place of the listed toppings, spread with 2 cups sliced cooked meatballs in seasoned tomato sauce, 1 cup shredded mozzarella, and $1/4$ cup grated Parmesan.
- In place of the listed toppings, brush with $1^1/2$ tablespoons olive oil, then sprinkle with $1^1/2$ cups sliced or crumbled cooked Italian sausage, 1 cup sliced roasted bell peppers, and 1 cup shredded mozzarella.

pepper and olive pan pizza

Cooking the pizza briefly over direct heat sets, crisps, and lightly blackens the crust in a way that the oven cannot do. If you have a cast-iron skillet, more the better, but this pizza will work just fine in any heavy-duty ovenproof skillet.

$2^1/_2$ tablespoons olive oil

2 teaspoons yellow cornmeal

One 10-ounce tube refrigerated pizza dough

3 garlic cloves, finely chopped

1 small red bell pepper, thinly sliced

1 small sweet onion, such as Vidalia, thinly sliced

$^1/_3$ cup sliced black olives

2 tablespoons chopped fresh oregano

1 cup shredded mozzarella cheese

2 tablespoons grated Parmesan cheese

1 Preheat the oven to 400°F. Coat a 12-inch ovenproof skillet with about $^1/_2$ tablespoon of the olive oil and sprinkle with the cornmeal.

2 Unroll the pizza dough and ease it into the skillet. The dough will be uneven and fit partway up the sides of the pan, which is fine, since the pizza is rustic and free form. Stir the garlic into the remaining 2 tablespoons olive oil and brush about half of the garlic oil onto the pizza dough. Scatter the red bell pepper, onion, olives, oregano, mozzarella, and Parmesan over the dough.

3 Set the pan over direct medium-high heat and cook until the dough begins to puff and the bottom becomes golden, about 2 minutes. Transfer the skillet to the preheated oven and bake until the cheese is melted, toppings are hot, and the pizza is rich golden brown and crusty, 15 to 18 minutes.

4 Serve the pizza, cut into wedges, directly from the skillet.

Pepper and Olive Pan Pizza **Tips**

- Remember that the skillet handle will be very hot right out of the oven. Be sure to use a potholder and drape it over the handle after it comes from the oven to remind you not to touch it.
- A good skillet that sits evenly on the burner works best for this, and all other skillet recipes as well. It's worth the investment.
- Cornmeal gives the crunchy bottom that is typical of a good pizza parlor pizza.

Pepper and Olive Pan Pizza **Variations**

- Any other combination of toppings, as long as they are not too heavy, works well here. Other quick-cooking vegetables, such as thin asparagus, sliced Roma tomatoes, or green bell peppers don't need to be precooked, but leftover cooked vegetables such as broccoli make a great pizza, too.
- Packaged shredded "4-cheese" pizza blends can be substituted for the mozzarella and Parmesan. They are found in the dairy/cheese section of the market.
- Flavored olive oils, such as garlic and/or herb oil can be used in place of plain olive oil.
- Substitute other herbs, such as basil, thyme, or marjoram, for the oregano.

herbed sausage calzones

Kids love these calzones as an after-school snack or light supper along with a bowl of mine-strone. Use sweet or hot, pork or turkey sausage—whatever you like. You could even use tofu sausage, but you would lose the kid appeal, of course.

1 tablespoon yellow cornmeal

$1/2$ pound bulk Italian sausage

$1^{1}/_{2}$ cups high-quality marinara sauce

$1/3$ cup ricotta cheese

3 tablespoons slivered fresh basil

1 egg, beaten

One 10-ounce tube refrigerated pizza dough

1 cup grated Italian Fontina or mozzarella cheese

1   Preheat the oven to 425°F. Lightly grease a baking sheet. Dust with the cornmeal.

2   In a medium skillet, cook the sausage over medium-high heat, stirring until no longer pink. Use a slotted spoon to transfer the sausage to a mixing bowl. Stir in $1/2$ cup of the marinara sauce, the cheese, basil, and one-half of the beaten egg. Season lightly with salt and pepper. Stir 1 tea-spoon water into the remaining beaten egg.

3   Unfold the dough on the prepared baking sheet. Gently stretch the dough to an 11- or 12-inch square, then cut it into 4 even squares. Divide the filling among the squares, spooning into the center of each. Top the filling with the cheese. Brush the edges of the dough with some of the remaining egg. Fold the dough over the filling to form triangles, press the edges to seal, then crimp the edges with the tines of a fork. Use a small knife to make 3 slits in the top of each cal-zone, then brush the tops with the remaining egg.

4   Bake until rich golden brown, 16 to 18 minutes. While the calzones are baking, heat the remain-ing marinara sauce. Serve the calzones warm with the sauce on the side.

Herbed Sausage Calzones **Tips**

- If you can only find sausage in casings, simply squeeze out the meat and discard the casings.
- Be sure the edges of the calzones are well sealed so that the filling does not seep out during baking.
- The calzones are best warm from the oven, but can be reheated on a baking sheet in a 300°F oven, if necessary.

Herbed Sausage Calzones **Variations**

- Practically anything can be used to fill the calzones, from leftover meatballs to roasted vegetables. The amount of filling should be about $1/4$ cup per calzone.
- For cheese calzones, fill with 1 cup ricotta mixed with $1/4$ cup grated Parmesan, $1/4$ cup chopped fresh basil, and 1 egg.
- For empanadas, a favorite throughout the Americas, fill the turnovers with shredded cooked chicken or pork mixed with a bit of sour cream, chopped fresh cilantro, and chili powder, using about $1/4$ cup filling for each empanada. Brush and bake as directed, then serve with salsa.
- For Indian-style samosas, fill the turnovers with a mixture of diced cooked potatoes (such as hash browns), green peas, ground lamb, and curry powder or chopped fresh cilantro, using about $1/4$ cup filling for each samosa. Brush and bake as directed, then serve with yogurt mixed with chopped fresh mint for dipping.
- For sweet fruit calzones, fill with drained cooked fruit, such as apples or pears.

grilled white clam pizza

Grilled pizza is astonishingly simple and very impressive. The important thing is to have a covered gas or charcoal grill, though in a pinch an outdoor "oven" can be approximated by tenting the pizzas with heavy-duty aluminum foil. The other qualification is to have light toppings that need no cooking, and to have them ready before you begin grilling, since the grilling itself takes only about 5 minutes. You might think the soft raw dough will fall through the grill grates. Trust me, it will be fine.

White clam pizza is a famous specialty from New Haven, Connecticut. If you've never had it, you really ought to try it. It's the next best thing to graduating from Yale.

3 tablespoons olive oil

4 large garlic cloves, finely chopped

$^1/_4$ teaspoon crushed hot red pepper flakes

$^2/_3$ cup chopped fresh clams or one 10-ounce can chopped clams, drained

$^1/_4$ cup chopped fresh basil

1 tablespoon chopped fresh oregano

One 10-ounce tube refrigerated pizza dough

2 teaspoons yellow cornmeal

2 tablespoons grated Parmesan cheese

1   **Prepare a medium-hot charcoal fire or preheat a gas grill. Oil the grill rack. In a small dish, combine the oil, garlic, and hot red pepper flakes. In another bowl, combine the clams, basil, and oregano. Have both bowls ready and near the grill.**

2   **Sprinkle a baking sheet with 1 teaspoon of the cornmeal. Unroll the pizza dough onto the baking sheet and press or roll to a rough 12 x 14-inch rectangle. Sprinkle with the remaining cornmeal, then cut the dough into 4 equal pieces.**

3   **Place the dough pieces directly on the grill rack. Cover and grill until the bottoms are rich golden brown with grill marks, 2 to 3 minutes. Use a spatula to turn the pizzas grilled side up, moving to the edge of the coals. Working quickly, brush the grilled side with most of the oil,**

sprinkle with the clam mixture, then the cheese. Dribble with the remaining oil. Move the pizzas back directly over the coals. Cover and grill until the bottom is rich golden brown, crisp, and with grill marks, 2 to 3 minutes.

4 Cut each piece of pizza in half to serve hot.

Grilled White Clam Pizza Tips

- If you don't want to light the grill, the pizzas can be baked on the baking sheet with the toppings in place in a 425°F oven for about 20 minutes until the crust is crisp and browned.
- The dough is easiest to work with if it is well chilled.
- Be sure to oil the grill rack so the dough does not stick to it.

Grilled White Clam Pizza Variations

- Other simple, light toppings can be used, such as diced fresh tomatoes, slivered fresh basil, and grated Parmesan.
- Grill the pizzas with only the flavored oil, then heap a room-temperature salad of diced tomatoes and fresh mozzarella tossed with a little balsamic vinegar on top of the hot pizza. Serve with a knife and fork.
- Substitute tiny shrimp for the clams.

MAKES 1
FLATBREAD;
16 PIECES,
SERVING 8
AS AN
APPETIZER

italian flag flatbread

This is a whimsical cross between pizza and focaccia. The flatbread can be made with only one of the toppings, but then it wouldn't resemble the red, white, and green of the Italian flag, of course. Serve it on a marble slab, cut into pieces for a fanciful start to an Italian supper.

One 10-ounce tube refrigerated pizza dough
1 tablespoon yellow cornmeal
$1/3$ cup basil pesto
$1/3$ cup sun-dried tomato pesto
$1/3$ cup spreadable herbed cheese, such as Boursin or Rondelé

1 Preheat the oven to 425°F. Slightly oil a large baking sheet, then sprinkle with the cornmeal.

2 Unroll the pizza dough onto the baking sheet, then press or roll to a 10 x 12-inch rectangle. Spread the basil pesto down one-third of the long side of the dough, spreading to within $1/2$ inch of the edge. Spread the sun-dried tomato pesto down one-third of the other side of the dough, spreading to within $1/2$ inch of the edge. Spread the cheese down the center third of the dough.

3 Bake until the dough is rich golden brown and well browned on the bottom, and the toppings are bubbly, 18 to 22 minutes. Use two large spatulas to transfer the flatbread to a wooden board or marble slab. Use a pizza cutter to cut into 16 pieces.

Italian Flag Flatbread **Tips**

- Bake the dough as soon as the toppings are spread on it so that the dough does not become soggy.
- The cornmeal helps to promote a crisp, nicely textured crust.
- Avoid baking on a dark metal sheet, which tends to cause overbrowning.

Italian Flag Flatbread **Variations**

- Use only one of the fillings, tripling the amount.
- Cut into larger pieces and serve as lunch or supper with a salad.
- Substitute soft herbed goat cheese or mascarpone mixed with 1 tablespoon chopped fresh herbs for the Boursin.

rosemary and sea salt focaccia

Focaccia is related to pizza, but is generally topped only with herbs and coarse salt. The dough is not as thin as pizza and is liberally brushed with olive oil, then dimpled with your fingers to make little pools for the oil during baking. Richer than Italian bread, but not quite a pizza, this has become a restaurant breadbasket favorite in recent years. Rosemary is the classic herb to sprinkle on the focaccia, but you can use almost anything you have on hand or a combination of herbs.

3 tablespoons fruity olive oil

1 tablespoon yellow cornmeal

One 10-ounce tube refrigerated pizza dough

$1^1/2$ tablespoons chopped fresh rosemary

2 teaspoons coarse sea salt or kosher salt

$^1/2$ teaspoon coarsely ground black pepper

1   Preheat the oven to 400°F. Brush a small baking sheet with about 2 teaspoons of the olive oil, then sprinkle with the cornmeal.

2   Unroll the pizza dough onto the baking sheet, but do not stretch or pull the dough. Brush the dough with the remaining oil, then sprinkle with the rosemary, salt, and pepper. Use your fingers to make dimpled indentations all over the dough.

3   Bake until the dough is rich golden brown and crusty, 15 to 20 minutes. Use a pizza cutter or sharp knife to cut the focaccia into rough 2 x 4-inch rectangles. Serve warm.

Rosemary and Sea Salt Focaccia **Tips**

- Don't stretch the dough as you would for a pizza. Focaccia is thicker than pizza.
- Use really good olive oil, since it is a major flavor in the focaccia.
- Focaccia is best right from the oven, but can be reheated in a 300°F oven for a few minutes.

Rosemary and Sea Salt Focaccia **Variations**

- Substitute other herbs, such as thyme or basil, for the rosemary.
- Add about $1/3$ cup thinly sliced sautéed onions to the topping.
- Omit the salt and pepper if you like a more Tuscan-style focaccia or are serving it with salty soups.

german bacon and onion flatbread

A German version of focaccia, this flatbread is made with French bread dough, which bakes up more crisp and less chewy. It is excellent served with choucroute garni or any grilled sausage or pork and sauerkraut variation. It is also terrific as an accompaniment to vegetable or cheese soup. As with focaccia and all other flatbreads, it can be topped with almost anything that you like.

8 strips bacon, cut into 1-inch pieces
1 large onion, thinly sliced
2 large garlic cloves, finely chopped
2 tablespoons crème fraîche or sour cream
1 tablespoon chopped fresh thyme
1 teaspoon caraway seeds
1 tablespoon olive oil
1 tablespoon yellow cornmeal
One 11-ounce loaf refrigerated French bread dough

1 In a large skillet, partially cook the bacon until barely limp. Transfer to a plate. In the bacon drippings, cook the onion over medium heat, stirring often, until softened, about 5 minutes. Add the garlic and cook for 1 minute. Remove the pan from the heat, stir in the crème fraîche, thyme, and caraway seeds. Let the mixture cool to lukewarm.

2 Preheat the oven to 400°F. Brush a large baking sheet with the oil, then sprinkle with the cornmeal. Carefully unroll the bread dough onto the baking sheet, stretching to a rough 9 x 12-inch rectangle. Spread the onion filling over the top of the dough, then sprinkle with the partially cooked bacon.

3 Bake until the bread is rich golden brown and crisp, and the bacon is crisp. Use a pizza cutter or sharp knife to cut the bread into rough 2 x 4-inch rectangles. Serve warm.

German Bacon and Onion Flatbread **Tips**

- The filling should be cooled before spreading on the bread dough.
- The filling can be made several hours ahead of time, refrigerated, and then returned to room temperature before using.
- The bread will bake to a very crisp texture, especially at the edges. Cut it as soon as it comes from the oven.

German Bacon and Onion Flatbread **Variations**

- Diced Canadian bacon (about 3 ounces) can be used in place of the bacon.
- Thinly sliced kielbasa or other cooked garlic sausage (about 4 ounces) can be used in place of the bacon.
- The flatbread can be sprinkled with about $1/2$ cup grated Swiss cheese in place of the bacon.

tandoor-style flatbread

Tandoor-baked breads are among the most popular foods in an Indian restaurant, and they are important to every meal in India. The tandoor, a clay oven that reaches very high temperatures, also produces moist chicken, lamb, and even seafood specialties; still, the day-to-day commonplace use of a tandoor is to bake the bread by sticking it to the sides of the hot oven. Though an American home oven will never be a tandoor, we can enjoy an excellent flatbread in the Indian tradition.

> 1 tablespoon yellow cornmeal
> One 10-ounce tube refrigerated pizza dough
> 2 teaspoons fennel seeds
> $\frac{1}{2}$ teaspoon kosher or sea salt
> 1 tablespoon unsalted butter, melted

1   Preheat the oven to 500°F. Sprinkle a large baking sheet with the cornmeal. Unroll the pizza dough on the baking sheet, stretching and rolling it as close to the edges of the baking sheet as possible. Sprinkle the dough with the seeds and salt.

2   Bake until the bread is rich golden brown with the thinnest parts well browned and charred, 6 to 8 minutes. Brush the hot breads with the melted butter.

3   Use a pizza cutter or sharp knife to cut the bread into rough squares, or simply tear the bread into pieces. Serve warm.

Tandoor-Style Flatbread **Tips**

- Do not oil the baking sheet. These breads should be very crisp and browned with little oil.
- When cooled, the breads will firm to almost a cracker consistency, so they can be easily broken into pieces to serve with soups or for snacks.
- Even if the stretched bread has a few tears, that is okay.

Tandoor-Style Flatbread **Variations**

- Substitute sesame, caraway, or poppy seeds for the fennel seeds.
- Spread the stretched dough with a thin layer (about $1/2$ cup) sautéed chopped onion.
- Brush the stretched dough with 1 tablespoon olive oil before sprinkling with the seeds, then omit the brushing with butter after baking.
- Make stuffed flatbreads by spreading half of the dough to within $1/2$ inch of the edges with about 2 cups of thinly sliced onions sautéed in about 2 tablespoons olive oil along with 2 or 3 minced garlic cloves and 2 table-spoons cumin seeds or chopped fresh cilantro or other herbs. Fold the dough over the filling, then bake until the bread is rich golden brown and crisp, 8 to 10 minutes.

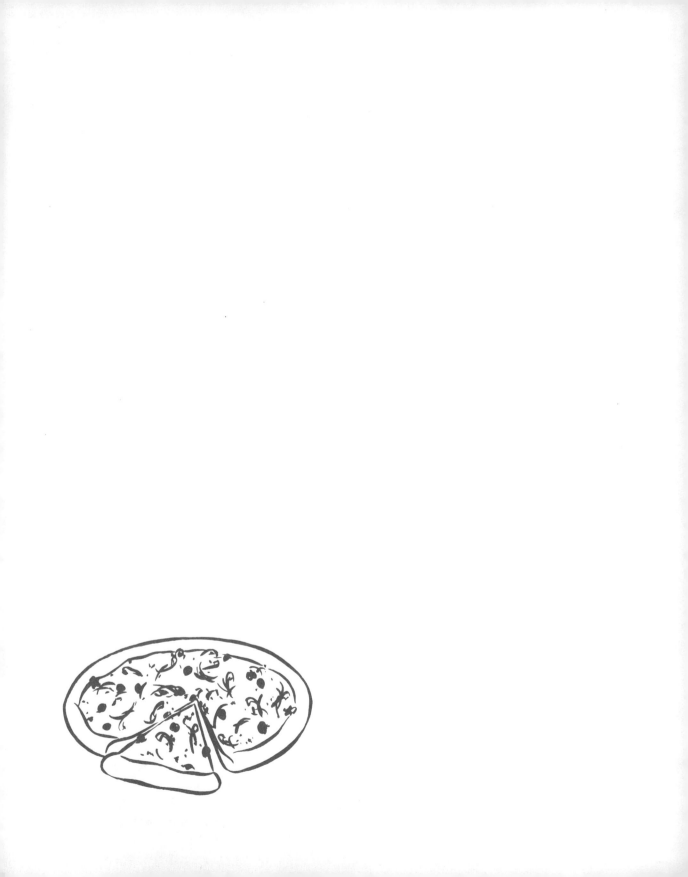

main dishes

Bread and pastry dough is an important part of international **main dishes**, from the classic Greek spanokopita to an **elegant** continental quiche, as well as all manner of savory Middle European strudels and American pot pies. Most are practically **one-dish meals**, easily rounded out with little more than a big green salad. All are well **loved**, and made unbelievably **quickly** with prepared doughs. Supper never looked, smelled, or tasted **this good** . . . well, not since we were kids and Mom was in the kitchen all day.

chicken and herb baked dumplings

These "baked" dumplings are a real improvement on the usual steamed dumplings, which are always too doughy for my taste. These are the best of both worlds—a golden crusted biscuit on top of a moist, flavorful stew. To make this most modern version of an old-fashioned American favorite even easier, look for presliced carrots and celery at the salad bar in your supermarket.

1 pound skinless, boneless chicken thighs, cut into $1^1/_2$-inch chunks

3 tablespoons unsalted butter

2 tablespoons all-purpose flour

$1^1/_2$ cups frozen pearl onions, thawed

3 carrots, thickly sliced (about $1^1/_2$ cups)

2 celery ribs, thickly sliced (about 1 cup)

$3^1/_2$ cups canned chicken broth

4 tablespoons chopped mixed fresh herbs, such as thyme, savory, and sage

3 tablespoons chopped parsley

One $7^1/_2$-ounce tube refrigerated biscuit dough, preferably buttermilk

1   Preheat the oven to 400°F. Season the chicken with salt and pepper. In a deep 10- or 12-inch ovenproof skillet or Dutch oven, heat the butter. Cook the chicken over medium-high heat, stirring often, until golden on all sides. Sprinkle with the flour, then cook and stir for 1 minute. Add the onions, carrots, celery, chicken broth, and 2 tablespoons each of the mixed herbs and parsley. Bring the liquid to a simmer.

2   Meanwhile, separate the dough into 10 biscuits. Cut each biscuit in half. Place the biscuits in a single layer on top of the simmering liquid. (The biscuits may be quite close together.) Sprinkle the biscuits with the remaining 2 tablespoons mixed herbs. Place the pan in the oven and bake until the biscuits are pale golden on top, 10 to 12 minutes.

3   Sprinkle with the remaining 1 tablespoon parsley and serve.

Chicken and Herb Baked Dumplings Tips

- Other types of biscuits can be used, but the total weight of the package should not exceed about 8 ounces.
- If the pan is too shallow, you might need a little more chicken broth.
- Chicken thighs are more flavorful than breasts.

Chicken and Herb Baked Dumplings Variations

- Chicken breast, turkey, boneless pork, or even a tender cut of beef can be used in place of the chicken. For beef, use beef broth in place of the chicken broth.
- Other aromatic vegetables, such as turnips, can be used in place of some of the carrot, celery, and onion.
- Vegetables and meat or poultry left over from another meal can be turned into a quick stew by simply bringing to a simmer with the liquid and herbs, then adding the biscuits and herbs, and baking as directed.

mustard beef and red wine in puff pastry

This is definitely a company-worthy meal, and especially so since it not only can be prepared ahead, it actually tastes better when the beef, wine, and aromatic herbs and vegetables have had a chance to mingle.

1 pound beef sirloin, cut into 1-inch pieces

4 tablespoons all-purpose flour

4 tablespoons unsalted butter

2 cups frozen pearl onions, thawed

$1^1/_2$ cups baby carrots, cut in half if large

1 medium parsnip, sliced

3 large garlic cloves, finely chopped

2 tablespoons Dijon mustard

2 tablespoons chopped fresh rosemary

$^3/_4$ cup red wine

$^3/_4$ cup beef broth, preferably reduced sodium

1 sheet frozen puff pastry from a 17.3-ounce package, thawed but
   well chilled

1 egg, beaten

1   Preheat the oven to 400°F. Season the beef with salt and pepper, then toss with 1 tablespoon of the flour.

2   In a large skillet, heat 2 tablespoons of the butter over medium-high heat. Cook the beef, turning often, until browned on all sides, about 5 minutes. Transfer the beef to a plate. Add the remaining 2 tablespoons butter to the skillet. Cook the onions, carrots, and parsnip over medium heat, stirring often, until golden and tender, about 5 minutes. Stir in the garlic and remaining 3 tablespoons flour. Cook and stir for 1 minute. Stir in the mustard and $1^1/_2$ tablespoons of the rosemary. Slowly stir in the wine and broth. Simmer, stirring often, until the sauce is thickened and bubbly, about 3 minutes. Return the beef and any accumulated juices to the skillet. Spoon the mixture into a shallow 2-quart baking dish, such as an 8-inch square dish.

3   On a lightly floured surface, roll the puff pastry to a 10-inch square, or to a size that is 2 inches in diameter larger than the top of the baking dish. Sprinkle the pastry with the remaining $1/2$ tablespoon rosemary, then lightly press it in with the rolling pin.

4   Place the pastry over the filling, crimping the edges just inside the rim of the baking dish. Use a sharp knife to cut several slits in the pastry. Brush lightly with the beaten egg.

5   Bake until the pastry is rich golden brown and the filling is bubbly, 20 to 25 minutes.

Mustard Beef and Red Wine in Puff Pastry Tips

- The filling can be made up to 6 hours ahead and refrigerated, but return to room temperature for baking. The puff pastry can also be rolled out up to 6 hours ahead and refrigerated on a baking sheet, tightly covered. Place the pastry on the beef just before baking.
- The slits allow steam to escape, thus keeping the bottom of the pastry from becoming soggy.

Mustard Beef and Red Wine in Puff Pastry Variations

- Boneless chicken or pork can be substituted for the beef.
- White wine can be substituted for red wine.
- 1 medium potato, peeled and diced, can be substituted for the parsnip.

pork, apple, and sweet potato lattice pie

For a simple, warming autumnal supper, this can't be beat. If you are having company, all you need is a big green salad to complete the meal. Breadsticks make a great lattice topping, since they don't need to be rolled out or shaped—just arranged on the filling.

> 1^1/$_2$ pounds pork tenderloin, cut into 1-inch pieces
>
> 6 tablespoons all-purpose flour
>
> 5 tablespoons vegetable oil
>
> 2 small tart apples, peeled and cut into ^{1}/$_2$-inch dice
>
> 1 large sweet potato, peeled and cut into ^{1}/$_2$-inch dice
>
> 1 large onion, coarsely chopped
>
> 1^1/$_2$ cups apple cider
>
> 3 tablespoons chopped fresh sage
>
> ^{1}/$_3$ cup applejack or Calvados or additional apple cider
>
> ^{1}/$_3$ cup chicken broth, preferably reduced sodium
>
> 1^1/$_2$ tablespoons cider vinegar
>
> One 11-ounce tube refrigerated breadstick dough

1   Preheat the oven to 400°F. Place the pork in a mixing bowl. Season with salt and pepper, then toss with 2 tablespoons of the flour.

2   In a large skillet, heat 1 tablespoon of the oil over medium-high heat. Cook half of the pork, stirring often, until browned, 3 to 5 minutes. Transfer to a plate. Add 1 more tablespoon oil and cook the remaining pork in the same way.

3   Add the remaining 3 tablespoons oil to the skillet. Cook the apples, sweet potato, and onion in the oil over medium heat, stirring often, for 3 minutes. Add ^{1}/$_2$ cup of the cider and reduce the heat to medium-low. Simmer the vegetables until just tender, 8 to 10 minutes. Sprinkle with the remaining 4 tablespoons flour and the sage. Cook and stir for 1 minute, then slowly stir in the remaining 1 cup cider until smooth and bubbly, about 2 minutes. Add the applejack, broth, and vinegar, stirring until thickened and bubbly, about 1 minute. Taste and add salt and pepper as needed. Return the pork and any accumulated juices to the skillet. Spoon the mixture into a

shallow 3-quart baking dish, such as a 9 x 13-inch rectangular dish.

4   Unroll the breadsticks and arrange them on top of the hot filling in a lattice pattern, twisting each to form a spiral and cutting to fit the baking dish.

5   Place in the oven and immediately reduce the temperature to 375°F. Bake until the breadsticks are rich golden brown and the filling is bubbly, 22 to 27 minutes. To serve, use a wide spoon to cut through the breadsticks and scoop out the filling.

Pork, Apple, and Sweet Potato Lattice Pie Tips

- The breadsticks bake best if arranged on a hot filling. If you make the filling ahead of time, place it in the baking dish and heat, covered, in the oven for about 15 minutes until hot. Then arrange the breadsticks on top.
- The pork filling can be prepared up to 6 hours ahead of time and refrigerated.
- Pork tenderloins are usually sold two to a package, and packages often weigh about 1^1/2 pounds. If it is slightly more or less, that is fine.

Pork, Apple, and Sweet Potato Lattice Pie Variations

- Boneless chicken or turkey can be substituted for the pork.
- Regular potatoes can be substituted for the sweet potatoes.
- Parmesan breadsticks can be used. Sprinkle the Parmesan topping on the breadsticks after arranging them on the filling.

chorizo, shrimp, and corn biscuit pot pies

The flavors here are reminiscent of jambalaya, gone a bit farther to the Southwest from Louisiana. Chorizo is a very peppery sausage; if you can't find it, you can substitute hot Italian sausage. Chipotles in adobo, found in the Mexican food section of the market, are also very hot, so use the smaller measurement if you are unfamiliar with them.

The recipe can be cut in half to serve 4 people, and you can bake the remaining biscuits to have for breakfast. The recipe can also be baked in a 3-quart baking dish if you don't have individual ramekins of the correct size.

1 tablespoon cumin seeds

$1^1/_2$ tablespoons corn oil

$^3/_4$ pound chorizo, sliced thinly, or bulk hot Italian sausage

1 medium red onion, chopped

3 cups diced mixed red, yellow, and green bell peppers

$1^1/_2$ cups fresh or frozen and thawed corn

1 to 2 chipotles in adobo sauce, chopped

1 tablespoon adobo sauce

$1^1/_2$ tablespoons yellow cornmeal

$^1/_4$ cup all-purpose flour

2 cups chicken broth, preferably reduced sodium

$^3/_4$ pound shelled and deveined uncooked medium shrimp

One 17.3-ounce tube refrigerated large-size cornmeal biscuits

1 Preheat the oven to 400°F. Have ready eight 10- to 12-ounce individual baking dishes or gratins, or a 3-quart rectangular or other shallow 3-quart baking dish. In a small dry skillet, toss the cumin seeds over medium heat until fragrant and a shade darker, about 1 minute. Transfer the seeds to a plate.

2 In a large skillet, heat the oil. Cook the chorizo over medium heat, stirring often, until browned, 4 to 5 minutes. Use a slotted spoon to transfer the chorizo to a plate. Increase the heat to medium-high and add the onion, bell peppers, and corn. Cook, stirring often, until the vegetables are just tender and pale golden. Stir in the chipotle, adobo sauce, cornmeal, and flour.

Cook, stirring, for 1 minute. Slowly stir in the broth until lightly thickened and simmering. Stir in the shrimp and cook, stirring, for about 1 minute. Stir in the chorizo and any accumulated juices. Divide the mixture among the individual baking dishes or spoon into a large dish.

3 Separate the dough into 8 biscuits, cutting each in half. Arrange the biscuits on the filling, 2 to each individual dish, or in an attractive pattern in the large baking dish. Bake until the biscuits are rich golden brown and the filling is bubbly, 20 to 25 minutes. Serve the individual dishes or use a spoon to scoop out filling and 2 biscuit halves for each portion from the large baking dish.

Chorizo, Shrimp, and Corn Biscuit Pot Pies Tips

- If you use Italian sausage links, squeeze out the sausage meat and discard the casings.
- The filling can be made up to 6 hours ahead of time, and reheated before adding the biscuits. Do not add the shrimp until just before baking so that it does not overcook.
- Chipotles in adobo are smoked jalapeño peppers in a rich, spicy brown sauce. They have myriad uses, and come several to a can. Freeze extra chipotles in adobo up to 6 months.
- Colorful bell peppers are usually part of the supermarket salad bar, which makes it easy to have an array of colors without buying 3 whole peppers.

(continued)

Chorizo, Shrimp, and Corn Biscuit Pot Pies
Variations

- Crabmeat or cooked chicken chunks can be substituted for the shrimp.
- Other biscuits, such as buttermilk or Southern-style, can be substituted for the cornmeal biscuits.
- The pot pies can also be baked with a refrigerated breadstick lattice topping, unrolling the breadsticks and arranging in a lattice fashion atop the filling in a 3-quart baking dish. Bake at 375°F until the breadsticks are rich golden, 22 to 27 minutes.

curried chicken pie

Flaky pastry is often used in Indian cooking, most commonly to make samosas. So the topping for this pie, although it could also be yeast breadsticks or puff pastry, just seems right as a piecrust. Serve this chicken pie accompanied by a spinach salad. Note that you can also make individual pies for an even more sophisticated presentation.

1 pound skinless and boneless chicken breasts, cut into 1-inch
    chunks

3 tablespoons all-purpose flour

2 tablespoons unsalted butter

1 large onion, coarsely chopped

1 small red bell pepper, cut into $1/2$-inch pieces

$1^1/2$ tablespoons curry powder

1 tablespoon finely chopped fresh ginger

2 medium (about 8 ounces total) red potatoes, cut into $1/2$-inch
    chunks

1 cup chicken broth, preferably reduced sodium

2 cups broccoli florets

2 cups cauliflower florets

$1/2$ cup unsweetened coconut milk

1 tablespoon lime juice

2 tablespoons chopped fresh cilantro

One-half 15-ounce package refrigerated folded piecrusts

1 egg, beaten

1   Preheat the oven to 425°F. Season the chicken with salt and pepper, then sprinkle with 1 tablespoon of the flour.

2   In a large skillet, heat $1^1/2$ tablespoons of the butter. Cook the chicken over medium-high heat, turning once or twice, until browned on all sides, about 5 minutes. Transfer the chicken to a plate. Add the remaining $1/2$ tablespoon butter to the skillet and cook the onion and bell pepper

over medium heat, stirring often, just until softened, about 4 minutes. Sprinkle with the remaining 2 tablespoons flour, the curry powder, and ginger. Cook, stirring for 1 minute. Stir in the potatoes and chicken broth. Bring to a simmer, stirring constantly, until thickened and bubbly. Cover and simmer for 4 minutes. Stir in the broccoli, cauliflower, coconut milk, lime juice, and 1 tablespoon of the cilantro. Return the chicken and any accumulated juices to the skillet. Spoon into a shallow 2-quart baking dish, such as an 8-inch square dish or a 10-inch round, deep pie plate.

3   On a lightly floured surface, sprinkle the piecrust with the remaining 1 tablespoon cilantro, then roll the piecrust just to smooth the seams and press in the cilantro. Use a small, sharp knife to cut several slits in the pastry. Place the crust on top of the filling, crimping the edges if desired.

4   Bake the pie for 20 minutes, then reduce the oven temperature to 400°F and continue to bake until the crust is rich golden brown and the filling is bubbly, 18 to 20 minutes more. To serve, use a large spoon to cut through the crust and scoop out the filling.

Curried Chicken Pie **Tips**

- If the piecrust is not the correct shape for your dish, cut into decorative shapes with large cookie cutters, or cut into wedges along the fold lines.
- Be sure to use a high-quality curry powder, and buy a new tin if yours is more than a year old. Curry powder loses potency fairly rapidly.
- Broccoli and cauliflower florets are available in bags in the produce section, and quite often at the salad bar.
- Be sure to use *unsweetened* coconut milk found in the Asian section of the market.

Curried Chicken Pie **Variations**

- Cooked chicken or turkey can be substituted for the chicken. Omit the browning of the chicken and instead just add it to the vegetables.
- Shrimp can be substituted for the chicken, adding the raw shrimp with the vegetables.
- The pies can be baked in 6 individual 8- to 10-ounce casseroles or gratin dishes. Cut the pastry into $3^{1}/_{2}$-inch circles or shapes to fit the dishes.

peppered pork tenderloin en croûte

MAKES
8 SERVINGS

Pork tenderloins weigh about 12 ounces each, and often come two to a package. One sheet of puff pastry is large enough to wrap both tenderloins, making this a really elegant meal for eight, the perfect number for a dinner party in my estimation. Additionally, the pork and pastry can and really should be assembled in advance, with nothing but the baking and serving to be done during the party.

> 2 pork tenderloins, each about 12 ounces
>
> 2 tablespoons Dijon mustard
>
> 2 teaspoons cracked black pepper
>
> 1 tablespoon olive oil
>
> 1 sheet frozen puff pastry from a 17.3-ounce package, thawed but well chilled
>
> 1 egg, beaten

1   Brush the pork on all sides with the mustard, then sprinkle with the pepper, patting it in if necessary. If the pork is too long to fit in a skillet, cut each tenderloin in half crosswise. In a large skillet, heat the oil over high heat. When the pan is hot, sear the pork, turning to brown on all sides, for 2 minutes total. Transfer the pork to a plate to cool completely.

2   On a lightly floured surface, roll the puff pastry to about $1/4$-inch thickness, taking care that it is at least 2 inches longer than the length of each tenderloin, about 12 x 14 inches. Use a sharp knife to cut the pastry in half lengthwise. Place each tenderloin in the center of the pastry. Fold over to enclose, pinching and tucking the ends together. The pastry should fold over by about $1/2$ inch; trim any excess pastry away. Brush the edges of the folds with beaten egg, then press and pinch together to seal. Place the wrapped pork tenderloins, seam side down and at least 3 inches apart, on a large baking sheet. Brush the tops and sides with more beaten egg. If there is excess pastry, shape into circles or twists or other decorative shapes, then "glue" it to the top by brushing with more beaten egg. Place the baking sheet in the refrigerator for at least 15 minutes and up to 4 hours, covered with plastic wrap.

3   Preheat the oven to 425°F. Bake for 10 minutes, then reduce the oven temperature to 400°F and bake until the pastry is rich golden brown, 10 to 12 minutes more. Use a spatula to transfer the tenderloins to a cutting board or platter. Let stand 5 minutes, then cut each on the diagonal into 4 pieces.

Peppered Pork Tenderloin en Croûte Tips

- The meat should be completely cooled before wrapping in the pastry.
- Good-quality Dijon mustard makes a big difference.
- Cracked black pepper can be freshly ground or found in the spice section of the market.

Peppered Pork Tenderloin en Croûte Variations

- If you wish to make individual servings of pork en croûte, cut the seared meat into 4 pieces, then wrap each in pastry. Reduce the baking time by about 2 minutes.
- Substitute flavored mustard, such as tarragon or honey, for the Dijon mustard.
- Use premarinated pork tenderloins, but pat them quite dry before searing.

broccoli, ham, and gruyère quiche

Quiche is about as 70s as you can get in the fast-forward food world. It has been so maligned that it is hard to remember that quiche Lorraine is, and has always been, one of the glories of French cooking from the Alsace-Lorraine region where the eggs and cheese are extraordinary. This version of the classic bacon-and-onion quiche uses Canadian bacon and adds a little broccoli for color. For other variations, see page 271.

One-half 15-ounce package refrigerated folded piecrusts

4 eggs, beaten

2 cups (about 6 ounces) small broccoli florets

1 tablespoon unsalted butter

4 ounces (1 cup) diced Canadian bacon

1 medium onion, chopped

1^1/$_3$ cups half-and-half or light cream

2 tablespoons chopped fresh thyme

^{3}/$_4$ teaspoon coarsely ground black pepper

4 ounces (1 cup) shredded Gruyère or Swiss cheese

1   Preheat the oven to 450°F. Unfold the piecrust and ease into a deep 9-inch pie plate, pressing together any breaks in the fold lines. Crimp the edges of the pastry. Lightly brush the bottom of the piecrust with about 2 teaspoons of the beaten eggs. Place the pie plate in the freezer for at least 15 minutes.

2   Meanwhile, cook the broccoli in boiling salted water until just tender, 3 to 5 minutes. Drain well. In a medium skillet, heat the butter and cook the bacon and onion over medium-high heat, stirring often, until golden and the onion is just softened.

3   Bake the pie shell directly from the freezer until golden, about 12 minutes. Cool on a rack for about 10 minutes. Reduce the oven temperature to 325°F.

4   In a mixing bowl, stir together the remaining eggs, broccoli, bacon-and-onion mixture, thyme, and pepper. Sprinkle the cheese over the bottom of the baked pie shell. Pour the egg mixture over the cheese.

5   Bake the quiche until the custard is set and no longer liquid, but is still soft in the center, 30 to 40 minutes. Transfer to a rack to cool for at least 10 minutes before cutting into wedges to serve.

Broccoli, Ham, and Gruyère Quiche Tips

- Don't prick the bottom of the pastry before baking. Placing it in the freezer is enough to keep it from shrinking.
- Brushing the bottom of the pastry with some of the egg will form a seal to prevent it from becoming soggy during baking with the custard.
- The custard keeps the fully baked pastry from overcooking during the second baking process.
- No salt is usually needed, since both the ham and cheese are salty. If yours are not, add about $1/2$ teaspoon salt to the recipe.

Broccoli, Ham, and Gruyère Quiche Variations

- Substitute cooked sliced asparagus, carrot, or potato, or 1 cup cooked and well-drained spinach for the broccoli.
- Substitute cooked thick-sliced bacon for the Canadian bacon.
- Substitute any other fresh herb, such as marjoram, oregano, or dill, for the thyme.

spanakopita

Spanakopita recipes are as varied as there are Greek cooks who make them. The spinach-and-cheese filling makes this dish a marvelous vegetarian main course, but if the "pie" is cut into smaller squares or diamonds, or the filling is fashioned in individual packets, it can also be a terrific appetizer or first course. Frozen spinach is fine here, but be sure to buy leaf spinach, not chopped spinach.

1 tablespoon olive oil

1 medium onion, chopped

One 10-ounce package frozen leaf spinach, thawed and squeezed
of excess moisture

$3/4$ cup ricotta cheese

$1/4$ cup crumbled feta cheese

2 tablespoons chopped fresh oregano

2 teaspoons lemon juice

1 teaspoon grated lemon zest

1 egg

8 sheets (12 x 17 inches) frozen phyllo dough, thawed according
to package directions

4 tablespoons unsalted butter, melted

1   Preheat the oven to 375°F.

2   In a small skillet, heat the oil and cook the onion over medium heat, stirring often, until it is soft-ened with golden edges, 4 to 5 minutes. Transfer the onion to a mixing bowl. Add the spinach, ricotta, feta, oregano, lemon juice and zest, and egg to the bowl. Stir to blend all the ingredi-ents well.

3   Place the phyllo sheets on a work surface, keeping them covered with a large tea towel. Brush an 8 x 8-inch baking dish with a little melted butter, then lay one sheet of phyllo in the dish, fit-ting one edge to the bottom of the dish. Almost half of the phyllo will extend over the dish. Brush the phyllo in the dish with melted butter, then fold over the other side, brushing it with

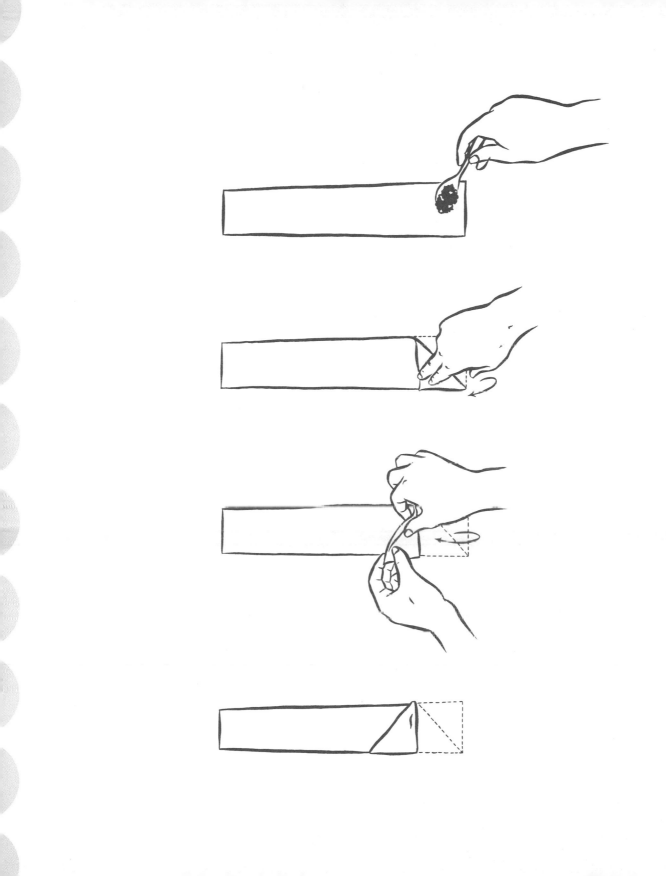

butter. Repeat the procedure to use a total of 4 phyllo sheets and about half of the melted butter. Spread the spinach filling evenly over the phyllo base, then repeat the layering and brushing to use the remaining 4 sheets phyllo and butter. With a knife, score the top few layers of phyllo into 4 to 6 squares or large diamond shapes.

4   Bake until the pastry is rich golden brown and crisp, 40 to 45 minutes. Let the spanakopita stand for 5 to 10 minutes before cutting through the scored marks and transferring with a spatula for serving.

Spanakopita Tips

- Use frozen leaf spinach, then pull it apart into shreds as you squeeze it of excess moisture. Chopped spinach is almost all water and is very hard to squeeze dry.
- Squeeze the spinach by placing it in a sieve, then pushing hard to squeeze out the water.
- Use whole milk or part-skim ricotta, and plain or herbed feta as desired.

Spanakopita Variations

- Add $\frac{1}{4}$ cup chopped sun-dried tomatoes to the filling.
- Make the spanakopita into individual packets by brushing and layering 2 sheets of phyllo on a work surface. Cut the stack into 4 lengthwise strips. Place a heaping tablespoon of filling on the top corner of each strip. Fold each strip as if folding a flag, making a triangular package.

dilled salmon in phyllo

MAKES 4 SERVINGS

Baking fish in pastry is a good idea for many reasons. The pastry seals in aromatic flavors, such as herbs, and the pastry keeps the delicate fish from drying out. Salmon is particularly attractive and flavorful done in this manner. Although fish can be wrapped in puff or flaky pastry, phyllo is even better, since it becomes ultracrisp during baking, which is a lovely contrast to the soft texture of the salmon.

5 tablespoons unsalted butter

$1/4$ cup chopped shallots

4 sheets (12 x 17 inches) frozen phyllo dough, thawed according
    to package directions

2 tablespoons unflavored dried bread crumbs

8 paper-thin slices fresh lemon

$1/4$ cup chopped fresh dill

4 pieces (5 to 6 ounces each) skinned salmon fillet

1   Preheat the oven to 375°F. In a medium skillet, heat 1 tablespoon of the butter. Cook the shallots over medium-low heat, stirring often until softened, about 2 minutes. In a small saucepan, melt the remaining butter.

2   Place the phyllo sheets on a work surface, keeping them covered with a tea towel. Transfer one sheet to another work surface, brush with about $1/2$ tablespoon of the melted butter. Add another sheet and brush with $1/2$ tablespoon butter and sprinkle with $1/2$ tablespoon crumbs. Cut the stack of phyllo in half lengthwise.

3   Season the fish with salt and pepper, then place one fillet at the top of one phyllo strip. Top the fish with about 1 tablespoon sautéed shallots, then 2 slices lemon, and finally 1 tablespoon of the chopped dill. Spread the topping to completely cover the top of the fish. Repeat with another piece of fish and the second length of phyllo. Wrap each piece of phyllo as if wrapping a flag, and ending with a large triangular folded package. Transfer to a large baking sheet, leaving at least 1 inch in between each package, and brushing the tops lightly with butter.

(continued)

4   Repeat the entire procedure to make 2 more fish packages, using all of the remaining ingredients. Bake until the phyllo is crisp and rich golden brown, 28 to 32 minutes. Transfer the packets to plates and serve immediately.

Dilled Salmon in Phyllo **Tips**

- Be sure to use salmon fillets, not steaks, which are full of bones.
- If you are not practiced in skinning fish, ask the fishmonger to do it.
- Fresh salmon should be sweet smelling and glistening.

Dilled Salmon in Phyllo **Variations**

- Substitute 2 tablespoons chopped fresh tarragon for the $\frac{1}{4}$ cup dill.
- Substitute boneless swordfish or tuna or halibut steaks of the same weight for the salmon.
- Brush the fish all over with Dijon mustard before placing on the phyllo sheets.

bacon, lettuce, and tomato tarts

It is well worth investing in 4- or 4 1/2-inch tart pans with removable bottoms. Their uses range from fancy first courses to individually presented main-dish pies, and even personal tart desserts. And the fillings are equally unlimited. Here, the tart filling is a fanciful take on an old favorite, the BLT sandwich. Brushing the tart bottom with a little mayonnaise before baking helps to seal the crust after baking. If you wish, bake as one 9-inch tart.

> **One-half 15-ounce package folded refrigerated piecrusts**
>
> **1/4 cup mayonnaise**
>
> **2 tablespoons slivered fresh basil**
>
> **1 cup seeded and diced plum tomatoes**
>
> **8 slices bacon, cooked until just crisp, drained, and coarsely crumbled**
>
> **4 tablespoons grated Fontina or mozzarella cheese**
>
> **8 sprigs watercress**

1   Unfold the pastry and cut into 4 pieces along the fold lines. Ease each piece into a 4 1/2-inch individual tart pan, pressing to the edges and trimming the excess to fill in any gaps. Trim the top to the edge of the pan. Brush the bottoms of each pastry with about 1 teaspoon mayonnaise. Place the tart pans in the freezer for at least 15 minutes. In a small dish, stir the basil into the remaining mayonnaise.

2   Preheat the oven to 450°F. Place the tart pans on a baking sheet and bake, directly from the freezer, until the pastry is golden, about 9 minutes. Remove from the oven. Reduce the oven temperature to 375°F.

3   Spread the bottoms of the baked shells with the mayonnaise, dividing equally with a generous 2 teaspoons each. Spoon the tomatoes onto the mayonnaise, then top with the bacon and finally the cheese. Bake until the cheese is melted and bubbly, 10 to 12 minutes. Carefully remove the tart pan sides and slide the tarts off the base onto plates. Serve warm, each topped with 2 watercress sprigs.

(continued)

Bacon, Lettuce, and Tomato Tarts **Tips**

- Use really good bacon. Remember, you usually get what you pay for, since cheap bacon is very fatty and without much flavor.
- Cook the bacon just short of very crisp. Some of the bacon drippings should drip onto the tomatoes for extra flavor during baking.
- If flavorful tomatoes are not in season, use drained diced canned tomatoes.

Bacon, Lettuce, and Tomato Tarts **Variations**

- Canadian bacon or good smoked ham can be used in place of the bacon.
- Other herbs, such as tarragon or cilantro, can be used in place of the basil.
- Other cheese, such as Swiss or Monterey Jack, can be used in place of the mozzarella.
- About 2 cups assorted sliced roasted vegetables, such as zucchini, eggplant, bell peppers, and onions, can replace the bacon and tomato, and $1/4$ cup prepared basil pesto can replace the mayonnaise mixture.

Index

ice cream sandwiches, 129
red/white/blueberry cookie shortcakes, 125–26
Ingredients to have on hand, 5–6
Italian fig-filled bars, 166–67
Italian flag flatbread, 248–49

J

Jams and jellies
baked jelly doughnuts, 196–97
jam thumbprints, 154–55
oatmeal pb&j streusel bars, 176–77

L

Lemons
blueberry citrus slump, 100–101
citrus custard tart, 46–47
lemon bars, 174–75
lemon cheese Danish twist, 198–99
mile-high lemon meringue pie, 31–33
Lettuce, bacon, and tomato tarts, 279–80

M

Mail-order sources for dough, 14
Main dishes
bacon, lettuce, and tomato tarts, 279–80
broccoli, ham, and Gruyère quiche, 272–73
chicken and herb baked dumplings, 258–59
chorizo, shrimp, and corn biscuit pot pies,
264–66
curried chicken pie, 267–69
dilled salmon in phyllo, 277–78
mustard beef and red wine in puff pastry, 260–61
peppered pork tenderloin en croûte, 270–71
pork, apple, and sweet potato lattice pie, 262–63
spanakopita, 274–76
Malted milk "balls," 144–45
Malted mousse cake, chocolate, 112–13
Maple walnut spice drops, 152–53
Marshmallows
s'more phyllo flowers, 82–83
Mascarpone and anise fig puff tarts, 59–60
Measuring cups and spoons, 4
Meringue pie, mile-high lemon, 31–33
Mint
chocolate mint strawberry tart, 57–58
Mixers, 4
Mixing spoons, 4
Molasses tuiles, 160–61
Mousse cake, chocolate malted, 112–13
Mustard beef and red wine in puff pastry, 260–61

N

Napoleons, double chocolate, 62–64
Nectarine five-spice tarts, 40–41
Nuts. *See* Almonds; Hazelnuts; Pecans; Walnuts

O

Oatmeal
oatmeal pb&j streusel bars, 176–77
oatmeal raisin snack cake, 121–22
Olive and pepper pan pizza, 242–43
Onions
German bacon and onion flatbread, 252–53
Oranges
blueberry citrus slump, 100–101
citrus custard tart, 46–47
fruit and nut holiday tart, 53–54
molten chocolate clementine brownie cakes, 117–18
orange gingerbread persons, 136–37
orange pecan sticky buns, 213–14

P

Palmiers, 72–73
Pandowdy, pear, 104–5
Panforte, 168–69
Parmesan crackers, flaky, 233
Pastries
chocolate cherry phyllo turnovers, 84–86
double chocolate napoleons, 62–64
eccles cakes, 65–66
fall fruit strudel, 76–78
gâteau pithiviers, 69–71
gianduja pillows, 67–68
palmiers, 72–73
puff pastry bear claws, 74–75
s'more phyllo flowers, 82–83
spiced baklava, 79–81
Peaches
old-fashioned peaches and cream pie, 21–23
puff pastry peach and cherry pot pies, 96–97
summer peach tart, 55–56
Peanut butter
double peanut butter and Concord grape shortcakes,
127–28
double peanut butter cookies, 146–47
oatmeal pb&j streusel bars, 176–77
Pears
apple-pear galette, 38–39
fall fruit strudel, 76–78
pear pandowdy, 104–5

© Anne Himmelright

MELANIE BARNARD has written or coauthored more than a dozen books, including *The American Medical Association Family Cookbook,* which won a James Beard Award; *Short & Sweet*; and, most recently, *A Flash in the Pan.* She is also the coauthor of the monthly *Bon Appétit* column "Every-Night Cooking," and appears frequently on local and national television. She lives in Connecticut with her husband.